Greg Byrd, Lynn Byrd and Chris Pearce

Cambridge Checkpoint

Mathematics

Coursebook

7

CAMBRIDGE
UNIVERSITY PRESS

CAMBRIDGE
UNIVERSITY PRESS

University Printing House, Cambridge CB2 8BS, United Kingdom

One Liberty Plaza, 20th Floor, New York, NY 10006, USA

477 Williamstown Road, Port Melbourne, VIC 3207, Australia

314–321, 3rd Floor, Plot 3, Splendor Forum, Jasola District Centre, New Delhi – 110025, India

79 Anson Road, #06–04/06, Singapore 079906

Cambridge University Press is part of the University of Cambridge.

It furthers the University's mission by disseminating knowledge in the pursuit of education, learning and research at the highest international levels of excellence.

Information on this title: education.cambridge.org

© Cambridge University Press 2012

First published 2012

20 19 18

Printed in Spain by GraphyCems

A catalogue record for this publication is available from the British Library

ISBN 978-1-107-64111-2 Paperback
ISBN 978-1-108-61589-1 Paperback with Cambridge Online Mathematics (1 Year)
ISBN 978-1-108-70914-9 Cambridge Online Mathematics Checkpoint 7 (1 Year)

Introduction

Welcome to Cambridge Checkpoint Mathematics stage 7

The *Cambridge Checkpoint Mathematics* course covers the Cambridge Secondary 1 mathematics framework and is divided into three stages: 7, 8 and 9. This book covers all you need to know for stage 7.

There are two more books in the series to cover stages 8 and 9. Together they will give you a firm foundation in mathematics.

At the end of the year, your teacher may ask you to take a **Progression test** to find out how well you have done. This book will help you to learn how to apply your mathematical knowledge to do well in the test.

The curriculum is presented in six content areas:

- Number
- Algebra
- Measure
- Handling data
- Geometry
- Problem solving.

This book has 19 units, each related to one of the first five content areas. Problem solving is included in all units. There are no clear dividing lines between the five areas of mathematics; skills learned in one unit are often used in other units.

Each unit starts with an introduction, with **key words** listed in a blue box. This will prepare you for what you will learn in the unit. At the end of each unit is a **summary** box, to remind you what you've learned.

Each unit is divided into several topics. Each topic has an introduction explaining the topic content, usually with worked examples. Helpful hints are given in blue rounded boxes. At the end of each topic there is an exercise. Each unit ends with a review exercise. The questions in the exercises encourage you to apply your mathematical knowledge and develop your understanding of the subject.

As well as learning mathematical skills you need to learn when and how to use them. One of the most important mathematical skills you must learn is how to solve problems.

 When you see this symbol, it means that the question will help you to develop your problem-solving skills.

During your course, you will learn a lot of facts, information and techniques. You will start to think like a mathematician. You will discuss ideas and methods with other students as well as your teacher. These discussions are an important part of developing your mathematical skills and understanding.

Look out for these students, who will be asking questions, making suggestions and taking part in the activities throughout the units.

Contents

Acknowledgements

The authors and publisher are grateful for the permissions granted to reproduce copyright materials. While every effort has been made, it has not always been possible to identify the sources of all the materials used, or to trace all the copyright holders. If any omissions are brought to our notice, we will be happy to include the appropriate acknowledgements on reprinting.

p. 19*t* The Granger Collection/TopFoto; p. 19*bl* Eiji Ueda Photography/Shutterstock; p. 19*br* sizov/ Shutterstock; p. 27*t* Ilin Sergey/Shutterstock; p. 31*mr* Joel Blit/Shutterstock; p. 31*bl* 3d brained/ Shutterstock; p. 39*m* Kurhan/Shutterstock; p. 44*tr* Rena Schild/Shutterstock; p. 44*mr* Kirill P/ Shutterstock; p. 45*b* Tyler Olson/Shutterstock; p. 46*tm* Georgis Kollidas/Shutterstock; p. 46*mr* Stefanie Timmermann/iStock; p. 46*br* Yuttasak Jannarong/Shutterstock; p. 49*m* Greg Byrd; p. 53*br* Mesopotamian/ The Art Gallery Collection / Alamy; p. 63*b* Adisa/Shutterstock; p. 65*t* Greg Byrd; p. 80*b* Denise Kappa/Shutterstock; p. 82*b* Gallo Images/Stringer/Getty Images Sport/Getty Images; p. 84*tm* Silvia Boratti/iStock; p. 84*mr* jobhopper/iStock; p. 85*b* Steve Broer/Shutterstock; p. 86*tm* S. Borisov/Shutterstock; p. 86*bl* Greg Byrd; p. 86*br* Greg Byrd; p. 97*ml* James Davies/Alamy; p. 97*br* Greg Byrd; p. 105*t* Michael Chamberlin/Shutterstock; p. 112*ml* Alhovik/shutterstock; p. 112*mr* kated/ Shutterstock; p. 114*m* Graça Victoria/iStock; p. 119*tl* Claude Dagenais/iStock; p. 119*mr* Michael Stokes/ Shutterstock; p. 119*br* Losevsky Pavel/Shutterstock; p. 128*b* USBFCO/Shutterstock; p. 136*t* Hulton Archive/iStock; p. 138*t* Maksim Toome/ Shutterstock; p. 142*b* charistoone-images/Alamy; p. 143*ml* Eastimages/shutterstock; p. 143*m* KtD/Shutterstock; p. 143*mr* Baloncici/Shutterstock; p. 152*bl* auremar/ Shutterstock; p. 152*br* m.bonotto/Shutterstock; p. 161*tl* Greg Byrd; p. 161*mr* Katarina Calgar/iStock; p. 161*br* Nickoloay Stanev/Shutterstock; p. 180*b* allekk/iStock

l = left, *r* = right, *t* = top, *b* = bottom, *m* = middle

The publisher would like to thank Ángel Cubero of the International School Santo Tomás de Aquino, Madrid, for reviewing the language level.

1 Integers

The first numbers you learn about are **whole numbers**, the numbers used for counting: 1, 2, 3, 4, 5, …, …

The whole number zero was only understood relatively recently in human history. The symbol 0 that is used to represent it is also a recent invention. The word 'zero' itself is of Arabic origin.

From the counting numbers, people developed the idea of **negative numbers**, which are used, for example, to indicate temperatures below zero on the Celsius scale.

In some countries, there may be high mountains and deep valleys. The height of a mountain is measured as a distance above sea level. This is the place where the land meets the sea. Sometimes the bottoms of valleys are so deep that they are described as 'below sea level'. This means that the distances are counted downwards from sea level. These can be written using negative numbers.

The lowest temperature ever recorded on the Earth's surface was −89 °C, in Antarctica in 1983. The lowest possible temperature is absolute zero, −273 °C.

Key words

Make sure you learn and understand these key words:

whole number
negative number
positive number
integer
multiple
common multiple
lowest common multiple
factor
remainder
common factor
divisible
prime number
sieve of Eratosthenes
product
square number
square root
inverse

When you refer to a change in temperature, you must always describe it as a number of degrees. When you write 0 °C, for example, you are describing the freezing point of water; 100 °C is the boiling point of water. Written in this way, these are exact temperatures.

To distinguish them from negative numbers, the counting numbers are called **positive numbers**. Together, the positive (or counting) numbers, negative numbers and zero are called **integers**.

This unit is all about integers. You will learn how to add and subtract integers and you will study some of the properties of positive integers. You will explore other properties of numbers, and different types of number.

You should know multiplication facts up to 10 × 10 and the associated division facts.
For example, 6 × 5 = 30 means that 30 ÷ 6 = 5 and 30 ÷ 5 = 6.
This unit will remind you of these multiplication and division facts.

1.1 Using negative numbers

When you work with negative numbers, it can be useful to think in terms of temperature on the Celsius scale.

Water freezes at 0 °C but the temperature in a freezer will be lower than that.

Recording temperatures below freezing is one very important use of negative numbers.

You can also use negative numbers to record other measures, such as depth below sea level or times before a particular event.

You can often show positive and negative numbers on a number line, with 0 in the centre.

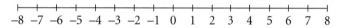

The number line helps you to put integers in order.

When the numbers 1, −1, 3, −4, 5, −6 are put in order, from lowest to highest, they are written as −6, −4, −1, 1, 3, 5.

> Positive numbers go to the right.
>
> Negative numbers go to the left.

Worked example 1.1

The temperature at midday was 3 °C. By midnight it has fallen by 10 degrees. What is the temperature at midnight?

The temperature at midday was 3 °C.

Use the number line to count 10 to the left from 3. Remember to count 0.

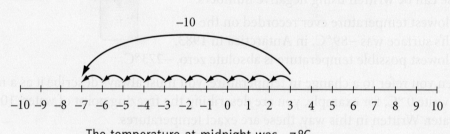

The temperature at midnight was −7 °C.

You can write the calculation in Worked example **1.1** as a subtraction: 3 − 10 = −7.

If the temperature at midnight was 10 degrees <u>higher</u>, you can write: 3 + 10 = 13.

◆ Exercise 1.1

1 Here are six temperatures, in degrees Celsius.

   6   −10   5   −4   0   2

Write them in order, starting with the lowest.

> Use the number line if you need to.

2 Here are the midday temperatures, in degrees Celsius, of five cities on the same day.

Moscow	Tokyo	Berlin	Boston	Melbourne
−8	−4	5	−2	12

    a Which city was the warmest?
    b Which city was the coldest?
    c What is the difference between the temperatures of Berlin and Boston?

3 Draw a number line from −6 to 6. Write down the integer that is halfway between the two numbers in each pair below.
    a 1 and 5   **b** −5 and −1   **c** −1 and 5   **d** −5 and 1

4 Some frozen food is stored at −8 °C. During a power failure, the temperature increases by 3 degrees every minute. Copy and complete this table to show the temperature of the food.

Minutes passed	0	1	2	3	4
Temperature (°C)	−8				

5 During the day the temperature in Tom's greenhouse increases from −4 °C to 5 °C.
What is the rise in temperature?

6 The temperature this morning was −7 °C. This afternoon, the temperature dropped by 10 degrees.
What is the new temperature?

7 Luigi recorded the temperature in his garden at different times of the same day.

Time	06 00	09 00	12 00	15 00	18 00	21 00
Temperature (°C)	−4	−1	5	7	1	−6

    a When was temperature the lowest?
    b What was the difference in temperature between 06 00 and 12 00?
    c What was the temperature difference between 09 00 and 21 00?
    d At midnight the temperature was 5 degrees lower than it was at 21 00.
       What was the temperature at midnight?

8 Heights below sea level can be shown by using negative numbers.
    a What does it mean to say that the bottom of a valley is at −200 metres?
    b A hill next to the valley in part **a** is 450 metres high.
       How far is the top of the hill above the bottom of the valley?

9 Work out the following additions.
    a −2 + 5   **b** −8 + 2   **c** −10 + 7
    d −3 + 4 + 5   **e** −6 + 1 + 5   **f** −20 + 19

> Think of temperatures going up.

10 Find the answers to these subtractions.
    a 4 − 6   **b** −4 − 6   **c** −8 − 7
    d 6 − 7 − 3   **e** −4 − 3 − 3   **f** 10 − 25

> Think of temperatures going down.

1.2 Adding and subtracting negative numbers

You have seen how to add or subtract a <u>positive</u> number by thinking of temperatures going up and down.

Examples: $-3 + 5 = 2$ $-3 - 5 = -8$

Suppose you want to add or subtract a <u>negative</u> number, for example, $-3 + -5$ or $-3 - -5$.

How can you do that?

You need to think about these in a different way.

To work out $-5 + -3$, start at 0 on a number line.

-5 means 'move 5 to the left' and -3 means 'move 3 to the left'.

The result is 'move 8 to the left'.

$-5 + -3 = -8$

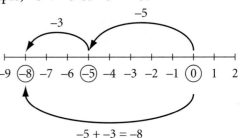

To work out $-3 - -5$ you want the <u>difference</u> between -5 and -3.

To go from -5 to -3 on a number line, move 2 to the right.

$-3 - -5 = 2$

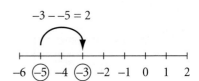

Worked example 1.2

Work these out.   **a** $2 + -6$ **b** $2 - -6$

a $2 + -6 = -4$ **b** $2 - -6 = 8$

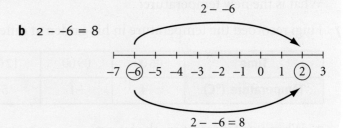

◆ Exercise 1.2

1 Work these out. ☐   **a** $-3 + 4$ **b** $3 + -6$ **c** $-5 + -5$ **d** $-2 + 9$

2 Work these out. ☐   **a** $3 - 7$ **b** $4 - -1$ **c** $2 - -4$ **d** $-5 - 8$

3 Work these out. ☐   **a** $3 + 5$ **b** $-3 + 5$ **c** $3 + -5$ **d** $-3 + -5$

4 Work these out. ☐   **a** $4 - 6$ **b** $4 - -6$ **c** $-4 - 6$ **d** $-4 - -6$

5 **a** Work these out.
　　i $3 + -5$ **ii** $-5 + 3$ **iii** $-2 + -8$ **iv** $-8 + -2$
　b If ▲ and ▼ are two integers, is it always true that ▲ + ▼ = ▼ + ▲?
　　Give a reason for your answer.

6 **a** Work these out.
　　i $5 - -2$ **ii** $-2 - 5$ **iii** $-4 - -3$ **iv** $-3 - -4$
　b If ▲ and ▼ are two integers, what can you say about ▲ − ▼ and ▼ − ▲?

1.3 Multiples

Look at this sequence. $1 \times 3 = 3$ $2 \times 3 = 6$ $3 \times 3 = 9$ $4 \times 3 = 12 \ldots, \ldots$

The numbers 3, 6, 9, 12, 15, … are the **multiples** of 3.

The multiples of 7 are 7, 14, 21, 28, …, …

The multiples of 25 are 25, 50, 75, …, …

> The dots … mean that the pattern continues.

Make sure you know your multiplication facts up to 10×10 or further.
You can use these to recognise multiples up to at least 100.

Worked example 1.3

What numbers less than 100 are multiples of both 6 and 8?

Multiples of 6 are 6, 12, 18, 24, 30, 36, 42, 48, 54, …, …
Multiples of 8 are 8, 16, 24, 32, 40, 48, …, …   The first number in both lists is 24.
Multiples of both are 24, 48, 72, 96, …, …   These are all multiples of 24.

Notice that 24, 48, 72 and 96 are **common multiples** of 6 and 8. They are multiples of <u>both</u> 6 and 8.

24 is the smallest number that is a multiple of both 6 and 8. It is the **lowest common multiple** of 6 and 8.

◆ Exercise 1.3

1 Write down the first six multiples of 7.

> Remember to start with 7.

2 List the first four multiples of each of these numbers.
   a 5   **b** 9   **c** 10   **d** 30   **e** 11

3 Find the fourth multiple of each of these numbers.
   a 6   **b** 12   **c** 21   **d** 15   **e** 32

4 35 is a multiple of 1 and of 35 and of two other numbers. What are the other two numbers?

5 The 17th multiple of 8 is 136.
   a What is the 18th multiple of 8? **b** What is the 16th multiple of 8?

6 **a** Write down four common multiples of 2 and 3.
   b Write down four common multiples of 4 and 5.

7 Find the lowest common multiple for each pair of numbers.
   a 4 and 6   **b** 5 and 6   **c** 6 and 9   **d** 4 and 10   **e** 9 and 11

8 Ying was planning how to seat guests at a dinner. There were between 50 and 100 people coming. Ying noticed that they could be seated with 8 people to a table and no seats left empty.
She also noticed that they could be seated with 12 people to a table with no seats left empty.
How many people were coming?

9 Mia has a large bag of sweets.

> If I share the sweets equally among 2, 3, 4, 5 or 6 people there will always be 1 sweet left over.

What is the smallest number of sweets there could be in the bag?

1.4 Factors and tests for divisibility

A **factor** of a whole number divides into it without a **remainder**. This means that 1 is a factor of every number. Every number is a factor of itself.

2, 3 and 12 are factors of 24. 5 and 7 are <u>not</u> factors of 24.

$24 \div 2 = 12$	$24 \div 3 = 8$
$24 \div 12 = 2$	
$24 \div 5 = 4$ remainder 1	
$24 \div 7 = 3$ remainder 4	

| 3 is a <u>factor</u> of 24 | 24 is a <u>multiple</u> of 3 |

These two statements go together.

> **Worked example 1.4**
>
> Work out all the factors of 40.
>
> | $1 \times 40 = 40$ | Start with 1. Then try 2, 3, 4, ... 1 and 40 are both factors. |
> | $2 \times 20 = 40$ | 2 and 20 are both factors. |
> | $4 \times 10 = 40$ | 3 is not a factor. $40 \div 3$ has a remainder. 4 and 10 are factors. |
> | $5 \times 8 = 40$ | 6 and 7 are not factors. $40 \div 6$ and $40 \div 7$ have remainders. 5 and 8 are factors. You can stop now. You don't need to try 8 because it is already in the list of factors. The factors of 40 are 1, 2, 4, 5, 8, 10, 20 and 40. |

1 is a factor of every whole number.

A **common factor** of two numbers is a factor of both of them.

> You don't have to list factors in order but it is neater if you do.

The factors of 24 are ①, ②, 3, ④, 6, ⑧, 12, 24.

| $1 \times 24 = 24$ | $2 \times 12 = 24$ | $3 \times 8 = 24$ | $4 \times 6 = 24$ |

The factors of 40 are ①, ②, ④, 5, ⑧, 10, 20, 40.

| $1 \times 40 = 40$ | $2 \times 20 = 40$ | $4 \times 10 = 40$ | $5 \times 8 = 40$ |

1, 2, 4 and 8 are common factors of 24 and 40.

Tests for divisibility

If one number is **divisible** by another number, there is no remainder when you divide the first by the second. These tests will help you decide whether numbers are divisible by other numbers.

Divisible by 2   A number is divisible by 2 if its last digit is 0, 2, 4, 6 or 8. That means that 2 is a factor of the number.

Divisible by 3   Add the digits. If the sum is divisible by 3, so is the original number.

Example   Is 6786 divisible by 3? The sum of the digits is $6 + 7 + 8 + 6 = 27$ and then $2 + 7 = 9$. This is a multiple of 3 and so therefore 6786 is also a multiple of 3.

Divisible by 4   A number is divisible by 4 if its last two digits form a number that is divisible by 4.

Example   3726 is not a multiple of 4 because 26 is not.

Divisible by 5   A number is divisible by 5 if the last digit is 0 or 5.

Divisible by 6   A number is divisible by 6 if it is divisible by 2 and by 3. Use the tests given above.

Divisible by 7   There is no simple test for 7. Sorry!

Divisible by 8   A number is divisible by 8 if its last three digits form a number that is divisible by 8.

    Example   17 816 is divisible by 8 because 816 is. 816 ÷ 8 = 102 with no remainder.

Divisible by 9   Add the digits. If the sum is divisible by 9, so is the original number. This is similar to the test for divisibility by 3.

    Example   The number 6786, used for divisibility by 3, is also divisible by 9.

Divisibility by 10 or 100   Multiples of 10 end with 0. Multiples of 100 end with 00.

◆ Exercise 1.4

1 The number 18 has six factors. Two of these factors are 1 and 18.
   Find the other four.

2 Find all the factors of each number.
     a 10   **b** 28   **c** 27   **d** 44
     e 11   **f** 30   **g** 16   **h** 32

3 The number 95 has four factors. What are they?

4 One of the numbers in the box is different from the rest.
   Which one, and why?

        13   17   21   23   29

5 The numbers 4 and 9 both have exactly three factors.
   Find two more numbers that have exactly three factors.

        Think about the factors of 4 and 9.

6 Find the common factors of each pair of numbers.
     a 6 and 10   **b** 20 and 25   **c** 8 and 15
     d 8 and 24   **e** 12 and 18   **f** 20 and 50

7 There is one number less than 30 that has eight factors.
   There is one number less than 50 that has ten factors.
   Find these two numbers.

8 **a** Find a number with four factors, all of which are odd numbers.
     b Find a number with six factors, all of which are odd numbers.

9 Use a divisibility test to decide which of the numbers in the box:
     a is a multiple of 3   **b** is a multiple of 6
     c is a multiple of 9   **d** has 5 as a factor.

        421   222   594   12 345   67 554

10 **a** Which of the numbers in the box:
       i   is a multiple of 10   **ii** has 2 as a factor
       iii has 4 as a factor   **iv** is a multiple of 8?

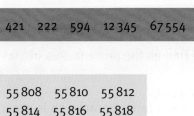

    55 808   55 810   55 812
    55 814   55 816   55 818

  b If the sequence continues, what will be the first multiple of 100?

1.5 Prime numbers

You have seen that some numbers have just two factors.

The factors of 11 are 1 and 11. The factors of 23 are 1 and 23.

Numbers that have just two factors are called **prime numbers** or just **primes**.

The factors of a prime are 1 and the number itself. If it has any other factors it is not a prime number.

There are eight prime numbers less than 20:

  2, 3, 5, 7, 11, 13, 17, 19

1 is <u>not</u> a prime number. It only has one factor and <u>prime numbers always have exactly two factors</u>.

All the prime numbers, except 2, are odd numbers.

9 is not a prime number because $9 = 3 \times 3$. 15 is not a prime number because $15 = 3 \times 5$.

The sieve of Eratosthenes

One way to find prime numbers is to use the **sieve of Eratosthenes**.

> Eratosthenes was born in 276 BC, in a country that is modern-day Libya. He was the first person to calculate the circumference of the Earth.

1 Write the counting numbers up to 100 or more.

2 Cross out 1.

3 Put a box around the next number that you have not crossed out (2) and then cross out all the multiples of that number ($4, 6, 8, 10, 12, \ldots, \ldots$)
You are left with $\boxed{2}$ 3   5   7   9   11   13   15   …   …

4 Put a box around the next number that you have not crossed off (3) and then cross out all the multiples of that number that you have not crossed out already ($9, 15, 21, \ldots, \ldots$)
You are left with $\boxed{2}$ $\boxed{3}$ 5   7   11   13   17   19   …   …

5 Continue in this way (next put a box around 5 and cross out multiples of 5) and you will be left with a list of the prime numbers.

> Did you know that very large prime numbers are used to provide secure encoding for sensitive information, such as credit card numbers, on the internet?

Worked example 1.5

Find all the prime factors of 30.

	You only need to check the prime numbers.
2 is a factor because 30 is even.	$2 \times 15 = 30$
3 is a factor.	$3 \times 10 = 30$
5 is a factor because the last digit of 30 is 0.	$5 \times 6 = 30$
The prime factors are 2, 3 and 5.	6 is in our list of factors (5×6) so you do not need to try any prime number above 6.

◆ **Exercise 1.5**

1 There are two prime numbers between 20 and 30. What are they?

2 Write down the prime numbers between 30 and 40. How many are there?

3 How many prime numbers are there between 90 and 100?

4 Find the prime factors of each number.
   a 10   **b** 15   **c** 25
   d 28   **e** 45   **f** 70

5 a Find a sequence of five consecutive numbers, none of which is prime.
   b Can you find a sequence of seven such numbers?

> Numbers such as 1, 2, 3, 4, 5 are consecutive. 2, 4, 6, 8, 10 are consecutive even numbers.

6 Look at this table.

1	2	3	4	5	6
7	8	9	10	11	12
13	14	15	16	17	18
19	20	21	22	23	24
25	26	27	28	29	30

   a i Where are the multiples of 3?   **ii** Where are the multiples of 6?
   b In one column all the numbers are prime numbers. Which column is this?
   c Add more rows to the table. Does the column identified in part **b** still contain only prime numbers?

7 Each of the numbers in this box is the **product** of two prime numbers.

> The product is the result of multiplying numbers.

   226   321   305   133

   Find the two prime numbers in each case.

8 Hassan thinks he has discovered a way to find prime numbers. Investigate whether Hassan is correct.

I start with 11 and then add 2, then 4, then 6 and so on.
The answer is a prime number every time.

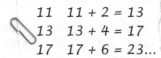

11   11 + 2 = 13
13   13 + 4 = 17
17   17 + 6 = 23...

9 a Find two different prime numbers that add up to:
   i 18   **ii** 26   **iii** 30.
   b How many different pairs can you find for each of the numbers in part **a**?

1.6 Squares and square roots

$1 \times 1 = 1 \qquad 2 \times 2 = 4 \qquad 3 \times 3 = 9 \qquad 4 \times 4 = 16 \qquad 5 \times 5 = 25$

The numbers 1, 4, 9, 16, 25, 36, … are called **square numbers**.

Look at this pattern.

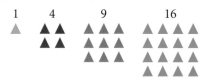

You can see why they are called square numbers.

The next picture would have 5 rows of 5 symbols, totalling 25 altogether, so the fifth square number is 25.

The square of 5 is 25 and the square of 7 is 49.

You can write that as $5^2 = 25$ and $7^2 = 49$.

Read this as '5 squared is 25' and '7 squared is 49'.

You can also say that the **square root** of 25 is 5 and the square root of 49 is 7.

The symbol for square root is $\sqrt{}$.

$\sqrt{25} = 5$ and $\sqrt{49} = 7$

$\sqrt{25} = 5$	means	$5^2 = 25$

> Be careful: 3^2 means 3×3, <u>not</u> 3×2.

> Adding and subtracting, and multiplying and dividing, are pairs of **inverse** operations. One is the 'opposite' of the other.
>
> Squaring and finding the square root are also inverse operations.

◆ Exercise 1.6

1 Write down the first ten square numbers.

2 Find 15^2 and 20^2.

3 List all the square numbers in each range.
   a 100 to 200 **b** 200 to 300 **c** 300 to 400

4 Find the missing number in each case.
   a $3^2 + 4^2 = \square^2$ **b** $8^2 + 6^2 = \square^2$
   c $12^2 + 5^2 = \square^2$ **d** $8^2 + 15^2 = \square^2$

5 Find two square numbers that add up to 20^2.

6 The numbers in the box are square numbers.
   a How many factors does each of these numbers have?
   b Is it true that a square number always has an odd number of factors? Give a reason for your answer.

16	25	36	49	81	100

7 Find:
   a the 20th square number **b** the 30th square number. **c** the 50th square number.

8 Write down the number that is the same as each of these.

a $\sqrt{81}$ **b** $\sqrt{36}$ **c** $\sqrt{1}$ **d** $\sqrt{49}$ **e** $\sqrt{144}$

f $\sqrt{256}$ **g** $\sqrt{361}$ **h** $\sqrt{196}$ **i** $\sqrt{29+35}$ **j** $\sqrt{12^2+16^2}$

> The square root sign is like a pair of brackets. You must complete the calculation inside it, before finding the square root.

9 Find the value of each number.

a **i** $\left(\sqrt{36}\right)^2$ **ii** $\left(\sqrt{196}\right)^2$ **iii** $\sqrt{5^2}$ **iv** $\sqrt{16^2}$

b Try to write down a rule to generalise this result.

10 Find three square numbers that add up to 125. There are two ways to do this.

11 Say whether each of these statements about square numbers is <u>always</u> true, <u>sometimes</u> true or <u>never</u> true.
   a The last digit is 5.   **b** The last digit is 7.
   c The last digit is a square number.   **d** The last digit is not 3 or 8.

Summary

You should now know that:

★ Integers can be put in order on a number line.

★ Positive and negative numbers can be added and subtracted.

★ Every positive integer has multiples and factors.

★ Two integers may have common factors.

★ Prime numbers have exactly two factors.

★ There are simple tests for divisibility by 2, 3, 4, 5, 6, 8, 9, 10 and 100.

★ 7^2 means '7 squared' and $\sqrt{49}$ means 'the square root of 49', and that these are inverse operations.

★ The sieve of Eratosthenes can be used to find prime numbers.

You should be able to:

★ Recognise negative numbers as positions on a number line.

★ Order, add and subtract negative numbers in context.

★ Recognise multiples, factors, common factors and primes, all less than 100.

★ Use simple tests of divisibility.

★ Find the lowest common multiple in simple cases.

★ Use the sieve of Eratosthenes for generating primes.

★ Recognise squares of whole numbers to at least 20 × 20 and the corresponding square roots.

★ Use the notation 7^2 and $\sqrt{49}$.

★ Consolidate the rapid recall of multiplication facts to 10 × 10 and associated division facts.

★ Know and apply tests of divisibility by 2, 3, 4, 5, 6, 8, 9, 10 and 100.

★ Use inverse operations to simplify calculations with whole numbers.

★ Recognise mathematical properties, patterns and relationships, generalising in simple cases.

End of unit review

1 Here are the midday temperatures one Monday, in degrees Celsius, in four cities.

Astana	Wellington	Kuala Lumpur	Kiev
−10	6	18	−4

    a Which city is the coldest?
    b What is the temperature difference between Kuala Lumpur and Kiev?
    c What is the temperature difference between Kiev and Astana?

2 At 9 p.m. the temperature in Kurt's garden was −2 °C.
   During the night the temperature went down 5 degrees and then it went up 10 degrees by midday the next day.
   What was the temperature at midday in Kurt's garden?

3 Work these out.
    a $6 - 11$ **b** $-5 - 4$ **c** $-8 + 6$ **d** $-3 + 18$

4 Work these out.
    a $-7 + -8$ **b** $6 - -9$ **c** $-10 - -8$ **d** $5 + -12$

5 Write down the first three multiples of each number.
    a 8   **b** 11   **c** 20

6 Find the lowest common multiple of each pair of numbers.
    a 6 and 9   **b** 6 and 10   **c** 6 and 11   **d** 6 and 12

7 List the factors of each number.
    a 25   **b** 26   **c** 27   **d** 28   **e** 29

8 Find the common factors of each pair of numbers.
    a 18 and 27   **b** 24 and 30   **c** 26 and 32

9 Look at the numbers in the box. From these numbers, write down:

                                        | 26 153   26 154   26 155   26 156   26 157 |

    a a multiple of 5
    b a multiple of 6
    c a multiple of 3 that is not a multiple of 9.

10 There is just one prime number between 110 and 120.
    What is it?

11 Find the factors of 60 that are prime numbers.

12 **a** What is the smallest number that is a product of three different prime numbers?
    b The number 1001 is the product of three prime numbers. One of them is 13.
        What are the other two?

2 Sequences, expressions and formulae

A famous mathematician called Leonardo Pisano was born around 1170, in Pisa in Italy. Later, he was known as Fibonacci.

Fibonacci wrote several books. In one of them, he included a number pattern that he discovered in 1202. The number pattern was named after him.

1 1 2 3 5 8 13 21 34 … …

Can you see the pattern?

To find the next number in the pattern, you add the previous two numbers.

So   1 + 1 = 2

             1 + 2 = 3

                 2 + 3 = 5

                     3 + 5 = 8

                         5 + 8 = 13 and so on.

Fibonacci (1170–1250).

Key words

Make sure you learn and understand these key words:

sequence
term
consecutive terms
term-to-term rule
infinite sequence
finite sequence
function
function machine
input
output
mapping diagram
map
unknown
equation
solution
expression
variable
formula (formulae)
substitute
derive

The numbers in the Fibonacci sequence are called the <u>Fibonacci numbers</u>.

The Fibonacci numbers often appear in nature. For example, the numbers of petals on flowers are often Fibonacci numbers.

The numbers of spirals in seed heads or pinecones are often Fibonacci numbers, as well.

A sunflower can have 34 spirals turning clockwise and 21 spirals turning anticlockwise.

A pinecone can have 8 spirals turning clockwise and 13 spirals turning anticlockwise.

In this unit you will learn more about number patterns.

2.1 Generating sequences (1)

3, 6, 9, 12, 15, … is a **sequence** of numbers.

Each number in the sequence is called a **term**. The first term is 3, the second term is 6 and so on.

Terms that follow each other are called **consecutive terms**. 3 and 6 are consecutive terms, 6 and 9 are consecutive terms and so on. Each term is 3 more than the term before, so the **term-to-term rule** is: 'Add 3.'

Three dots written at the end of a sequence show that the sequence continues for ever. A sequence that carries on for ever is called an **infinite sequence**.

If a sequence doesn't have the three dots at the end, then it doesn't continue for ever. This type of sequence is called a **finite sequence**.

Worked example 2.1

> **a** Write down the term-to-term rule and the next two terms of this sequence.
>   2, 6, 10, 14, … , …
> **b** The first term of a sequence is 5.
>   The term-to-term rule of the sequence is: 'Multiply by 2 and then add 1.'
>   Write down the first three terms of the sequence.

a Term-to-term rule is: 'Add 4.'	You can see that the terms are going up by 4 every time as 2 + 4 = 6, 6 + 4 = 10 and 10 + 4 = 14.
Next two terms are 18 and 22.	You keep adding 4 to find the next two terms: 14 + 4 = 18 and 18 + 4 = 22.
b First three terms are 5, 11, 23.	Write down the first term, which is 5, then use the term-to-term rule to work out the second and third terms. Second term = 2 × 5 + 1 = 11, third term = 11 × 2 + 1 = 23.

Exercise 2.1

1 For each of these infinite sequences, write down:
  i the term-to-term rule **ii** the next two terms.
  a 2, 4, 6, 8, …, …   **b** 1, 4, 7, 10, …, …   **c** 5, 9, 13, 17, …, …
  d 3, 8, 13, 18, …, …   **e** 30, 28, 26, 24, …, …   **f** 17, 14, 11, 8, …, …

2 Write down the first three terms of each of these sequences.

	First term	Term-to-term rule
a	1	Add 5
b	6	Add 8
c	20	Subtract 3
d	45	Subtract 7
e	6	Multiply by 2 and then subtract 3
f	60	Divide by 2 and then add 2

3 Copy these finite sequences and fill in the missing terms.

   a 2, 5, ☐, 11, ☐, 17, 20   **b** 5, 11, 17, ☐, ☐, 35, ☐

   c 26, 23, ☐, ☐, 14, ☐, 8   **d** 90, 82, ☐, 66, ☐, 50, ☐

   e 8, ☐, ☐, 32, 40, ☐, ☐   **f** ☐, ☐, 28, 23, ☐, ☐, 8

4 Write down whether each of these sequences is finite or infinite.

   a 4, 6, 8, 10, …   **b** 3, 5, 7, 9, 11, 13, 15

   c 85, 75, 65, 55, 45, 35   **d** 100, 97, 94, 91, 88, …

5 Copy this table.

First term	Sequence	Term-to-term rule
3	11, 14, 17, 20, …, …	Subtract 2
80	17, 15, 13, 11, …, …	Divide by 2
64	3, 6, 12, 24, …, …	Multiply by 5 then add 1
11	80, 40, 20, 10, …, …	Multiply by 2
17	1, 6, 31, 156, …, …	Divide by 2 then add 4
1	64, 36, 22, 15, …, …	Add 3

Draw a line connecting the sequence on the left with the first term in the middle, then with the term-to-term rule on the right. The first one has been done for you.

6 Shen and Zalika are looking at this number sequence:
4, 8, 20, 56, 164, …, …

I think the term-to-term rule is: 'Add 4.'

I think the term-to-term rule is: 'Multiply by 2.'

Is either of them correct? Explain your answer.

7 Ryker is trying to solve this problem. Work out the answer to the problem. Explain how you solved it.

The second term of a sequence is 13. The term-to-term rule is: 'Multiply by 2 then subtract 3.' What is the first term of the sequence?

8 Arabella is trying to solve this problem. Work out the answer to the problem. Explain how you solved it.

The third term of a sequence is 48. The term-to-term rule is: 'Subtract 2 then multiply by 3.' What is the first term of the sequence?

2.2 Generating sequences (2)

Here is a pattern of shapes made from dots.

The numbers of dots used to make each pattern form the sequence 3, 5, 7, …, …

You can see that, as you go from one pattern to the next, one extra dot is being added to each end of the shape. So, each pattern has two more dots than the pattern before. The term-to-term rule is 'add 2.'

The next pattern in the sequence has 9 dots because 7 + 2 = 9.

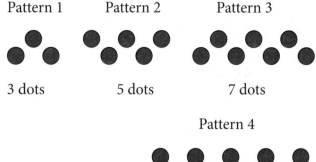

Pattern 1   Pattern 2   Pattern 3

3 dots   5 dots   7 dots

Pattern 4

9 dots

Worked example 2.2

Here is a pattern of triangles made from matchsticks.

Pattern 1   Pattern 2   Pattern 3

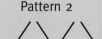   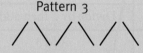

3 matchsticks   6 matchsticks   9 matchsticks

a   Draw the next pattern in the sequence.
b   Write down the sequence of numbers of matchsticks.
c   Write down the term-to-term rule.
d   Explain how the sequence is formed.

a	The next pattern will have another triangle added to the end. So pattern 4 has 12 matchsticks.
b 3, 6, 9, 12, … , …	Write down the number of matchsticks for each pattern.
c Add 3	Each term is 3 more than the previous term.
d An extra triangle is added, so 3 more matchsticks are added.	Describe in words how the pattern grows from one term to the next.

◆ Exercise 2.2

1   This pattern is made from dots.

Pattern 1   Pattern 2   Pattern 3

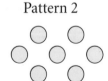   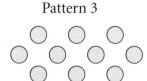

   a   Draw the next two patterns in the sequence.
   b   Write down the sequence of numbers of dots.
   c   Write down the term-to-term rule.
   d   Explain how the sequence is formed.

2 This pattern is made from squares.

Pattern 1   Pattern 2   Pattern 3

  a Draw the next two patterns in the sequence.

  b Copy and complete the table to show the number of squares in each pattern.

Pattern number	1	2	3	4	5
Number of squares	5	8	11		

  c Write down the term-to-term rule.

  d How many squares will there be in: **i** Pattern 8   **ii** Pattern 10?

3 This pattern is made from blue triangles.

Pattern 1   Pattern 2   Pattern 3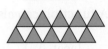

  a Draw the next two patterns in the sequence.

  b Copy and complete the table to show the number of blue triangles in each pattern.

Pattern number	1	2	3	4	5
Number of blue triangles					

  c Write down the term-to-term rule.

  d How many blue triangles will there be in: **i** Pattern 10   **ii** Pattern 15?

 4 Jacob is using dots to draw a sequence of patterns.
He has spilled tomato sauce over the first
and third patterns in his sequence.

Pattern 1   Pattern 2   Pattern 3   Pattern 4

  a Draw the first and the third patterns of Jacob's sequence.

  b How many dots will there be in Pattern 7?

5 Harsha and Jake are looking at this sequence of patterns made from squares.

Pattern 1   Pattern 2   Pattern 3   Pattern 4

5 squares   7 squares   9 squares   11 squares

I think there are 43 squares in Pattern 20 because, if I multiply the pattern number by 2 and add 3, I always get the number of squares. 20 × 2 + 3 = 43.

I think there are 22 squares in Pattern 20 because the pattern is going up by 2 each time, and 20 + 2 = 22.

Who is correct? Explain your answer.

2.3 Representing simple functions

A **function** is a relationship between two sets of numbers.

A function can be shown as a **function machine** like this.

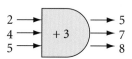

> This function machine adds 3 to any number that goes into the machine.

The numbers that you put into the function machine are called the **input**.

The numbers that you get out of the function machine are called the **output**.

A function can also be shown as a **mapping diagram** like this.

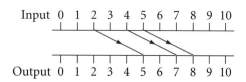

> We say that 2 **maps** to 5,
> 4 maps to 7 and
> 5 maps to 8.

Worked example 2.3

a Find the missing inputs and outputs in this function machine.

Input   Output

```
1 →          → ...
3 →   × 2    → ...
... →        → 10
```

b Draw a mapping diagram to show the function in part **a**.

a Input   Output

```
1 →          → 2
3 →   × 2    → 6
5 →          → 10
```

To work out the outputs, multiply the inputs by 2.
$1 \times 2 = 2$, $3 \times 2 = 6$
To work out the input, work backwards and divide the output by 2.
$10 \div 2 = 5$

b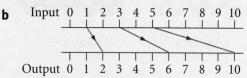

> 1 maps to 2, 3 maps to 6
> and 5 maps to 10.

Exercise 2.3

1 Copy these function machines and work out the missing inputs and outputs.

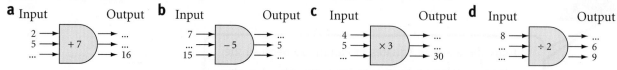

2 Copy these function machines and work out the missing inputs and outputs.

a Input / Output
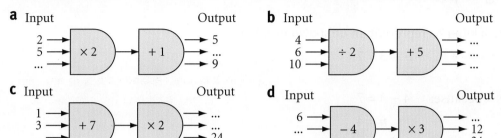

b Input / Output

3 a Work out the rule to complete each of these function machines.
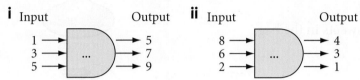

b Make two copies of the diagram below.

Input 0 1 2 3 4 5 6 7 8 9 10

Output 0 1 2 3 4 5 6 7 8 9 10

Draw a mapping diagram for each of the functions in part **a**.

4 Tanesha and Dakarai look at this function machine.
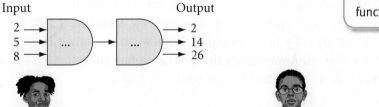

Test the input numbers in each of their functions to see if either of them is correct.

I think the function is: 'Multiply by 3 then take away 4.'

I think the function is: 'Multiply by 4 then take away 6.'

Is either of them correct? Explain your answer.

5 Chin-Mae draws this mapping diagram and function machine for the same function.
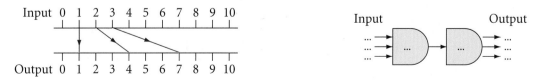

Input 0 1 2 3 4 5 6 7 8 9 10

Output 0 1 2 3 4 5 6 7 8 9 10

Input / Output

Fill in the missing numbers and the rule in the function machine.

2.4 Constructing expressions

In algebra you can use a letter to represent an **unknown** number.

Example: $n + 3 = 7$

You can see that the
value of the letter n is 4 because: $4 + 3 = 7$

So you can write: $n = 4$

To solve problems you sometimes have to use a letter to represent an unknown number.

Example: Here is a bag of sweets. You don't know how many
sweets there are in the bag.

n sweets

Let n represent the unknown number of sweets in the bag.

Three sweets are taken out of the bag.

Now there are $n - 3$ sweets left in the bag.

$n - 3$ is called an **expression** and the letter n is called the **variable**.

An expression can contain numbers and letters but <u>not</u> an equals sign.

$n - 3$ sweets

Worked example 2.4

Mathew is x years old. David is 4 years older than Mathew. Adam is 2 years younger than Mathew. Kathryn is 3 times older than Mathew. Ella is half Mathew's age.
Write down an expression for each of their ages.

Mathew is x years old.	This is the information you are given to start with.
David is $x + 4$ years old.	You are told David is 4 years older than Mathew, so add 4 to x.
Adam is $x - 2$ years old.	You are told Adam is 2 years younger than Mathew, so subtract 2 from x.
Kathryn is $3x$ years old.	You are told Kathryn is 3 times as old as Mathew, so multiply 3 by x. You write $3 \times x$ as $3x$. Always write the number before the letter.
Ella is $\frac{x}{2}$ years old.	You are told Ella is half Mathew's age, so divide x by 2. You write $x \div 2$ as $\frac{x}{2}$.

Exercise 2.4

1   Avani has a bag that contains n counters.
    Write an expression for the total number of counters she has in the bag when:
    a she puts in 2 more   **b** she takes 3 out.

2   The temperature on Tuesday was $t°C$.
    Write an expression for the temperature when it is:
    a 2 Celsius degrees higher than it was on Tuesday   **b** twice as warm as it was on Tuesday.

3 Write an expression for the answer to each of these.

  a David has *x* DVDs. He buys 6 more.
  How many DVDs does he now have?

  b Molly is *m* years old and Barney is *b* years old.
  What is the total of their ages?

  c Ted can store *g* photographs on one memory card.
  How many photographs can he store on 3 memory cards
  of the same size?

4 Maliha thinks of a number, *x*.
Write an expression for the number Maliha gets when she:

  a multiplies the number by 3   **b** multiplies the number by 4 then adds 1

  c divides the number by 3   **d** divides the number by 2 then subtracts 9.

5 The cost of an adult's ticket into a theme park is $*a*.
The cost of a child's ticket into the same theme park is $*c*.
Write an expression for the total cost for each group.

  a 1 adult and 1 child   **b** 2 adults and 1 child   **c** 4 adults and 5 children

6 This is part of Shashank's homework.

> **Question**
>
> Adrian thinks of a number, *n*.
> Write an expression for the number Adrian gets when he:
> **a** adds 2 to the number then multiplies by 5
> **b** subtracts 3 from the number then divides by 2.
>
> **Solution**
> **a** $(n + 2) \times 5$ which can be written as $5(n + 2)$
> **b** $(n - 3) \div 2$ which can be written as $\dfrac{n - 3}{2}$

> You must use brackets if you add or subtract before multiplying or dividing.

Use Shashank's method to write an expression for the number Adrian gets when he:

  a adds 5 to the number then multiplies by 3   **b** adds 7 to the number then divides by 4

  c subtracts 2 from the number then divides by 5   **d** subtracts 9 from the number then multiplies by 8.

7 Match each description (in the left-hand column) to the correct expression (in the right-hand column).

  a Multiply *n* by 3 and subtract from 2   **i** $2 + 3n$

  b Add 2 and *n* then multiply by 3   **ii** $2 + \dfrac{n}{3}$

  c Multiply *n* by 3 and subtract 2   **iii** $2 - 3n$

  d Multiply *n* by 3 and add 2   **iv** $3n - 2$

  e Add 2 and *n* then divide by 3   **v** $3(n + 2)$

  f Divide *n* by 3 and add 2   **vi** $2 - \dfrac{n}{3}$

           vii $\dfrac{n + 2}{3}$

Write a description for the expression that is left over.

2.5 Deriving and using formulae

A **formula** is a mathematical rule that shows the relationship between two quantities (variables).

You can write a formula using words: Area of rectangle = length × width

or using letters: $A = l \times w$

You can **substitute** numbers into expressions and formulae.

When $l = 5$ cm and $w = 4$ cm $A = 5 \times 4 = 20$ cm^2

You can write or **derive** your own formulae to help you solve problems.

Worked example 2.5

a Work out the value of the expression $a + 3b$ when $a = 2$ and $b = 4$.
b Write a formula for the number of days in any number of weeks, in:
  i words **ii** letters.
c Use the formula in part **b** to work out the number of days in 8 weeks.

a $a + 3b = 2 + 3 \times 4$ Substitute 2 for a and 4 for b in the expression.
  $= 2 + 12$ Remember that multiplication comes before
  $= 14$ addition.

> Remember the order of operations: division and multiplication must be done before addition and subtraction.

b i number of days
  $= 7 \times$ number of weeks There are 7 days in a week, so multiply
  the number of weeks by 7.
  ii $d = 7w$ Choose d for days and w for weeks and
  write $7 \times w$ as $7w$.

> Always write the number before the letter, so write $7w$ not $w7$.

c $d = 7 \times 8$ Substitute $w = 8$ into the formula.
  $= 56$

◆ Exercise 2.5

1 Work out the value of each expression.
  a $a + 5$ when $a = 3$
  b $x - 9$ when $x = 20$
  c $f + g$ when $f = 7$ and $g = 4$
  d $m - n$ when $m = 100$ and $n = 25$
  e $3k$ when $k = 5$
  f $p + 2q$ when $p = 5$ and $q = 3$
  g $\frac{y}{4}$ when $y = 32$
  h $c - 4d$ when $c = 10$ and $d = 2$
  i $2h + 3t$ when $h = 8$ and $t = 5$
  j $\frac{w}{2} + v$ when $w = 16$ and $v = 9$
  k $\frac{30}{c} - 2$ when $c = 6$
  l $\frac{x + y}{2}$ when $x = 19$ and $y = 11$

2 a Write a formula for the number of minutes in any number of hours, in:
  i words **ii** letters.
  b Use your formula in part **a ii** to work out the number of minutes in 5 hours.

3 Use the formula $V = IR$ to work out V when:
  a $I = 3$ and $R = 7$ **b** $I = 4$ and $R = 9$.

> IR means $I \times R$

4   Landon uses this formula to work
    out the pay of his employees. How
    much does he pay each
    of these employees?
    a   Cole: works 20 hours at $22 per
        hour and gets a $30 bonus.
    b   Avery: works 32 hours at $20 per
        hour and gets a $50 bonus.

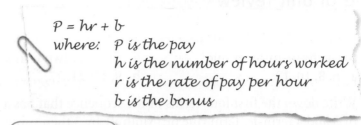

$P = hr + b$
where: P is the pay
         h is the number of hours worked
         r is the rate of pay per hour
         b is the bonus

hr means $h \times r$

5   What value of k can you substitute into each of these expressions to give you the <u>same</u> answer?

    $k + 10$ $3k$ $4k - 5$

6   A cookery book shows how long it takes, in minutes, to cook a joint of meat.

Electric oven	time = (66 × weight in kg) + 35
Microwave oven	time = (26 × weight in kg) + 15

    a   Compare the two formulae for cooking times. If a joint of meat takes about 2 hours to cook in
        an electric oven, roughly how long do you think it would take in a microwave oven?
    b   i   Work out how much quicker is it to cook a 2 kg joint of meat in a microwave oven than in an
            electric oven.
        ii Does your answer to part **a** seem sensible?

Summary

You should now know that:

★ Each number in a sequence is called a term and
  terms next to each other are called consecutive
  terms.

★ A sequence that continues for ever is called an
  infinite sequence.

★ A sequence that doesn't continue for ever is called
  a finite sequence.

★ Number sequences can be formed from patterns
  of shapes.

★ The numbers that go into a function machine are
  called the input. The numbers that come out of a
  function machine are called the output.

★ In algebra you can use a letter to represent an
  unknown number.

★ Equations and expressions contain numbers and
  letters. Only an equation contains an equals sign.

You should be able to:

★ Generate terms of an integer sequence and find a
  term, given its position in the sequence.

★ Find the term-to-term rule of a sequence.

★ Generate sequences from patterns and describe
  the general term in simple cases.

★ Use function machines and mapping diagrams to
  represent functions.

★ Work out input and output numbers of function
  machines.

★ Construct simple algebraic expressions.

★ Derive and use simple formulae.

★ Substitute positive integers into simple linear
  expressions and formulae.

★ Identify and represent information or unknown
  numbers in problems.

★ Recognise mathematical properties, patterns and
  relationships, generalising in simple cases.

End of unit review

1 For each of these infinite sequences, work out:
  i the term-to-term rule   **ii** the next two terms   **iii** the tenth term.
  a 6, 8, 10, 12, …, …   **b** 9, 15, 21, 27, …, …   **c** 28, 25, 22, 19, …, …

2 Write down the first four terms of the sequence that has a first term
  of 5 and a term-to-term rule of: 'Multiply by 3 then subtract 5.'

3 Sally is trying to solve this problem.
  Work out the answer to the problem.
  Explain how you solved the problem.

> The third term of a sequence is 19 and
> the fifth term is 11.
> The term-to-term rule is: 'Subtract a
> mystery number.'
> What is the first term of the sequence?
> What is the mystery number?

4 This pattern is made from squares.

  Pattern 1   Pattern 2   Pattern 3

     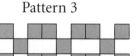

  a Draw the next pattern in the sequence.
  b Copy and complete the table to show the number of squares in each pattern.

Pattern number	1	2	3	4	5
Number of squares	5	10			

  c Write down the term-to-term rule.
  d How many squares will there be in Pattern 10?

5 Copy these function machines and work out the missing inputs and outputs.

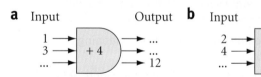

6 Ahmad looks at this function machine.

  Is Ahmad correct? Explain your answer.

7 Nimrah thinks of a number, n.
  Write an expression for the number Nimrah gets each time.
  a She multiplies the number by 4.   **b** She subtracts 6 from the number.
  c She multiplies the number by 3 then adds 5.   **d** She divides the number by 6 then subtracts 1.

8 Work out the value of each expression.
  a $a + 3$ when $a = 8$ **b** $p + 3q$ when $p = 3$ and $q = 4$.

2 Sequences, expressions and formulae

3 Place value, ordering and rounding

The decimal system is a number system based on 10. All the numbers can be written by using just the ten digits 0, 1, 2, 3, 4, 5, 6, 7, 8 and 9.

The world's earliest decimal system used lines to represent numbers, so their digits 1 to 9 looked something like this.

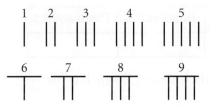

Before the symbol for zero (0) was invented, people used a blank space to represent it.

Many countries in the world use a decimal system for their currency, where each unit of currency is based on a multiple of 10.

For example:

UK, 1 pound = 100 pence (£1 = 100p)

Europe, 1 euro = 100 cents (€1 = 100c)

USA, 1 dollar = 100 cents ($1 = 100c)

Gambia, 1 dalasi = 100 bututs

China, 1 yuan = 100 fen

Thailand, 1 baht = 100 satang

When you travel to different countries you need to use different currencies. It is easier to understand new currencies if they are based, like your own, on the decimal system.

In this unit you will learn more about understanding and using decimal numbers.

> **Key words**
>
> **Make sure you learn and understand these key words:**
>
> decimal number
> decimal point
> decimal places
> place-value table
> round
> approximate
> short division
> estimate
> inverse operation

3.1 Understanding decimals

A **decimal number** always has a **decimal point**.

Example: 12.56 is a decimal number.

It has two **decimal places** because there are two numbers after the decimal point.

You can write the number 12.56 in a **place-value table**, like this. The position of a digit in the table shows its value.

Hundreds	Tens	Units	•	Tenths	Hundredths	Thousandths
	1	2	•	5	6	

The digit 1 represents 1 ten and the digit 2 represents 2 units. Together they make 12, which is the whole-number part of the decimal number.

The digit 5 represents 5 tenths and the digit 6 represents 6 hundredths. Together they make 56 hundredths, which is the fractional part of the decimal number.

Worked example 3.1

The diagram shows a parcel that weighs 3.465 kg.

Write down the value of each of the digits in the number.

3.465 kg

The digit 3 has the value 3 units.
The digit 4 has the value 4 tenths.
The digit 6 has the value 6 hundredths.
The digit 5 has the value 5 thousandths.

◆ **Exercise 3.1**

1 Here are some decimal numbers.

| 32.55 | 2.156 | 323.5 | 4.777 | 9.85 | 0.9 | 87.669 | 140.01 |

Write down all the numbers that have   **a** one decimal place   **b** three decimal places.

2 Write down the value of the red digit in each of these numbers.

   a 42.673   **b** 136.92   **c** 0.991
   d 32.07   **e** 9.998   **f** 2.4448

> In part **f**, to work out the value of the 8, extend the place-value table one more column to the right.

3

> 'The number 8.953 is bigger than 8 but smaller than 9'.

Is Xavier correct? Explain your answer.

4 Sham has a parcel that weighs 4 kilograms and 5 hundredths of a kilogram.
Write the weight of Sham's parcel as a decimal number.

3.2 Multiplying and dividing by 10, 100 and 1000

When you multiply a whole number or a decimal number by 10, the number becomes ten times bigger. This means that all the digits in the number move one place to the <u>left</u> in the place-value table.

$24 \times 10 = 240$

Hundreds	Tens	Units	•	Tenths	Hundredths
	2	4	•		
2	4	0	•		

> An empty space before the decimal point must be filled with a zero.

$0.24 \times 10 = 2.4$

Hundreds	Tens	Units	•	Tenths	Hundredths
		0	•	2	4
		2	•	4	

> An empty space at the end of the number, after the decimal point, does not need to be filled with a zero.

When you multiply by 100 all the digits move two places to the left.

When you multiply by 1000 all the digits move three places to the left.

Worked example 3.2A

Work out the answer to each of the following.

a 45×100 **b** 3.79×10

Solution

Thousands	Hundredths	Tenths	Units	•	Tenths
		4	5	•	
4	5	0	0	•	

a $45 \times 100 = 4500$ Move the digits two places to the left and fill the empty spaces with zeros.

b $3.79 \times 10 = 37.9$ Move the digits one place to the left. There are no empty spaces to fill with zeros.

Similarly, when you divide a whole number or a decimal number by 10 all the digits in the number move one place to the <u>right</u> in the place-value table.

$24 \div 10 = 2.4$

> An empty space before the first digit does not need to be filled with a zero.

Tens	Units	•	Tenths	Hundredths
2	4	•		
	2	•	4	

$0.24 \div 10 = 0.024$

> An empty space before the decimal point should be filled with a zero.

Tens	Units	•	Tenths	Hundredths	Thousandths
	0	•	2	4	
	0	•	0	2	4

When you divide by 100 all the digits move two places to the right.

When you divide by 1000 all the digits move three places to the right.

Worked example 3.2B

Work out the answer to each of the following: **a** $32 \div 1000$ **b** $47.96 \div 10$

Solution

a $32 \div 1000 = 0.032$ Move the digits three places to the right and fill the empty spaces with zeros.

b $47.96 \div 10 = 4.796$ Move the digits one place to the right. There are no empty spaces to fill with zeros.

◆ Exercise 3.2

1 Work these out.

   a 4.6×10 **b** 0.389×10 **c** 2.5×100 **d** 0.07×100

   e 6.5×1000 **f** 0.0389×1000 **g** $700 \div 10$ **h** $4.22 \div 10$

   i $620 \div 100$ **j** $43 \div 100$ **k** $420 \div 1000$ **l** $8.1 \div 1000$

2 Hannah works out $52 \div 10$ and 4.6×100.
She checks her answers by working backwards.
Work out the answers to these questions.
Check your answers by working backwards.

   a 3.7×10 **b** 0.42×1000

   c $6.7 \div 10$ **d** $460 \div 100$

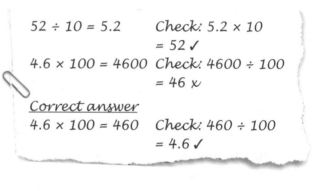

$52 \div 10 = 5.2$ *Check:* 5.2×10
                              $= 52$ ✓

$4.6 \times 100 = 4600$ *Check:* $4600 \div 100$
                                $= 46$ ✗

Correct answer
$4.6 \times 100 = 460$ *Check:* $460 \div 100$
                              $= 4.6$ ✓

3 Which symbol, $\times$ or $\div$, goes in each box to make the statement correct?

   a $45 \square 10 = 4.5$ **b** $3.2 \square 100 = 320$

   c $0.02 \square 1000 = 20$ **d** $0.3 \square 100 = 0.003$

   e $560 \square 1000 = 0.56$ **f** $0.09 \square 10 = 0.9$

4 Which of 10, 100 or 1000 goes in each box to make the statement correct?

   a $3.8 \times \square = 38$ **b** $0.002 \times \square = 0.02$ **c** $0.05 \times \square = 50$

   d $6.12 \times \square = 6120$ **e** $21 \div \square = 0.21$ **f** $730 \div \square = 7.3$

   g $56 \div \square = 0.056$ **h** $0.2 \div \square = 0.002$ **i** $0.8 \div \square = 0.08$

5 Use the numbers from the box to complete these calculations.
You can only use each number once. You should have no
numbers left at the end.

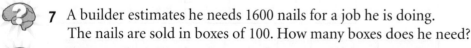

   0.047 8.2 0.04 110 0.3 0.82 300 3.2

   a $11 \times 10 = \square$ **b** $4 \div 100 = \square$ **c** $\square \times 100 = 320$

   d $47 \div 1000 = \square$ **e** $\square \div 10 = \square$ **f** $\square \times 1000 = \square$

6 In a supermarket lemons are sold in bags of 10 for $3.50.
How much does each lemon cost?

7 A builder estimates he needs 1600 nails for a job he is doing.
The nails are sold in boxes of 100. How many boxes does he need?

8 Alexi thinks of a number. He multiplies his number by 10, and
then divides the answer by 100. He then multiplies this answer by 1000
and gets a final answer of 67. What number does Alexi think of first?

3 Place value, ordering and rounding

3.3 Ordering decimals

To order decimal numbers you must write them in order of size, from the smallest to the largest.

Different whole-number parts

First compare the whole-number part of the numbers.

Look at these three decimal numbers. 8.9, 14.639, 6.45

If you highlight just the whole-number parts you get: 8.9, 14.639, 6.45

Now you can see that 14 is the biggest and 6 is the smallest of the whole numbers.

So, in order of size, the numbers are: 6.45, 8.9, 14.639

Same whole-number parts

When you have to put in order numbers with the <u>same</u> whole-number part, you must first compare the tenths, then the hundredths, and so on.

Look at these three decimal numbers. 2.82, 2.6, 2.816

They all have the same whole number of 2. 2.82, 2.6, 2.816

If you highlight just the tenths you get: 2.82, 2.6, 2.816

Now you can see that 2.6 is the smallest, but the other two both have 8 tenths, so highlight the hundredths. 2.6, 2.82, 2.816

You can now see that 2.816 is smaller than 2.82.

So, in order of size, the numbers are: 2.6, 2.816, 2.82

> Put the 2.6 at the start as you now know it's the smallest number.

Worked example 3.3

Write the decimal numbers in each set in order of size.
 a 6.8, 4.23, 7.811, 0.77 b 4.66, 4.6, 4.08

a 0.77, 4.23, 6.8, 7.811 All these numbers have a different whole-number part, so you don't need to compare the decimal part. Simply write them in order of their whole-number parts, which are 0, 4, 6 and 7.

b 4.08, 4.6, 4.66 All these numbers have the same whole-number part, so start by comparing the tenths. 4.08 comes first as it has the smallest number of tenths (zero tenths). 4.6 and 4.66 have the same number of tenths, so compare the hundredths. 4.6 is the same as 4.60 so it has 0 hundredths. 4.6 comes before 4.66 which has 6 hundredths.

Exercise 3.3

1 Write down which is the smaller decimal number from each pair.
   a 13.5, 9.99 b 4.32, 3.67 c 12.56, 21.652
   d 127.06, 246.9 e 0.67, 0.72 f 3.4, 3.21
   g 18.54, 18.45 h 0.05, 0.043 i 0.09, 0.1

2 Write these decimal numbers in order of size, starting with the smallest.
   a 3.46, 2.6, 3.31, 3.49 b 0.71, 0.52, 0.77, 0.59 c 6.9, 6.82, 6.8, 6.97
   d 5.212, 5.2, 5.219, 5.199 e 32.448, 32.42, 32.441, 32.4 f 9.08, 9.7, 9.901, 9.03, 9.99

3 Greg uses the symbols < and > to show
that one number is smaller than or larger
than another.
Write the correct sign, < or >, between
each pair of numbers.

> 4.07 is smaller than 4.15, so 4.07 < 4.15
>
> 2.167 is bigger than 2.163, so 2.167 > 2.163

a 6.03 ☐ 6.24   **b** 9.35 ☐ 9.41   **c** 0.49 ☐ 0.51   **d** 18.05 ☐ 18.02

e 9.2 ☐ 9.01   **f** 2.19 ☐ 2.205   **g** 0.072 ☐ 0.06   **h** 29.882 ☐ 29.88

> The symbol < means 'is smaller than'.
>
> The symbol > means 'is bigger than'.

4 Ulrika uses a different method
to order decimals. Her method
is shown on the right.

Use Ulrika's method to write
the decimal numbers in each
set in order of size, starting
with the smallest.

a 2.7, 2.15, 2.009
b 3.45, 3.342, 3.2
c 17.05, 17.1, 17.125, 17.42

> Question
> Write the decimal numbers 4.23, 4.6 and 4.179
> in order of size, starting with the smallest.
> Solution
> 4.179 has the most decimal places, so give all
> the other numbers three decimal places by
> adding zeros at the end: 4.230, 4.600, 4.179
> Now compare 230, 600 and 179:   179 is
> smallest, then 230 then 600
> Numbers in order of size are: 4.179, 4.23, 4.6

5 The table shows six of the fastest times run by women in the 100 m sprint.

Name	Country	Date	Time (seconds)
Kerron Stewart	Jamaica	2009	10.75
Marion Jones	USA	1998	10.65
Merlene Ottey	Jamaica	1996	10.74
Carmelita Jeter	USA	2009	10.64
Shelley-Ann Fraser	Jamaica	2009	10.73
Florence Griffith-Joyner	USA	1988	10.49

Who is the fourth fastest woman runner? Explain how you worked out your answer.

6 Brad puts these decimal number cards in order of size, starting with the smallest.
He has spilt tea on the middle card.

| 3.07 | | 3. 🍵 | | 3.083 |

Write down three possible numbers that could be on the middle card.

3.4 Rounding

Sometimes you need to **round** numbers. When you round a number you get an **approximate** value.

To round a number:

- to the nearest 10, look at the digit in the units column
- to the nearest 100, look at the digit in the tens column
- to the nearest 1000, look at the digit in the hundreds column.

> If the value of the digit is 5 or more, round up. If the value is less than 5, round down.

Worked example 3.4A

Round 12 874 to the nearest: **a** 10   **b** 100   **c** 1000.

a 12 874 = 12 870 (to the nearest 10)   The digit in the units column is 4. As 4 is less than 5, round down. The 7 in the tens column stays the same.

b 12 874 = 12 900 (to the nearest 100)   The digit in the tens column is 7. As 7 is more than 5, round up. The 8 in the hundreds column is replaced by 9.

c 12 874 = 13 000 (to the nearest 1000)   The digit in the hundreds column is 8. As 8 is more than 5, round up. The 2 in the thousands column is replaced by 3.

To round a decimal number:
- to the nearest whole number, look at the digit in the tenths column
- to one decimal place, look at the digit in the hundredths column.

Worked example 3.4B

Round 13.524 cm: **a** to the nearest whole number   **b** to one decimal place.

a 13.524 cm = 14 cm (to the nearest whole number)   The digit in the tenths column is 5 so round up. The 3 in the units column becomes a 4.

b 13.524 cm = 13.5 cm (to one decimal place)   The digit in the hundredths column is 2. As 2 is less than 5, round down. The 5 in the tenths column stays the same.

Exercise 3.4

1 Round each number to the nearest 10.
    a 32   **b** 78   **c** 145   **d** 363   **e** 1479   **f** 3804

2 Round each number to the nearest 1000.
    a 1200   **b** 2550   **c** 3707   **d** 8090   **e** 13892   **f** 792

3 Razi says: 'If I round 496 to the nearest 10 and to the nearest 100, I get the same answer!'
 Is Razi correct? Explain your answer.

4 Round each number to one decimal place.
    a 0.63   **b** 8.27   **c** 2.461   **d** 9.194   **e** 12.861   **f** 0.066

5 Kylie and Jason are both rounding 23.981 to one decimal place.
 Kylie gets an answer of 24 and Jason gets an answer of 24.0.
 Who is correct? Explain your answer.

3.5 Adding and subtracting decimals

When you add and subtract decimal numbers <u>mentally</u>, there are different methods you can use.

- When you are adding, you can break down the numbers into their whole-number and decimal parts. Then add the whole-number parts, add the decimal parts, and finally add the whole-number answer to the decimal answer.
- When you are subtracting, you can break down the number you are subtracting into its whole-number part and decimal part. Then subtract the whole-number part first and subtract the decimal part second.
- If one of the numbers you are adding or subtracting is close to a whole number, you can round it to the nearest whole number, do the addition or subtraction, then adjust your answer at the end.

Worked example 3.5A

Work these out mentally.   **a** $2.3 + 7.8$ **b** $6.9 + 12.4$ **c** $13.3 - 5.8$

a $2.3 + 7.8 = 2 + 7 + 0.3 + 0.8$	Break the numbers into whole-number and decimal parts.
$= 9 + 1.1$	Add the whole-number parts and add the decimal parts.
$= 10.1$	Add the whole-number answer to the decimal answer.
b $6.9 + 12.4 = 7 + 12.4 - 0.1$	Round 6.9 up to 7 and subtract 0.1 later.
$= 19.4 - 0.1$	Add 7 to 12.4.
$= 19.3$	Subtract 0.1.
c $13.3 - 5.8 = 13.3 - 6 + 0.2$	Round 5.8 up to 6 and add 0.2 later.
$= 7.3 + 0.2$	Subtract 6 from 13.3.
$= 7.5$	Add 0.2.

When you use a <u>written method</u> to add and subtract decimal numbers, always write the calculation in columns, with the decimal points vertically in line. Then add and subtract as normal but remember to write the decimal point in your answer.

Worked example 3.5B

Work these out.   **a** $27.52 + 4.8$ **b** $43.6 - 5.45$

a
```
    2 7 . 5 2
  +   4 . 8
  -----------
    3 2 . 3 2
      1   1
```

Start with the hundredths column: $2 + 0 = 2$.
Next add the tenths: $5 + 8 = 13$; write down the 3, carry the 1.
Now add the units: $7 + 4 + 1 = 12$; write down the 2, carry the 1.
Finally add the tens: $2 + 1 = 3$.

b
```
   ³4̶ ¹3 . ⁵6̶ ¹0
  -    5 . 4 5
  -----------
    3 8 . 1 5
```

First write 43.6 as 43.60.

Start by subtracting in the hundredths column: you can't take 5 from 0 ($0 - 5$), so borrow from the 6 tenths, then work out $10 - 5 = 5$.

Now subtract the tenths: $5 - 4 = 1$.
Now the units: you can't take 5 from 3 ($3 - 5$), so borrow from the 4 tens, then work out $13 - 5 = 8$.
Finally the tens: $3 - 0 = 3$.

3 Place value, ordering and rounding

◆ Exercise 3.5

1 Use a mental method to work out the answers to these.

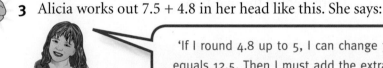

a 3.5 + 4.2   **b** 4.6 + 3.7   **c** 12.7 + 4.5

d 4.9 − 1.5   **e** 12.6 − 5.2   **f** 14.6 − 6.8

> Break the numbers into their whole-number parts and their decimal parts.

2 Use a different mental method to work out the answers to these.

a 4.9 + 7.3   **b** 9.6 + 8.9   **c** 22.8 + 3.3

d 5.4 − 1.9   **e** 14.9 − 4.4   **f** 21.1 − 6.7

> Use the method of rounding one of the numbers to a whole number.

3 Alicia works out 7.5 + 4.8 in her head like this. She says:

> 'If I round 4.8 up to 5, I can change 7.5 + 4.8 to 7.5 + 5, which equals 12.5. Then I must add the extra 0.2, which gives me 12.7.'

Is Alicia correct? Explain your answer.

4 Use a written method to work these out.

a 5.79 + 4.15   **b** 25.81 + 58.4   **c** 8.76 − 4.14   **d** 38.9 − 19.78

5 At the cinema, Priya spends $4.75 on a ticket, $1.75 on sweets and $0.85 on a drink.

a How much does she spend altogether?

b Priya pays with a $10 bill.
How much change does she receive?

6 Jed is a plumber.
He has four lengths of pipe that measure
1.8 m, 3.5 m, 2.45 m and 0.85 m.

a What is the total length of the four pipes?

b Jed needs 10 m of pipe altogether.
How much more pipe does he need to buy?

7 Moira went on a diet. She recorded her weight at the start and end of every month.
Here are her records for June and July.

	Weight (kg)		Weight (kg)
Start of June	95.45	End of June	91.92
Start of July	91.92	End of July	88.35

a During which month, June or July, did Moira lose more weight?

b At the start of August Moira weighed 88.35 kg. During August she lost 1.82 kg.
How much did Moira weigh at the end of August?

8 Work out the missing digits in these calculations.

a
```
  □ 2 . □ 1
+ 2 □ . 3 □
─────────────
  6 9 . 1 6
```

b
```
  6 □ . 6 4
− □ 9 . 5 □
─────────────
  3 8 . □ 6
```

3.6 Multiplying decimals

When you multiply a decimal number, you must remember the decimal place-value table.

Follow these steps when you multiply a decimal by a single-digit number.

Units	•	Tenths	Hundredths	Thousandths
1	•	$\frac{1}{10}$	$\frac{1}{100}$	$\frac{1}{1000}$

- At first, ignore the decimal point and work out the multiplication.
- Finally, put the decimal point in the answer. There must be the same number of digits after the decimal point in the answer as there were in the question.

Worked example 3.6

a Work these out mentally.   **i** 0.2 × 4   **ii** 0.6 × 2
b Use a written method to work out 4 × 2.16.

a i   2 × 4 = 8   Ignore the decimal point and work out 2 × 4.
   0.2 × 4 = 0.8   Put the decimal point back into the answer. There's 1 digit after the decimal point in the question, so there must be 1 digit after the decimal point in the answer.

ii 6 × 2 = 12   Ignore the decimal point and work out 6 × 2.
   0.6 × 2 = 1.2   Put the decimal point back into the answer. There's 1 digit after the decimal point in the question, so there must be 1 digit after the decimal point in the answer.

b   2   1   6   Ignore the decimal point and work out 216 × 4.
    ×   4
   ─────────────
     8   6   4
         ₂   Put the decimal point back into the answer. There are 2 digits after the
                         decimal point in the question, so there must be 2 digits after the decimal
   4 × 2.16 = 8.64   point in the answer.

◆ **Exercise 3.6**

1   Use a mental method to work these out.
   a 0.1 × 8   **b** 0.3 × 3   **c** 0.5 × 5   **d** 0.7 × 6   **e** 0.9 × 2

2   Use a written method to work these out.
   a 5 × 2.7   **b** 8 × 3.6   **c** 3 × 9.8   **d** 3.15 × 2

3   Use the numbers from the box to complete these calculations.
   You can only use each number once. You should have no
   numbers left at the end.

   | 18.3 2 36.8 |
   | 0.6 6.1 7 0.7 |

   a 0.1 × 6 = ☐   **b** 0.4 × ☐ = 2.8   **c** ☐ × 5 = 3.5
   d 4.3 × ☐ = 8.6   **e** 9.2 × 4 = ☐   **f** ☐ × 3 = ☐

4   Anders and Jake both work out the answer to 0.8 × 5.
   Anders says: 'The answer is 4.0.' Jake says: 'The answer is 4.'
   Are they both correct? Explain your answer.

3.7 Dividing decimals

When you divide a decimal number by a single-digit number:
- use **short division**
- keep the decimal point in the question and write the decimal point in the answer above the decimal point in the question.

Worked example 3.7

Work these out.   **a** 4.86 ÷ 2   **b** 29.35 ÷ 5

a
```
      2
  2)4 . 8 6
```
First of all work out 4 ÷ 2 = 2. Write the 2 above the 4.

```
      2
  2)4 . 8 6
```
Now write the decimal point in the answer.

```
    2 . 4 3
  2)4 . 8 6
```
Now work out 8 ÷ 2 = 4 and write the answer above the 8.
Finally work out 6 ÷ 2 = 3 and write the answer above the 6.

b
```
       5
  5)2 9 . ⁴3 5
```
First, try to work out 2 ÷ 5. You can't do it, so work out 29 ÷ 5 = 5 remainder 4.
Write the 5 above the 9 and carry the 4 across to before the 3.

```
       5 .
  5)2 9 . ⁴3 5
```
Now write the decimal point in the answer.

```
       5 . 8
  5)2 9 . ⁴3 ³5
```
Now work out 43 ÷ 5 = 8 remainder 3.
Write the 8 above the ⁴3 and carry the 3 across to before the 5.

```
       5 . 8 7
  5)2 9 . ⁴3 ³5
```
Now work out 35 ÷ 5 = 7.
Write the 7 above the ³5.

Exercise 3.7

1 Work these out.
  a 6.3 ÷ 3   **b** 4.6 ÷ 2   **c** 4.9 ÷ 7   **d** 8.4 ÷ 3   **e** 9.1 ÷ 7

2 Work these out.
  a 8.26 ÷ 2   **b** 6.93 ÷ 3   **c** 4.84 ÷ 4   **d** 18.66 ÷ 6   **e** 45.05 ÷ 5

3 Shen sees this sign in a supermarket.
What is the cost of one chicken? | 5 chickens for $18.25 |

4 Maggie pays $9.28 for 8 m of ribbon.
What is the cost of the ribbon per metre?

5 Copy and complete these divisions.

  a
```
    □ .  1 □
  2)6 .  □ ¹8
```
  b
```
    2 .  □ 5
  3)□ .  ¹9 □
```
  c
```
      5 .  □ 9
  □)3 5 . ⁵3 □
```

3.8 Estimating and approximating

When solving a problem, it is always a good idea to start with a rough **estimate** of what the answer should be.

To use an estimate to check if your answer is correct, follow these steps.

1 Round each of the numbers in the question.

Round: numbers in the thousands to the nearest 1000

numbers in the hundreds to the nearest 100

numbers in the tens to the nearest 10

numbers between 1 and 10 to the nearest 1.

For example:
- round 4390 to 4000
- round 185 to 200
- round 32 to 30
- round 2.82 to 3.

2 Complete the calculation, using the rounded numbers to give you an approximate answer.

3 Work out the accurate answer.

4 If your approximate answer is close to your accurate answer, you have probably got the answer right!

> **Worked example 3.8A**
>
> Work these out. **a** $6210 \div 276$ **b** $\dfrac{213 \times 3.97}{19}$
>
> **a** Estimate: $6000 \div 300 = 20$
> Accurate: $6210 \div 276 = 22.5$
>
> Round 6210 to 6000 and 276 to 300 and then divide.
> Work out the accurate answer.
> 20 is close to 22.5, so the answer is probably correct.
>
> **b** Estimate: $\dfrac{200 \times 4}{20} = 40$
>
> Round 213 to 200, 3.97 to 4 and 19 to 20.
> Multiply 200 by 4 to give 800, then divide 800 by 20.
>
> Accurate: $\dfrac{213 \times 3.97}{19} = 44.5$ (1 d.p.)
>
> Work out the accurate answer.
> 40 is close to 44.5 so the answer is probably correct.

Another way to check if an answer is correct is to use an **inverse operation**.

To check if your answer is correct using an inverse operation, simply follow one of these steps.

1 If your calculation involved an <u>addition</u>, check the answer by doing a <u>subtraction</u>.

2 If your calculation involved a <u>subtraction</u>, check the answer by doing an <u>addition</u>.

3 If your calculation involved a <u>multiplication</u>, check the answer by doing a <u>division</u>.

4 If your calculation involved a <u>division</u>, check the answer by doing a <u>multiplication</u>.

> **Worked example 3.8B**
>
> Work these out. **a** $723 + 476$ **b** 2.76×9
>
> **a** $723 + 476 = 1199$
> Check: $1199 - 476 = 723$
>
> Work out the accurate answer.
> Check the addition by doing a subtraction.
>
> Or use $1199 - 723 = 476$
>
> **b** $2.76 \times 9 = 24.84$
> Check: $24.84 \div 9 = 2.76$
>
> Work out the accurate answer.
> Check the multiplication by doing a division.
>
> Or use $24.84 \div 2.76 = 9$

When you are asked to solve a problem, as well as using an estimate or an inverse operation to check your answer, you should present your work clearly and neatly.

When you are writing out your solution, imagine someone else is looking over your shoulder. Make sure that when they read your work they can understand <u>exactly</u> what you have done and why.

Worked example 3.8C

a Madai runs in a marathon. The total distance is 26.2 miles. After 1 hour Madai has run 8.7 miles. How much further has she got to run?

b There are 1125 portable toilets along the marathon route. They are arranged into 12 toilet blocks. How many toilets should be in each toilet block?

a $26.2 - 8.7 = 17.5$	Work out the answer and make sure you write down the complete calculation
She has to run another 17.5 miles.	Write your answer in a sentence that explains what you have worked out. Make sure you include the units (miles).
Check: $17.5 + 8.7 = 26.2$ ✓	Use an inverse operation to check your answer.
b $1125 \div 12 = 93.75$	Work out the answer and make sure you write down the complete calculation.
There will be about 94 toilets in each toilet block.	Write your answer in a sentence that explains what you have worked out. Make sure your answer is sensible.
	You can't have 93.75 toilets so choose 93 or 94 as your answer.
Check: $1000 \div 10 = 100$ ✓	Use estimation to check your answer. 100 is close to 94 so the answer is probably right.

◆ Exercise 3.8

1 Work out an estimate for each calculation.

a $69 + 47$	**b** $81 - 38$	**c** 72×49	**d** $63 \div 18$
e $137 + 912$	**f** $292 - 64$	**g** 289×23	**h** $672 \div 21$

> Don't work out the accurate answer yet.

2 Work out the accurate answer for each of the parts of question 1.
Compare your estimates with your accurate answers to check your accurate answers are correct.

3 For each of these questions:
  i work out an estimate of the answer
  ii work out the correct answer, to one decimal place
  iii compare your estimate with the accurate answer to check your answer is correct.

a $\dfrac{194 + 45.7}{14}$	**b** $\dfrac{618.2 - 78.5}{39}$	**c** $\dfrac{36.5 \times 4}{76}$	**d** $\dfrac{8 \times 58.27}{23}$

4 For each of these questions:
  i work out the accurate answer
  ii use an inverse operation to check your answer.

  a $27.9 + 132.5$ **b** $67.09 - 39.52$ **c** 7×13.8 **d** $46.29 \div 3$

In questions 5 to 7:
   i   solve the problem
   ii explain what you have worked out
   iii check your answer by estimation or using an inverse operation
   iv make sure your workings are clear and neatly presented.

5 Daha is training for a bicycle race.
    On Monday he cycles 16.6 km and on Wednesday
    he cycles 24.8 km.
    a What is the total distance he has cycled?
    b Daha wants to cycle a total of 70 km every week.
       How much further does he have to cycle this week?

6 Aamina is an electrician. She charges $28 an hour.
    a It takes Aamina 6.5 hours to do one job. What is the
       total amount she charges for this job?
    b To do another job she charges a total of $343. How many
       hours did this job take her?

7 Hannah writes a recipe book. The recipe book uses 36 sheets of
    paper. She wants to produce 75 copies of the book. There are 500
    sheets of paper in one pack. How many packs of paper does she need?

Summary

You should now know that:

★ A decimal number always has a decimal point.

★ The digits to the left of the decimal point represent the whole-number part of a decimal number.

★ The digits to the right of the decimal point represent the fractional part of a decimal number.

★ When you multiply a number by 10, 100 or 1000 the digits move to the left one, two or three places.

★ When you divide a number by 10, 100 or 1000 the digits move to the right one, two or three places.

★ It is always a good idea to estimate the answer to a question before you work it out, so that you know whether your answer is realistic or not.

★ To work out an approximate answer, round all your numbers to the nearest 10, 100, … before doing the calculation.

★ Checking your work should help you find any errors before anyone else does.

★ Presenting your work neatly helps you and anyone else understand what you have done.

You should be able to:

★ Describe the value of each digit in a decimal number.

★ Multiply and divide whole numbers and decimals by 10, 100 and 1000.

★ Write decimals in order of size from the smallest to the largest.

★ Round whole numbers to the nearest 10, 100 or 1000.

★ Round decimals, including measurements, to the nearest whole number or one decimal place.

★ Add and subtract integers and decimals.

★ Multiply and divide decimals with one or two places by single-digit numbers.

★ Work out estimates or approximate answers to questions.

★ Use inverse operations and estimation to check working.

End of unit review

1 Here are some decimal numbers.

| 5.012 | 0.66 | 19.8 | 123.01 | 2.39 | 23.1 |

Write down all the numbers that have two decimal places.

2 Write down the value of the green digit in each of these numbers.
   a 132.5   **b** 69.27   **c** 4.882   **d** 61.05

3 a Work these out.   **i** 49 × 10   **ii** 2.3 ÷ 10   **iii** 0.034 × 1000   **iv** 876 ÷ 100
   b Use an inverse operation to check all your answers to part **a**. Show your working.

4 Copy and complete these calculations by filling in the empty boxes.
   a 2.5 × □ = 250   **b** 3.2 ÷ □ = 0.0032   **c** 0.17 □ 10 = 1.7

5 Write these numbers in order of size, starting with the smallest: 5.49, 4.2, 5.3, 5.498

6 Round 4753:   **a** to the nearest 10   **b** to the nearest 100   **c** to the nearest 1000.

7 Round 76.189:   **a** to the nearest whole number   **b** to one decimal place.

8 This is part of Dafydd's homework.
   a Explain what Dafydd has done wrong.
   b Write the correct answer.

> *Question*
> Round 39.47 to the nearest whole number.
>
> *Solution*
> The 7 rounds the 4 up to a 5 so 39.47 = 39.5
> Then the 5 rounds the 39 up to 40.
> So, 39.47 = 40 (to the nearest whole number)

9 Work these out.
   a 13.45 + 9.3   **b** 8 + 9.76 + 23.45   **c** 45.95 − 23.7   **d** 239.8 − 47.64

10 Shona goes for a run four times a week.
   During one week she runs 3.6 km, 4.85 km, 10.5 km and 7.45 km.
   How far did Shona run in this week?

11 Work these out.
   a 2 × 0.2   **b** 0.9 × 4   **c** 8 × 3.8   **d** 6 × 4.17

12 Sion sees this sign in a supermarket.
   What is the cost of one jar of coffee?

   3 jars of coffee for $13.89

13 For each part of this question:
   i work out an estimate of the answer
   ii work out the correct answer
   iii compare your estimate with the accurate answer to check your answer is correct.
   a 36 + 68 + 212   **b** 322 × 19

14 Andreas is training for a swimming competition.
   The table shows the number of lengths of the
   swimming pool that he swims during one week.
   The swimming pool has a length of 25 m.
   How far does Andreas swim this week?
   Use estimation to check your answer.

	Monday	Wednesday	Friday
No. of lengths	62	78	56

4 Length, mass and capacity

The metric system that is used today was developed in France, in the late 18th century, by Antoine Lavoisier.

At the time, different countries used different units for measuring, which was very confusing. The modern metric system is called the International System of Units (SI) and is now used by about 95% of the world's population.

Antoine Lavoisier (1743–1794).

Some countries that use the metric system, however, still use some of their old units as well as the metric units. A good example of this is the UK and the USA, where miles, not kilometres, are shown on road signs.

In everyday life people are often measuring and weighing. In many jobs it is vital that measurements are done accurately.

A chef needs to weigh the ingredients needed in the recipe.

If these measurements are wrong, bread and cakes may not rise or the food may not taste very nice.

An athletics track must be measured accurately.

One circuit of the running track must be exactly 400 m. The length of the sprint track must be exactly 100 m.

New world, Olympic or national records can only be set if distances are accurately measured.

In this unit you will learn more about reading scales on measuring instruments and using metric measurements.

4.1 Knowing metric units

You can use a tape measure or a ruler to measure distances.

The **metric units** of **length** are the **millimetre (mm)**, **centimetre (cm)**, **metre (m)** and **kilometre (km)**.

You can use scales to weigh objects.

The metric units of **mass** are the **gram (g)**, **kilogram (kg)** and **tonne (t)**.

You can use a measuring jug to measure how much liquid there is in a container.

The metric units of **capacity** are the **millilitre (ml)** and **litre (l)**.

You need to know these conversion factors.

Units of length	Units of mass	Units of capacity
10 mm = 1 cm	1000 g = 1 kg	1000 ml = 1 l
100 cm = 1 m	1000 kg = 1 t	
1000 m = 1 km		

You can convert between different metric units by multiplying or dividing by 10, 100 or 1000.

When you are converting a smaller unit into a bigger one you <u>divide</u> by the conversion factor.

Example: To change metres to kilometres, grams to kilograms or millilitres to litres, divide by 1000.

When you are converting a bigger unit into a smaller one you <u>multiply</u> by the conversion factor.

Example: To change kilometres to metres, kilograms to grams or litres to millilitres, multiply by 1000.

When you order decimal numbers that involve measurements, you must make sure all your measurements are in the <u>same units</u>.

Worked example 4.1

a Convert these measures. **i** 3.2 km into metres **ii** 750 g into kilograms
b Write the following lengths in increasing order of size. 50 cm, 0.4 m, 345 mm

a i 1 km = 1000 m The conversion factor is 1000.
　3.2 × 1000 = 3200 m You are changing from a bigger unit (km) to a smaller one (m) so multiply by the conversion factor.

ii 1000 g = 1 kg The conversion factor is 1000.
　750 ÷ 1000 = 0.75 kg You are changing from a smaller unit (g) to a bigger one (kg) so divide by the conversion factor.

b 0.4 m = 40 cm Change the measurements so that they are all in centimetres.
345 mm = 34.5 cm
50 cm, 40 cm, 34.5 cm Rewrite the question with all the lengths in centimetres.
34.5 cm, 40 cm, 50 cm Now compare the lengths and write them in order.
345 mm, 0.4 m, 50 cm Finally write the lengths in the units in which they were given.

◆ Exercise 4.1

1 Write down the appropriate letter, A, B, C or D, for the correct method for each conversion.
   a m to cm   **A** × 100   **B** ÷ 100   **C** × 1000   **D** ÷ 1000
   b ml to l   **A** × 100   **B** ÷ 100   **C** × 1000   **D** ÷ 1000
   c kg to g   **A** × 100   **B** ÷ 100   **C** × 1000   **D** ÷ 1000
   d kg to t   **A** × 100   **B** ÷ 100   **C** × 1000   **D** ÷ 1000

2 Convert these lengths into the units shown.
   a 80 mm = ☐ cm   **b** 12 cm = ☐ mm   **c** 3 m = ☐ cm
   d 5000 m = ☐ km   **e** 560 cm = ☐ m   **f** 45 mm = ☐ cm
   g 4.3 km = ☐ m   **h** 1.8 m = ☐ cm   **i** 895 m = ☐ km

3 Convert these masses into the units shown.
   a 8000 kg = ☐ t   **b** 2 kg = ☐ g   **c** 3.4 t = ☐ kg
   d 5400 g = ☐ kg   **e** 0.8 kg = ☐ t   **f** 425 g = ☐ kg

4 Convert these capacities into the units shown.
   a 9000 ml = ☐ l   **b** 4 l = ☐ ml   **c** 5.2 l = ☐ ml
   d 3200 ml = ☐ l   **e** 0.5 l = ☐ ml   **f** 680 ml = ☐ l

5 a Copy and complete these conversions. All the answers are in the box.
   i 4.3 t × ☐ = 4300 kg   **ii** 8.5 ☐ × 10 = 85 mm
   iii 67 mm ☐ 10 = 6.7 cm   **iv** 0.43 m × 100 = ☐ cm
   v ☐ ml ÷ 1000 = 0.67 l   **vi** 850 ☐ ÷ 1000 = 0.85 ☐

43	kg	32	cm	670
g	×	÷	10	1000

   b There are three answers in the box that haven't been used.
      Write your own conversion that includes these three answers.

6 Write the decimal measurements in each set in order of size, starting with the smallest.
   a 35 cm, 0.38 m, 270 mm   **b** 4.2 l, 795 ml, 0.8 l
   c 0.125 kg, 0.08 kg, 95 g   **d** 6250 m, 6.2 km, 6.05 km

7 This is part of Mouna's homework.
   Is Mouna correct? Explain your answer.

Question Convert 2.3 m into mm.
Solution 2.3 × 1000 = 2300 mm

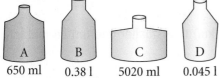

8 Shadi has four bottles.

A	B	C	D
650 ml	0.38 l	5020 ml	0.045 l

The bottles hold 650 ml, 0.38 l, 5020 ml and 0.045 l.

Shadi want to use the bottle that holds closest to $\frac{1}{2}$ litre.

Which bottle should he use? Show your working.

9

I am thinking of a length. My length is a whole number of
centimetres. It is smaller than 0.328 m but larger than 315 mm.

What length is Sasha thinking of?

4.2 Choosing suitable units

You should always choose appropriate units of measurement to measure and **estimate** length, mass and capacity.

Worked example 4.2

a Which units would you use to measure:
 i the height of a chair **ii** the mass of a dog?
b Ajani estimates the height of the door in his classroom to be 1.4 m.
 Is this estimate sensible? Give a reason for your answer.

a i cm   A chair is usually less than 1 m high, so centimetres would be the best unit to use.
 ii kg   Most dogs weigh more than 1 kg, so kilograms would be the best unit to use.
b No, an average adult is about 1.7 m tall, so 1.4 m would be too small.
   Compare Ajani's estimate with a height that you know then make a decision and
   give a reason.

Exercise 4.2

1 Which metric units would you use to measure the following?
  a the length of a football pitch   **b** the mass of an apple
  c the mass of an adult elephant   **d** the capacity of a mug
  e the width of a pencil   **f** the mass of a person
  g the length of this maths book   **h** the capacity of the petrol
                       tank of a car

2 Which measurement, A, B or C, do you think is most likely to be the correct one for each object?
  a the width of a computer screen   **A** 32 mm   **B** 32 cm   **C** 32 m
  b the mass of a banana   **A** 20 g   **B** 2 kg   **C** 200 g
  c the capacity of a bucket   **A** 5 l   **B** 50 l   **C** 50 ml
  d the height of a bus   **A** 300 mm **B** 30 m   **C** 3 m
  e the capacity of a teaspoon   **A** 500 ml **B** 5 l   **C** 5 ml
  f the mass of a horse   **A** 600 kg **B** 6 t   **C** 60 kg

3 Jayla has a brother who is 8 years old. She estimates his weight to be 65 kg. Is this estimate sensible?
 Give a reason for your answer.

4 Deion has a new pencil. He estimates that the length of the pencil is 16 cm. Is this estimate sensible?
 Give a reason for your answer.

5 Jamar has these cards.

| 80 | m | mass of a full suitcase | 10 | 1 |

capacity of a can of cola   cm

330   g   length of a toothbrush

kg   length of a house

25

mass of a mobile phone   18   capacity of a bath tub   ml   125

Sort the cards into their correct groups. Each group must contain one green, one pink
and one blue card.

4.3 Reading scales

When you read a **scale** you need to work out what each **division** on the scale represents.

On this scale there are four divisions between 0 and 100 g.

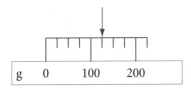

Each division represents 100 ÷ 4 = 25 g, so the arrow is pointing at 125 g.

Worked example 4.3

a Write down the value shown on this scale.

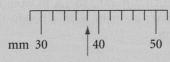

b Estimate the reading on this scale.

a 10 ÷ 5 = 2   There are 5 divisions between 30 and 40. Each division represents 2 mm.
   Value = 38 mm   30 + 8 = 38 or 40 − 2 = 38
b 10 ÷ 2 = 5 kg   There are 2 divisions between 40 and 50. Each division represents 5 kg.
   Estimate = 42 kg   The reading is almost halfway between 40 and 45, so 42 is a good estimate.

◆ **Exercise 4.3**

> Don't forget to include the units with each answer.

1 Write down the value shown on each of these scales.

a    **b** 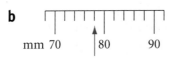   **c**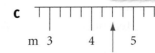

d 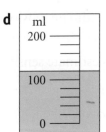   **e**    **f**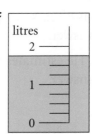

2 Anil says that this scale shows a mass of 6.2 kg.
   Is Anil correct?
   Explain your answer.

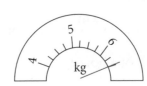

3 Estimate the readings on each of these scales.

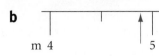

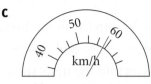

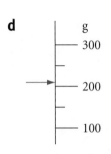

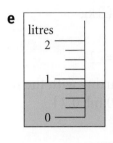

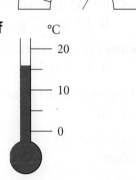

4 Mirai has two measuring jugs, A and B.

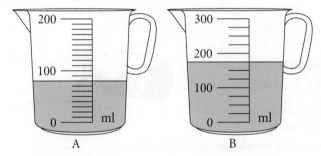

She pours water into the measuring jugs to the levels shown.
How much water does she need to add to measuring jug A so
that there is the same amount of water in both jugs?

Summary

You should now know that:

★ The conversion factors for length are:
10 mm = 1 cm, 100 cm = 1 m, 1000 m = 1 km
★ The conversion factors for mass are:
1000 g = 1 kg, 1000 kg = 1 t
★ The conversion factors for capacity are:
1000 ml = 1 l
★ When you are converting a smaller unit into a bigger one, you divide by the conversion factor.
★ When you are converting a bigger unit into a smaller one, you multiply by the conversion factor.
★ When you order decimal numbers that involve measurements, you must make sure all the measurements are in the same units.
★ When you read a scale you must start by working out what each division on the scale represents.

You should be able to:

★ Use abbreviations for the metric units of length, mass and capacity.
★ Convert between kilometres, metres, centimetres and millimetres.
★ Convert between tonnes, kilograms and grams.
★ Convert between litres and millilitres.
★ Choose suitable units of measurement to estimate, calculate and solve problems in everyday contexts.
★ Read the scales on a range of measuring instruments.
★ Understand everyday systems of measurement and use them to estimate, measure and calculate.
★ Work logically and draw simple conclusions.

End of unit review

1 Convert these lengths into the units shown.
   a 75 mm = ☐ cm   **b** 1.2 km = ☐ m   **c** 120 cm = ☐ m

2 Convert these masses into the units shown.
   a 2000 kg = ☐ t   **b** 3.2 kg = ☐ g   **c** 0.25 t = ☐ kg

3 Convert these capacities into the units shown.
   a 8000 ml = ☐ l   **b** 4.2 l = ☐ ml   **c** 650 ml = ☐ l

4 Write these decimal measurements in order of size, starting with the smallest.
   a 325 m, 850 cm, 0.2 km   **b** 3.6 l, 880 ml, 0.7 l

5 This is part of Xanti's homework.
   Is Xanti correct? Explain
   your answer.

Question *Convert 5650 mm into metres.*
Solution *5650 ÷ 1000 = 5.65 m*

6 Tiago has a 0.3 l bottle of medicine.
   He is told to take two 5 ml spoonfuls of medicine three times a day.
   How many days will the medicine last? Show your working.

7 Which metric units would you use to measure the following?
   a the length of a classroom   **b** the mass of a ship
   c the length of an eyelash   **d** the capacity of a breakfast cereal bowl.

8 Teresa's maths teacher is really tall. She estimates his height to be 2.5 m.
   Is this estimate sensible? Give a reason for your answer.

9 Write down the value shown on each of these scales.

   a

   cm 8   9   10

   b

   c
   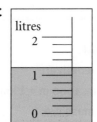

10 Estimate the readings on each of these scales.

   a

   cm 60   70

   b
   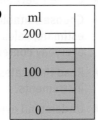

   c
   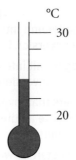

5 Angles

When you measure lengths you use different units, including millimetres, metres and kilometres. But length is not the only type of measurement you need to make when you are looking at flat shapes. Sometimes, you need to change direction, for example, if you turn a corner.

A turn between one direction and another is called an **angle**. You measure angles in **degrees**. One whole turn is 360 degrees, written as 360°.

Humans have needed to measure angles for a long time. When early astronomers looked at stars in the sky, they wanted to describe their positions relative to one another. The natural way to do this was to use angles. We know that the ancient Babylonians and Egyptians divided a whole turn into 360 parts, as long ago as 1500 BC.

Why are there 360 degrees in a whole turn?

A clay tablet excavated in Shush, in what is now modern-day Iran, shows that Babylonians divided a whole turn into 360 units. One reason could be that many simple fractions of a whole turn of 360°, including $\frac{1}{2}, \frac{1}{3}, \frac{1}{4}, \frac{1}{5}$ and $\frac{1}{6}$, can be written as a whole number of degrees. It may also be because there are approximately 360 days in a year.

The angles of a triangle

The sum or total of the angles of a triangle is always 180°.

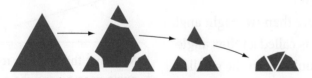

In this unit you will learn about other angle facts and use them to solve problems.

Ancient Babylonian tablet recording measurements.

5.1 Labelling and estimating angles

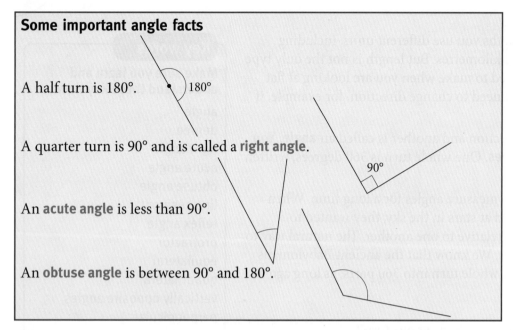

Some important angle facts

A half turn is 180°.   180°

A quarter turn is 90° and is called a **right angle**.   90°

An **acute angle** is less than 90°.

An **obtuse angle** is between 90° and 180°.

This diagram shows parts of lines between two points, AB, AC and AD.

You can label a line segment by writing down the letters of the points at each end of the line.

You can write the points in any order: AB and BA are two different ways to label the same line segment.

If you look again at the diagram, you can see several angles.

The angle between AB and AC is called <u>angle BAC</u> or <u>angle CAB</u>. The letter of the point of the angle is always in the middle.

Here is part of the diagram again.

There are <u>two</u> angles at A between AB and AC.

One is an acute angle. The other angle is more than two right angles.

An angle that is more than two right angles is called a **reflex angle**.

Normally, if you refer to 'angle BAC', you would mean the smaller of the two angles. If you want to refer to the other one, you must call it 'reflex angle BAC'.

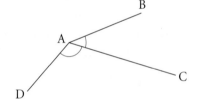

Note that the arc for a reflex angle goes around the outside.

Worked example 5.1

Angle CDE is a right angle. How big is reflex angle CDE?

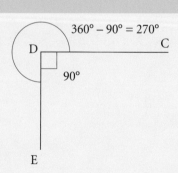

$360° - 90° = 270°$

Reflex angle CDE is 270°.
The two angles at D add up to 360°; $360° - 90° = 270°$.

Exercise 5.1

1 This diagram shows triangle ABC.
   a Sketch the triangle.   **b** Mark angle CBA.
   c Give a three-letter name for each of the other two angles.

2 Say whether each of these angles is acute, right, obtuse or reflex.

   a

   b

   c

   d

   e

   f

3 Here are the sizes of some angles. Say whether each one is acute, right, obtuse or reflex.
   a 120°   **b** 60°   **c** 200°   **d** 300°   **e** 10°   **f** 170°

4 Angle ABC is a right angle.
   Angles ABD and DBC are equal.

   Find the size of:

   a angle ABD
   b reflex angle ABC
   c reflex angle ABD
   d reflex angle CBD.

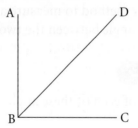

5 Every angle in each of the triangles in this diagram is 60°.
   Find the size of these angles.

   a ABC
   b AMC
   c MDE
   d reflex angle BMD
   e reflex angle AMF

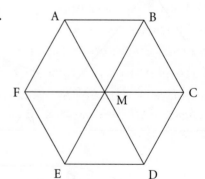

6 Each of these angles is a multiple of 30°. State the size of each one. Do not measure the angles.

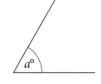

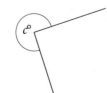

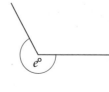
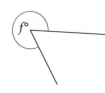

5.2 Drawing and measuring angles

You need to use a **protractor** to draw and measure reflex angles.

How to draw an angle of 245°

If you have a protractor that measures angles up to 360° you can measure 245° directly. If your protractor only goes up to 180°, use one of these methods.

Method 1: 245° – 180° = 65°. Measure 180° (half a turn) and then another 65°.

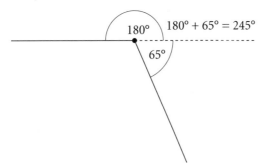

Method 2: A whole turn is 360° and 360° – 245° = 115°.

Measure an obtuse angle of 115° and the reflex angle between the two lines will be 245°.

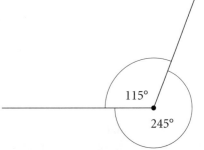

You can use a similar method to measure a reflex angle. Either divide it into 180° + another angle, or measure the smaller angle between the two line segments and subtract it from 360°.

◆ Exercise 5.2

1 Estimate the size of each of these angles. Then measure each one to see how close you were to the correct answer.

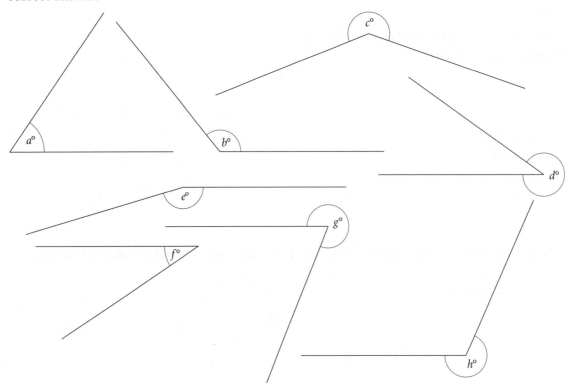

2 Draw angles of the following sizes.

   a 62°   **b** 157°   **c** 200°   **d** 295°   **e** 19°   **f** 111°   **g** 342°   **h** 233°

3 a Measure the angles labelled $x°$, $y°$ and $z°$.

> When we use small italic letters to label angles, each letter stands for a <u>number of degrees</u>.

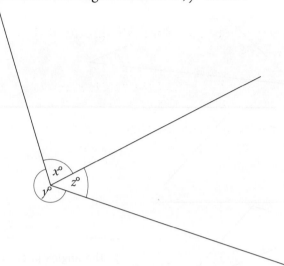

   b Explain why the angles should add up to 360°. Use this fact to check your accuracy.

4 a Measure the angles labelled $r°$, $s°$ and $t°$.

   b The angles should add up to 900°. Use this fact to check your accuracy.

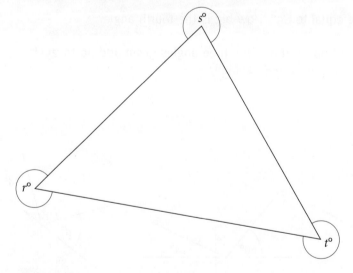

   c If the triangle was **equilateral**, what would be the values of r, s and t? Give a reason for your answer.

5 The angles of a triangle are 125°, 37° and 18°.

   a What are the reflex angles at the corners of this triangle?

   b Can you draw a triangle where one of the angles of the triangle is a reflex angle?

5.3 Calculating angles

Important angle facts

The angles round a point add up to 360°.

The angles on a straight line add up to 180°.

The three angles of a triangle add up to 180°.

$x + y + z = 180$

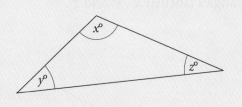

A four-sided shape is called a **quadrilateral**.

What can you say about the angles of a quadrilateral?

By adding another line, you can divide the quadrilateral into two triangles.

The six angles of the two triangles combine to make up the four angles of the quadrilateral.

The angles of a quadrilateral add up to $2 \times 180° = 360°$.

> The angles in each triangle add up to 180°.

Worked example 5.3

Three of the angles of a four-sided shape are equal to 85°. How big is the fourth angle?

$3 \times 85° = 255°$ All four angles add up to 360°. The three angles given add up to 255°.
The fourth angle is 105°.   The fourth angle is $360° - 255° = 105°$.

◆ Exercise 5.3

1 Calculate the sizes of the lettered angles.

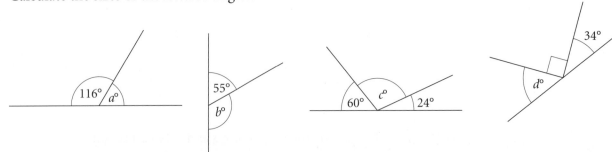

2 Calculate the sizes of the lettered angles.

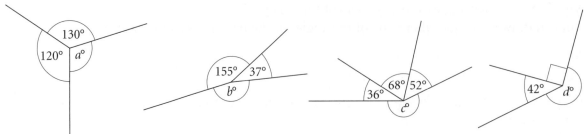

3 The angles in each of these diagrams are all the same size. How big is each one?

a  **b**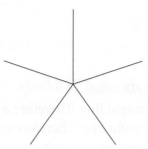

4 Calculate the size of angle ABC in each of these triangles.

a 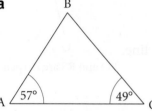 **b** 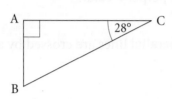 **c**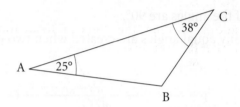

5 Calculate the size of angle BCD in each of these diagrams.

a 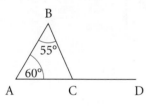 **b** 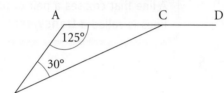 **c**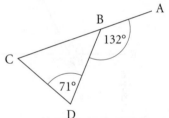

6 Three angles of a quadrilateral are 60°, 80° and 110°. How big is the fourth angle?

7 Calculate the sizes of the lettered angles in these quadrilaterals.

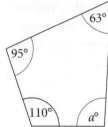

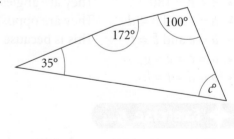

8 If all the angles of a quadrilateral are equal, what can you say about the quadrilateral?

9 Maha measures three of the angles of a quadrilateral.

> The angles are 125°, 160° and 90°.

How do you know she has made a mistake?

10 One angle of a quadrilateral is 150°. The other three angles are all the same size as each other. How big are they?

Section 5.4 Solving angle problems

This diagram shows two straight lines crossing.

Angles labelled $a°$ and $c°$ are **vertically opposite angles**. Angles labelled $b°$ and $d°$ are also opposite angles.

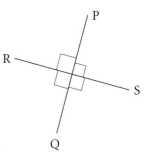

You can prove that <u>vertically opposite angles are equal</u>, as follows.

- $a + d = 180$ because they are angles on a straight line. Therefore $a = 180 - d$.
- $c + d = 180$ because they are angles on a straight line. Therefore $c = 180 - d$.
- Since a and c are both equal to $180 - d$, this means that $a = c$.

In the same way, you can show that $b = d$.

A special case of this is when two lines are **perpendicular**.

All the angles are 90°.

Many equal angles are created when two **parallel** lines are crossed by a third line.

PQ and RS are perpendicular.

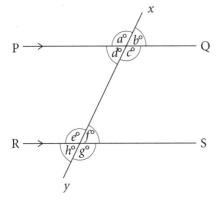

> A line that crosses a pair of parallel lines is called a **transversal**.

The arrows drawn on the diagram show that PQ and RS are parallel. XY is a straight line.

Check the following facts.

- $a + b = 180$ They are angles on a straight line.
- $a = c$ and $b = d$ They are opposite angles.
- $a = e$ and $b = f$ This is because PQ and RS are parallel.
- $a = c = e = g$
- $b = d = f = h$

> If you know one of the eight angles, you can find the other seven.

◆ Exercise 5.4

1 Prove angle APC = angle DPB.

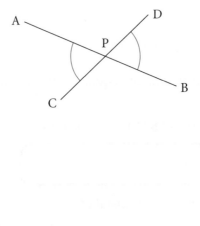

2 Three straight lines cross at one point.

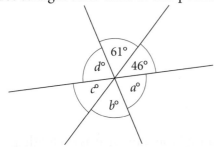

Calculate the values of a, b, c and d. Give reasons for your answers.

3 Lines WX and YZ are parallel.

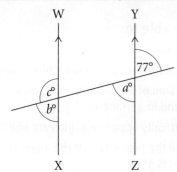

One angle of 77° is marked. Find the values of *a*, *b* and *c*.

4 This diagram shows four identical triangles.

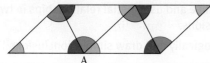

Look at the angles at point A.
Explain why this shows that the angles of a triangle add up to 180°.

5 ABC is an isosceles triangle. AB = BC and angle BAC = 40°.

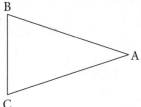

> An **isosceles** triangle
> has two equal sides and
> two equal angles.

Calculate the other two angles of the triangle.

6 Calculate the value of *a*.

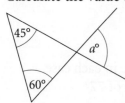

7 Explain why AB and AC are equal in length.

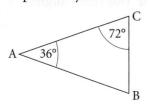

Summary

You should now know that:

★ Lines, angles and shapes can be identified by putting letters on the corners.

★ Reflex angles are greater than 180°.

★ A protractor can be used to measure angles.

★ The sum of the angles meeting at a point on one side of a straight line is 180°.

★ The sum of the angles in a triangle is 180° and this fact can be used to calculate angles.

★ The angles at a point add up to 360° and this fact can be used to calculate angles.

★ Vertically opposite angles are equal.

★ There are connections between the angles formed when a transversal crosses parallel lines.

You should be able to:

★ Label lines, angles and shapes.

★ Estimate, measure and draw angles of any size.

★ Calculate the sum of angles at a point, on a straight line and in a triangle.

★ Prove that vertically opposite angles are equal.

★ Derive and use the property that the angle sum of a quadrilateral is 360°.

★ Solve simple angle problems, and explain reasoning.

★ Start to recognise the angular connections with parallel lines.

★ Recognise and use spatial relationships in two dimensions.

★ Work logically and draw simple conclusions.

End of unit review

1 Write down the size of each of these angles.
  a angle ADC   **b** angle DBC
  c reflex angle AEB   **d** BCD

2 **a** Draw angles of the following sizes.
     i 47°   **ii** 147°   **iii** 247°   **iv** 347°
  b State whether each angle is acute, obtuse or reflex.

3 **a** Two angles of a triangle are given. Calculate the third angle in each case.
     i 45° and 75°   **ii** 8° and 11°
     iii 54° and 54°   **iv** 138° and 21°
  b Which of the triangles have two sides the same length?

4 Each of these sets are three angles of a quadrilateral. Calculate the fourth angle in each case.
  a 72°, 97° and 113°   **b** 55°, 55° and 155°   **c** three angles of 77°

5 Can a quadrilateral have:
  a four acute angles   **b** three obtuse angles   **c** one reflex angle   **d** two reflex angles?
  Justify your answer in each case.

6 AB and CD are parallel. Calculate the values of *s* and *t*.

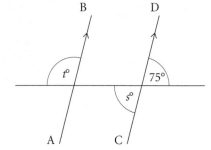

6 Planning and collecting data

What is **data**? Another word for data is **information**.

Many people work in jobs for which they need to collect information. For example, companies need to collect information from customers to see how they can improve their products or services. Doctors and nurses need to collect information to see how their patients are improving after taking certain medicines.

A scientist may carry out an experiment and use the results from the experiment to prove a new theory. They may be testing new medicines to see if they work. They may be testing new light bulbs to see if they last longer. Whatever they are testing, they are collecting information or data.

When you go on holiday, you may be asked to complete a questionnaire at the end of it. The holiday company likes to know what you thought about the services they provided. If everyone thought the hotel food was poor, then the hotel management needs to know so that they can talk to the chef. If everyone thought the cleanliness of their room was excellent, then the hotel manager needs to thank the cleaners for doing a great job. Any data they collect will help them improve their services.

> **Key words**
>
> **Make sure you learn and understand these key words:**
>
> data
> information
> primary data
> secondary data
> questionnaire
> data-collection sheet
> frequency table
> grouped frequency table
> class interval

Please tick one box for each question.

1   What did you think of the hotel facilities?
    ☐ Poor   ☐ Average   ☑ Good   ☐ Excellent

2   What did you think of the hotel food?
    ☑ Poor   ☐ Average   ☐ Good   ☐ Excellent

3   What did you think of the cleanliness of your room?
    ☐ Poor   ☐ Average   ☐ Good   ☑ Excellent

A company that makes a product, such as shoes, needs to collect information on the number of shoes that they sell. They need to know which sizes, colours and styles are the most popular, so they know which ones to produce the most of. It's not very sensible if they make more size 39 shoes than any other if most of the customers want a size 36! Whatever data they collect will help them decide which products are selling well and which aren't.

In this unit you will learn about collecting data.

6.1 Planning to collect data

When you want to answer questions or solve problems that need information, you need to know where to collect or find the data that you need. There are two types of data.

Primary data is information that you collect yourself. You can carry out a survey and ask people questions, or you can carry out an experiment and write down your results.

Secondary data is data that someone else has already collected. You can look on the internet or in books, newspapers and magazines to find this type of data.

Worked example 6.1

a If you were doing a survey, which units would you use to measure:
 i the weight of 12-year-old children
 ii the amount of time for which people are not at work due to illness?

b Where would you get data to help answer the following questions?
 i How many students are there in your school?
 ii Which ocean is the largest in the world?

c Would you collect primary data or secondary data to answer the following questions?
 i What is the favourite colour of the students in your class?
 ii What is the most popular make of car in your country?

d Mysha wants to know if the teachers in her school prefer to do a number puzzle or a crossword puzzle. She only asks the maths teachers. Will the results of her survey give a fair result?

a	**i** kg	Weights of children and adults are usually measured in kilograms.
	ii days	Records usually show how many days people take off work due to illness.
b	**i** School records	You could ask the school secretary, head teacher or class teacher to check the school records to find out how many students there are in your school.
	ii Encyclopaedia	You could look in an encyclopaedia, a fact book, a geography book or on the internet to find the answer to this question.
c	**i** Primary data	You would need to ask the students in your class what their favourite colour is to find the answer to the question.
	ii Secondary data	You wouldn't be able to collect this information yourself. You would need to find the information from somewhere else, such as government records, survey results or car company records.
d	No	She needs to ask teachers of all subjects. Maths teachers are probably more likely to do number puzzles than crossword puzzles since they like maths.

◆ Exercise 6.1

1 If you were doing a survey, which units shown on the right would you use to measure:
 a the time it takes to for a person to run 100 m
 b the distance a person can cycle in 1 hour
 c the length of time a person sleeps at night
 d the length of a person's thumbnail?

millilitres   kilometres   kilograms   days   seconds   millimetres   hours   metres

2 Where would you get data to help you answer the following questions?

   a How many loaves of bread does your local shop sell every day?

   b How many cars are sold in the world every year?

   c Which country has the highest mountain in the world?

   d How many students cycle to your school?

   e How many people live in your village or town?

3 Would you collect primary data or secondary data to answer the following questions?

   a What is the favourite football team of the students in your class?

   b Which football team has the biggest stadium in the world?

   c Which sport is played by the most students in your school?

   d How often do the members of your family eat fruit?

   e How many people live in your country?

4 When you collect primary data you can either

   i carry out a survey and ask people questions   or

   ii carry out an experiment and write down your results.

For each of the following questions, decide whether you should carry out a survey or an experiment. Write **i** or **ii** for each answer. The first one is done for you.

   a How many times does a dice land on '1' when it is rolled 50 times?   Answer: **ii**

   b What is the favourite song of students in your class?

   c How many brothers and sisters do students in your class have?

   d How many times does a coin land on 'heads' when it is flipped 20 times?

   e What is the most common shoe size of the students in your school?

   f What is the most common total score when you roll two dice?

   g How often do the members of your class visit the doctor?

5 Odita wants to know if the students in her school like to play cricket.

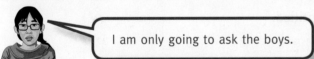

I am only going to ask the boys.

Will the results of her survey give a fair result?
Give a reason for your answer.

6 Taji wants to know when people prefer to do their shopping. He stands outside the supermarket on a Saturday and asks people as they come out of the shop.
Will the results of his survey give a fair result? Give a reason for your answer.

7 Taya wants to find out people's favourite sports. Every evening for one week she stands outside the swimming pool and asks people as they go in.
Will the results of her survey give a fair result? Give a reason for your answer.

6.2 Collecting data

One way of collecting data is to carry out a survey and ask people questions.

To do this you can use a **questionnaire**.

This is a list of questions that you want to know the answer to.

You must write the questions very carefully and try to follow these rules.

> A questionnaire is a form, with questions, that people fill in.

1 Ask short questions and use simple language. Give people boxes to tick whenever possible.

> *Are you* ☐ *male* ☐ *female*

2 Try to use questions that have a 'Yes' or 'No' answer.

> *Do you have any pets?*
> ☐ *yes* ☐ *no*

3 When there is a choice of answers, make sure there are no overlapping groups and that all possible answers are included.

> *How many pets do you have?*
> ☐ *0* ☐ *1-2* ☐ *3-4* ☐ *5 or more*

4 Make sure questions are specific. Do not use words such as 'sometimes', 'often', 'regularly' and 'occasionally'.

> *How many times do you usually go swimming each month?*
> ☐ *never* ☐ *1-4 times*
> ☐ *5-8 times* ☐ *9 times or more*

5 Never ask a personal question as many people won't answer it or will give a false answer. For example don't ask people to write down their age, but give them ranges of ages they can tick.

> *How old are you?*
> ☐ *under 20 years* ☐ *21-40 years*
> ☐ *41-60 years* ☐ *Over 60*

6 Never ask a leading question as people may tick the box they think you want them to, rather than the one they should. This is an example of a leading question.

> *Do you agree that eating junk food is bad for you?*
> ☐ *yes* ☐ *no* ☐ *don't know*

7 Never ask people to put their names on a questionnaire. They might not want to be identified.

8 Finally, don't ask too many questions. If your questionnaire is too long people won't want to answer it.

Worked example 6.2

This is a question about diet.
a Give two reasons why the question is not appropriate for a questionnaire.
b Re-write the question so that it is suitable for a questionnaire.

> *Do you agree that eating fresh fruit is good for you?*
> ☐ *agree* ☐ *strongly agree* ☐ *don't know*

a (1) It is a leading question.   The question is trying to get you to agree.
  (2) There is no 'disagree' box.   If you do disagree there is no box for you to tick.
b Do you think that eating fresh fruit is good or bad for you?
   ☐ good   ☐ bad   ☐ don't know

> This question is not leading but is asking for your opinion.

Exercise 6.2

1 Eira asks people in her village to fill in a questionnaire about their local dentist.
These are four of the questions she writes.

> 1 What is your name? ....
> 2 What is your date of birth? ....
> 3 Do you agree that the local dentist provides an excellent service?
>   ☐ yes   ☐ not sure   ☐ don't know
> 4 How many times did you visit the dentist last year?
>   ☐ 0 times   ☐ 1-3 times   ☐ 3-5 times   ☐ more than 4 times

a Explain why each question is unsuitable.
b Re-write questions 2, 3 and 4 to make them suitable for a questionnaire.

2 Sham asks people in his neighbourhood to fill in a questionnaire about diet.
These are two of the questions he asks.

> 1 How often do you buy junk food?
>   ☐ very often   ☐ often   ☐ not very often
> 2 How many times in one week do you usually eat fresh vegetables?
>   ☐ 0 times   ☐ 1-3 times   ☐ 4-6 times   ☐ 7 or more times

a Give one reason why question 1 is unsuitable.
b Give two reasons why question 2 is suitable.

3 Annika is carrying out a survey on the number of hours
students in her school sleep. This is one of her questions:
'How many hours, on average, do you sleep each night?'
Design a response section for Annika's question.

> When you are designing a response
> section, remember that everyone
> must be able to tick a box.

4 Lars is carrying out a survey on the way students in his class
travel to school.
This is one of his questions: 'What method do you usually use to travel to school?'
Design a response section for his question.

6.3 Using frequency tables

Another way of collecting data is to use a **data-collection sheet**.

This is a table in which you use tally marks to fill in responses.

For example, you could use this data collection sheet if you were asking students in your class how many brothers and sisters they had.

Number of brothers and sisters	0	1	2	3	4	5 or more

Every time you asked a student, you would put a tally mark in the table.

If the first ten students gave you answers of 0, 2, 1, 2, 1, 2, 2, 3, 5 and 2, your table would look like this.

Number of brothers and sisters	0	1	2	3	4	5 or more
	/	//	ĦĦ	/		/

Notice that the fifth tally mark is a diagonal line across the previous four. This makes it easier at the end to add up all the tally marks, as you can count them in groups of five – if you know your tables!

A **frequency table** is another type of data-collection sheet. It usually has three columns: the first is for the list of the items you are going to count, the second is for the tally marks and the third is for writing the total number of tallies, which is the <u>frequency</u>.

Worked example 6.3

Here are the grades awarded to 30 students for their science project.

A	C	D	C	B	B	A	B	B	C
D	E	A	A	C	C	C	B	C	D
E	D	C	C	B	B	B	B	A	C

a   Put the results into a frequency table.
b   How many students had Grade A?
c   What was the most common grade?

a
Grade	Tally	Frequency
A	ĦĦ	5
B	ĦĦ ////	9
C	ĦĦ ĦĦ	10
D	////	4
E	//	2
	Total:	30

When you draw a frequency table, always make sure the tally column is quite wide to make sure all the tallies will fit.

b   5 students   The frequency for Grade A is 5.
c   Grade C   The highest frequency is 10, so C is the most common grade.

⬥ **Exercise 6.3**

1 Twenty students were asked to choose their favourite colour out of red (R), blue (B), green (G), yellow (Y), pink (P) or other (O). The results are below.

| R | G | G | B | Y | G | R | G | R | Y |
| B | O | O | R | B | Y | R | R | O | P |

a Copy and complete the data-collection sheet to show this information.

Favourite colour	Red (R)	Blue (B)	Green (G)	Yellow (Y)	Pink (P)	Other (O)

b Which colour was the most popular?

2 The students in one class were divided into three groups, A, B and C.
There were 10 students in each group.
Each member of the group had to answer as many maths questions as they could in 10 seconds.
Here are the numbers of questions that each student answered correctly.

Group A: 2, 1, 3, 2, 2, 1, 2, 2, 3, 4
Group B: 2, 2, 3, 4, 0, 1, 0, 1, 2, 4
Group C: 4, 0, 2, 3, 2, 1, 1, 1, 1, 0

Copy and complete the data-collection sheet to show the information above.
The scores for the first six students from group A have been done for you.

		Group		
		A	B	C
Score	0			
	1	/		
	2	////		
	3	/		
	4			

3 Thirty students were asked to choose their favourite subject out of maths (M), science (S), art (A), history (H) or other (O). The results are below.

S	S	A	S	M	M	S	H	M	H
M	A	M	O	H	M	M	S	S	M
H	H	M	H	S	S	M	M	M	O

a Copy and complete the frequency table to show this information.

Subject	Tally	Frequency
Maths (M)		
Science (S)		
Art (A)		
History (H)		
Other (O)		
	Total:	

b What was the most popular subject?

4 Some people were asked to choose their favourite sport out of football (F), rugby (R), basketball (B), hockey (H) and tennis (T). The results are below.

RRBF, FFHF, RTTR, BFTT, RFRH, BRRT

   a Draw a frequency table to show this information.
   b What is the most popular sport?
   c How many people were asked?

5 Mrs Gupta gave her class a spelling test. These are the students' scores, marked out of 20.

   12,19,7,18   15,2,6,20   8,12,10,17   16,12,5,11   13,11,4,9   18,8,16,13   14,19,9,18

   a Copy and complete the grouped frequency table.

Score	Tally	Frequency
1–5		
6–10		
11–15		
16–20		
	Total:	

> In this **grouped frequency table** tallies for the scores 1, 2, 3, 4 and 5 all go in the first group. Tallies for the scores 6, 7, 8, 9 and 10 all go in the second group, and so on.

> The **class interval** 16–20 includes all the scores from 16 to 20 inclusive.

   b How many students are there in Mrs Gupta's class?
   c How many students had a score in the class interval 16–20?
   d How many students got more than half the spellings correct? Explain how you worked out your answer.

6 Jasmine has a spinner with the numbers 1 to 12. She spins the spinner 24 times and records the results. These are the results she gets.

   2,1,12,10   2,6,4,8   7,6,3,12   5,11,8,4   9,8,3,6   9,9,7,1

   a Draw a grouped frequency table to show this information. Use the groups 1–3, 4–6, 7–9 and 10–12.
   b Do you think this is a fair spinner? Explain your answer.

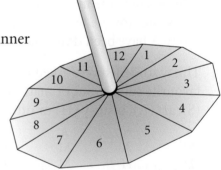

Summary

You should now know that:

★ There are two types of data: primary data and secondary data.

★ Primary data is data that you collect yourself.

★ Secondary data is data that has already been collected by someone else.

★ You can use a questionnaire or a data-collection sheet to collect data.

★ A frequency table is a type of data-collection sheet. The first column is for the list of the items you are going to count, the second is for the tally marks and the third is for the frequency.

You should be able to:

★ Decide which data would be relevant to a question and collect and organise the data.

★ Design and use a questionnaire for a simple survey.

★ Design and use a data-collection sheet for a simple survey.

★ Construct and use frequency tables to gather discrete data, grouped, where appropriate, into equal class intervals.

★ Record and explain your methods and conclusions.

★ Communicate findings effectively.

End of unit review

1 In a survey, which units would you use to measure:
 a the distance a person can swim in 10 minutes
 b the length of time a person takes to have a shower?

2 Would you collect primary data or secondary data to answer the following questions?
 a Which countries in the world have active volcanoes?
 b What is the favourite fruit of students in your class?

3 Should you carry out a survey or an experiment to collect the primary data for these questions?
 a How many times does a dice land on '6' when it is rolled 30 times?
 b Who is the favourite sports personality of the students in your class?

4 Tara wants to know if the students in her school like to listen to music. She asks five boys and five girls from each class. Will the results of her survey give a fair result? Give a reason for your answer.

5 Eira asks people in her village to fill in a questionnaire about their local shop.
 These are three of the questions she writes.
 a Explain why each question is unsuitable.
 b Re-write Eira's questions 2 and 3 to make them suitable for a questionnaire.

> 1 What is your age? .... years
> 2 Do you agree that the local shop has a good selection of products?
> ☐ agree ☐ strongly agree ☐ not sure
> 3 How many times do you visit the local shop each month?
> ☐ 1-3 times ☐ 3-6 times ☐ 6-9 times ☐ more than 10 times

6 Some people were asked to choose their favourite drink out of tea (T), coffee (C), fruit juice (F) and water (W). The results are below.

T W F C T W T F C C W W T F C W T W

 a Draw a frequency table to show this information.
 b What is the most popular drink?

7 Mr Stephens gave his class a mental maths test. On the right are the students' scores, out of 15.

Score	Tally	Frequency
1–5		
6–10		
11–15		
	Total:	

12	9	7	8	5	12
5	11	13	11	14	9
3	8	5	12	9	8
15	6	4	15	3	10
9	8	14	10	6	13

 a Copy and complete the grouped frequency table.
 b How many students are there in Mr Stephen's class?
 c Can you tell from the frequency table how many students got more than half of the questions correct? Explain your answer.

7 Fractions

The word 'fraction' originally comes from the Latin word *fractio* which means 'breaking into pieces'. This makes sense as when you break something up into smaller parts you have fractions of it!

From as early as 1800 BC, the Egyptians were writing fractions. They used pictures, called hieroglyphs, to write words and numbers.

Here are the hieroglyphs they used for some numbers.

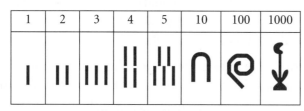

The Egyptians wrote all their fractions with a numerator (number at the top) of 1. To show they were writing a fraction they drew a mouth picture, which meant 'part', above the number.

So, 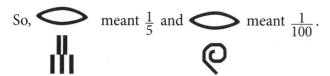 meant $\frac{1}{5}$ and meant $\frac{1}{100}$.

Can you use Egyptian hieroglyphs to write the fraction shaded in each of these diagrams?

 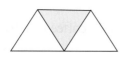 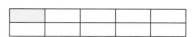

You see fractions all the time in everyday life, from signs showing distances, to posters in shops and recipes in cookery books.

Nolton 2³/₄ miles

Sale
¹/₄ off all prices in store!

Ingredients
250 g butter
500 g flour
¹/₂ tsp salt
2¹/₂ tsp baking powder
3 eggs

In this unit you will learn more about using and calculating with fractions.

> **Key words**
>
> **Make sure you learn and understand these key words:**
> numerator
> denominator
> equivalent fraction
> simplify
> common factor
> cancel
> simplest form
> lowest terms
> highest common factor
> terminating
> recurring
> proper fraction
> improper fraction
> top-heavy fraction
> mixed number
> divisor
> dividend
> remainder

7.1 Simplifying fractions

Look at these three rectangles.

In the first rectangle $\frac{1}{4}$ of the shape is shaded.

In the second rectangle $\frac{2}{8}$ of the shape is shaded.

In the third rectangle $\frac{4}{16}$ of the shape is shaded.

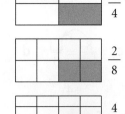

> The number at the top of the fraction is the **numerator**; the number at the bottom is the **denominator**.

You can see that in all three rectangles the same fraction of the shape is shaded. This shows that $\frac{1}{4}$, $\frac{2}{8}$ and $\frac{4}{16}$ are **equivalent fractions**. You can **simplify** fractions into equivalent fractions by dividing the numerator and denominator by the same number. This number must be a **common factor** of the numerator and denominator.

For example
$$\overset{\div 2}{\frac{4}{16}} = \underset{\div 2}{\frac{2}{8}} \quad \text{and} \quad \overset{\div 2}{\frac{2}{8}} = \underset{\div 2}{\frac{1}{4}}$$

> Simplifying fractions is also called **cancelling** fractions.

When you have simplified a fraction to give the smallest possible numerator and denominator, the fraction is in its **simplest form** or **lowest terms**.

When you simplify a fraction, if you divide the numerator and denominator by their **highest common factor**, your answer will be in its simplest form in one step.

Worked example 7.1

a Write the fraction $\frac{6}{10}$ in its simplest form.

b Cancel the fraction $\frac{12}{18}$ to its lowest terms.

a

2 is the highest common factor of 6 and 10, so $\frac{3}{5}$ is in its simplest form.

> Don't worry if you don't know the highest common factor. Just cancel one step at a time. You will end up with the same answer.
>
> then

b

6 is the highest common factor of 12 and 18, so $\frac{2}{3}$ is in its lowest terms.

◆ Exercise 7.1

1 Copy and complete these equivalent fractions.

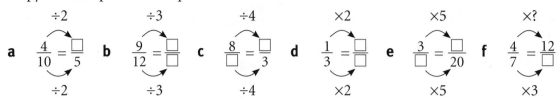

2 Write each fraction in its simplest form.

a $\dfrac{2}{10}$ b $\dfrac{15}{25}$ c $\dfrac{6}{9}$ d $\dfrac{14}{21}$ e $\dfrac{22}{77}$ f $\dfrac{25}{75}$

3 Write each fraction in its lowest terms.

a $\dfrac{4}{6}$ b $\dfrac{12}{30}$ c $\dfrac{9}{27}$ d $\dfrac{24}{40}$ e $\dfrac{24}{36}$ f $\dfrac{15}{18}$

4 Copy and complete the equivalent fractions in these spider diagrams.

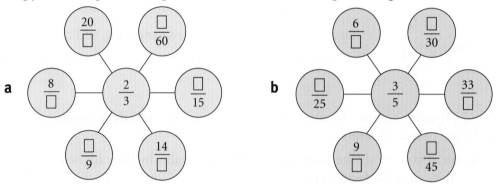

5 Each fraction in a pink star has an equivalent fraction in a blue star.
   a Match each pink star with the correct blue star.
     There should be three blue stars left over. Which are they?

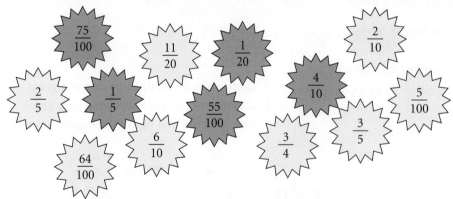

   b Cancel the fraction in the blue star that is left over to its lowest terms.

6 Harsha says:

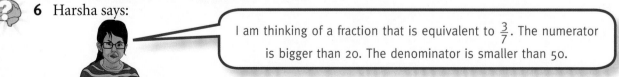

I am thinking of a fraction that is equivalent to $\dfrac{3}{7}$. The numerator is bigger than 20. The denominator is smaller than 50.

What fraction is Harsha thinking of?

7.2 Recognising equivalent fractions, decimals and percentages

In Unit 3 you saw the connection between decimal numbers and fractions.

Hundreds	Tens	Units	•	Tenths	Hundredths	Thousandths
100	10	1	•	$\frac{1}{10}$	$\frac{1}{100}$	$\frac{1}{1000}$

> Remember the decimal place-value table.

The decimal number 0.1 can be written as the fraction $\frac{1}{10}$.

The decimal number 0.2 can be written as the fraction $\frac{2}{10}$, 0.3 as $\frac{3}{10}$ and so on.

Similarly, 0.01 can be written as $\frac{1}{100}$, 0.05 as $\frac{5}{100}$, 0.15 as $\frac{15}{100}$ and so on.

> All these decimal numbers are called **terminating** decimals because they come to an end.

To write a terminating decimal as a fraction, follow these steps.

- Write the number in the place-value table and look at the value (tenths, hundredths, ...) of the last digit.
- Write this value as the denominator of your fraction.
- Write as the numerator the digits that come after the decimal point.
- Cancel the fraction to its simplest form.

Worked example 7.2A

Write the following decimal numbers as fractions in their simplest form.
a 0.7   **b** 0.26   **c** 0.045

a $0.7 = \frac{7}{10}$ The 7 is in the tenths column of the place value table. $\frac{7}{10}$ cannot be cancelled.

b $0.26 = \frac{26}{100}$ The 6 is in the hundredths column of the place-value table.

$\frac{26}{100} = \frac{13}{50}$ $\frac{26}{100}$ can be cancelled by dividing 26 and 100 by 2.

c $0.045 = \frac{45}{1000}$ The 5 is in the thousandths column of the place-value table.

$\frac{45}{1000} = \frac{9}{200}$ $\frac{45}{1000}$ can be cancelled by dividing 45 and 1000 by 5.

Percentages can be written as fractions with a denominator of 100, as the words 'per cent' mean 'out of 100'.

$$8\% = \frac{8}{100}, \ 14\% = \frac{14}{100}$$

You need to be able to recognise equivalent fractions, decimals and percentages.

The diagram shows the ones that are most commonly used.

Learn these and it will help you answer all sorts of questions in the future!

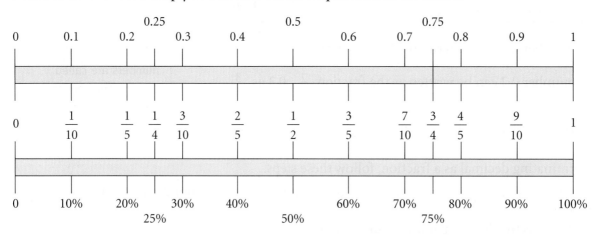

Worked example 7.2B

a Write the following percentages as fractions.   **i** 5%   **ii** 83%
b Write 20% as: **i** a fraction   **ii** a decimal.

a   **i** $5\% = \frac{5}{100}$ 5 per cent means 5 out of 100.

      $\frac{5}{100} = \frac{1}{20}$ $\frac{5}{100}$ can be cancelled by dividing 5 and 100 by 5.

   ii $83\% = \frac{83}{100}$ 83 per cent means 83 out of 100 $\frac{83}{100}$ cannot be cancelled.

B   **i** $20\% = \frac{1}{5}$ 20% is a commonly used percentage, 20% as a fraction is $\frac{20}{100} = \frac{1}{5}$.

   ii $20\% = 0.2$ 20% as a decimal is 0.2.

Exercise 7.2

1 Write these decimal numbers as fractions in their simplest form.
   a 0.3   **b** 0.9   **c** 0.2   **d** 0.6   **e** 0.8
   f 0.17   **g** 0.35   **h** 0.84   **i** 0.07   **j** 0.04
   k 0.139   **l** 0.125   **m** 0.826   **n** 0.042   **o** 0.006

2 Write these percentages as fractions.
   a 9%   **b** 27%   **c** 81%   **d** 69%   **e** 11%

3 Use the numbers from the box to complete the following.
You can only use each number once.
You should have no numbers left at the end.

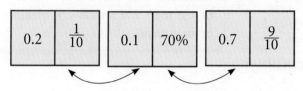
$\frac{1}{10}$ 80% $\frac{3}{4}$ 50%   0.3   0.12 $\frac{4}{5}$

a $0.5 = \square$ **b** $\frac{3}{10} = \square$ **c** $\square = 75\%$

d $0.1 = \square$ **e** $12\% = \square$ **f** $\square = \square$

4 In the game of dominoes players lay out their dominoes end to end.
The touching ends must be the same number, even if it is not in the same form.
For example these three dominoes could be arranged like this.

| 0.2 | $\frac{1}{10}$ | | 0.1 | 70% | | 0.7 | $\frac{9}{10}$ |

$\frac{1}{10}$ is the same as 0.1.   70% is the same as 0.7.

Work out how to arrange these ten dominoes, end to end.

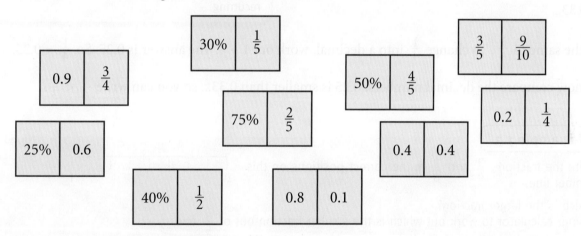

| 0.9 | $\frac{3}{4}$ |

| 30% | $\frac{1}{5}$ |

| $\frac{3}{5}$ | $\frac{9}{10}$ |

| 50% | $\frac{4}{5}$ |

| 25% | 0.6 |

| 75% | $\frac{2}{5}$ |

| 0.2 | $\frac{1}{4}$ |

| 0.4 | 0.4 |

| 40% | $\frac{1}{2}$ |

| 0.8 | 0.1 |

5 In a maths test, Archie got $\frac{1}{5}$ of the questions wrong.

a What was Archie's percentage score?
b Explain why it is not possible to work out his actual score.

7.3 Comparing fractions

There are several different ways that you can compare two fractions. One way is to use diagrams like these.

In the first rectangle $\frac{1}{3}$ is shaded.

In the second rectangle $\frac{1}{4}$ is shaded.

You can see that $\frac{1}{4}$ is smaller than $\frac{1}{3}$, so you write $\frac{1}{4} < \frac{1}{3}$.

Or you can say that $\frac{1}{3}$ is bigger than $\frac{1}{4}$, so you write $\frac{1}{3} > \frac{1}{4}$.

> Remember that < means 'is smaller or less than' and > means 'is greater or more than'.

Another way to compare two fractions is to use your calculator.

Take the fraction $\frac{1}{3}$. To change $\frac{1}{3}$ into a decimal, work out $1 \div 3$. The answer is 0.33...

0.33... is called a **recurring** decimal. The three dots at the end show that the number goes on for ever.

So $\frac{1}{3} = 0.33...$

> You can also write 0.33... as $0.\dot{3}$. The dot above the 3 shows that the number is recurring.

Now do the same to $\frac{1}{4}$. To change $\frac{1}{4}$ into a decimal, work out $1 \div 4$. The answer is 0.25. So $\frac{1}{4} = 0.25$.

You can now compare the decimal numbers. 0.25 is smaller than 0.33... so you can write $\frac{1}{4} < \frac{1}{3}$.

Worked example 7.3

a i Write the fractions $\frac{3}{4}$ and $\frac{7}{8}$ in the correct positions on this number line.

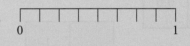

ii Which is the larger fraction?

b Use your calculator to work out which is the smaller fraction out of $\frac{3}{5}$ and $\frac{2}{3}$.

a i

The black lines show the eighths and the red lines show the quarters.

ii $\frac{7}{8}$ is the larger. $\frac{7}{8}$ is closer to 1 than $\frac{3}{4}$, so is the bigger of the two.

b $\frac{3}{5} = 3 \div 5 = 0.6$ Divide the numerator by the denominator.

$\frac{2}{3} = 2 \div 3 = 0.66...$ Write down the first two decimal places then ... to show the decimal carries on.

$\frac{3}{5}$ is the smaller.

◆ Exercise 7.3

1 a Copy the number line.

Write the fractions $\frac{1}{2}$ and $\frac{2}{3}$ in the correct positions on the number line.

b Which is the larger fraction?

2 a Copy the number line.

Write the fractions $\frac{4}{5}$ and $\frac{7}{10}$ in the correct positions on the number line.

b Which is the larger fraction?

3 In each part of the question copy the shapes, then:
- shade in the fraction that is shown next to each shape
- write down which is the smaller of the two fractions.

a   **b**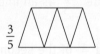

c  **d**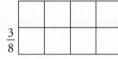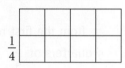

4 Use your calculator to work out which is the larger of the two fractions in each pair.

a $\frac{1}{4}$ and $\frac{3}{10}$ **b** $\frac{5}{8}$ and $\frac{13}{20}$ **c** $\frac{1}{6}$ and $\frac{2}{15}$ **d** $\frac{2}{7}$ and $\frac{3}{8}$

5 Write the symbol < or > between each pair of fractions.

a $\frac{3}{4}$ ... $\frac{7}{8}$ **b** $\frac{2}{5}$ ... $\frac{3}{7}$ **c** $\frac{7}{15}$ ... $\frac{11}{25}$ **d** $\frac{8}{11}$ ... $\frac{12}{15}$

 6 '$\frac{1}{8}$ is bigger than $\frac{1}{7}$ because 8 is bigger than 7'. Is this correct? Explain your answer.

7 This is part of Roman's homework. Is he right? Explain your answer.

> *Question Which is larger, $\frac{6}{31}$ or $\frac{9}{47}$?*
>
> *Solution $\frac{6}{31}$ = 6 ÷ 31 = 0.19 $\frac{9}{47}$ = 9 ÷ 47 = 0.19*
>
> *Neither is larger as they are both the same size.*

 8 Hassan says: 'I am thinking of a fraction. My fraction is bigger than $\frac{2}{5}$ but smaller than $\frac{2}{3}$.

When I divide the numerator by the denominator I get an answer of 0.533.'
What fraction is Hassan thinking of?

7.4 Improper fractions and mixed numbers

In a **proper fraction** the numerator is smaller than the denominator.
Example: $\frac{2}{3}$

In an **improper fraction** the numerator is bigger than the

denominator. **Example:** $\frac{4}{3}$

An improper fraction can be written as a **mixed number.**

> An improper fraction is sometimes called a **top-heavy fraction.**
>
> An improper fraction can be written as a **mixed number.**

> A mixed number contains a whole number and a fraction.

Worked example 7.4

a Write the fraction shaded in this diagram as:

   i a mixed number   **ii** an improper fraction.

b **i** Write $\frac{5}{2}$ as a mixed number.   **ii** Write $4\frac{2}{3}$ as an improper fraction.

---

a **i** $1\frac{1}{4}$ 1 complete rectangle and $\frac{1}{4}$ of the second rectangle are shaded.

   ii $\frac{5}{4}$ $\frac{4}{4}$ from the first rectangle and $\frac{1}{4}$ from the second gives a total of 5 quarters or $\frac{5}{4}$.

b **i** $\frac{5}{2} = 2\frac{1}{2}$ $\frac{5}{2}$ is 5 halves. 4 halves makes 2 whole units and there is 1 half left.

   ii $4\frac{2}{3} = \frac{14}{3}$ Change 4 whole units into thirds: 4 × 3 = 12 so there are 12 thirds.
Then add the extra 2 thirds: 12 + 2 = 14 thirds.

◆ Exercise 7.4

1 Write down the fraction shaded in each of these diagrams as:

   i a mixed number   **ii** an improper fraction.

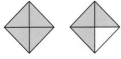

2 Write each improper fraction as a mixed number.   **a** $\frac{7}{2}$ **b** $\frac{13}{4}$ **c** $\frac{6}{5}$

3 Write each mixed number as an improper fraction.   **a** $4\frac{1}{2}$ **b** $2\frac{1}{3}$ **c** $4\frac{3}{4}$

4 Sita made 5 cakes for a birthday party. She cut each cake into 12 pieces.
At the end of the party there were 7 pieces of cake that had <u>not</u> been eaten.
Write the amount of cake that <u>was</u> eaten as:

   a a mixed number   **b** an improper fraction.

7.5 Adding and subtracting fractions

To add or subtract fractions you want the denominators to be the same.

When you add or subtract fractions follow these steps.

- If the denominators are the same, simply add or subtract the numerators.
- If the denominators are different, write the fractions as equivalent fractions with the same denominator, then add or subtract the numerators.
- Cancel your answer to its simplest form.
- If your answer is an improper fraction, write it as a mixed number.

> Once the denominators are the same, add the numerators but <u>do not</u> add the denominators.

Worked example 7.5

Work these out. **a** $\frac{4}{5} - \frac{3}{5}$ **b** $\frac{7}{8} + \frac{5}{8}$ **c** $\frac{5}{6} + \frac{1}{3}$

a $\frac{4-3}{5} = \frac{1}{5}$ The denominators are the same, so simply subtract the numerators.

b $\frac{7+5}{8} = \frac{12}{8}$ The denominators are the same, so simply add the numerators.

$\frac{12}{8} = 1\frac{4}{8}$ $\frac{12}{8}$ is an improper fraction, so re-write it as a mixed number.

$1\frac{4}{8} = 1\frac{1}{2}$ Finally, cancel the $\frac{4}{8}$ to its simplest form.

c $\frac{5}{6} + \frac{1}{3} = \frac{5}{6} + \frac{2}{6}$ The denominators are not the same so change the $\frac{1}{3}$ into $\frac{2}{6}$.

$\frac{5+2}{6} = \frac{7}{6}$ The denominators are now the same, so add the numerators.

$\frac{7}{6} = 1\frac{1}{6}$ $\frac{7}{6}$ is an improper fraction, so re-write it as a mixed number.

◆ Exercise 7.5

1 Work these out.

a $\frac{1}{5} + \frac{2}{5}$ **b** $\frac{3}{7} + \frac{3}{7}$ **c** $\frac{5}{7} - \frac{2}{7}$ **d** $\frac{8}{9} - \frac{4}{9}$

2 Work out these additions. Write each answer in its simplest form and as a mixed number.

a $\frac{3}{4} + \frac{3}{4}$ **b** $\frac{3}{8} + \frac{7}{8}$ **c** $\frac{9}{10} + \frac{7}{10}$ **d** $\frac{11}{14} + \frac{5}{14}$

3 Work out the answers to these additions.
Write each answer in its simplest form and as a mixed number.

a $\frac{4}{5} + \frac{13}{20}$ **b** $\frac{5}{8} + \frac{11}{16}$ **c** $\frac{3}{7} + \frac{13}{14}$ **d** $\frac{5}{6} + \frac{11}{18}$

4 Mia adds together two <u>proper</u> fractions. The fractions have <u>different</u> denominators.

She gets an answer of $1\frac{2}{5}$.

Write down two fractions that Mia may have added.

7.6 Finding fractions of a quantity

You work out a unit fraction of a quantity by dividing the quantity by the denominator of the fraction.

Example: To work out $\frac{1}{3}$ of 18 cm, divide 18 cm by 3. So $\frac{1}{3}$ of 18 cm = 18 ÷ 3 = 6 cm.

To work out a more complicated fraction such as $\frac{2}{3}$, divide the quantity by the denominator <u>and then</u> multiply your answer by the numerator.

Example: To work out $\frac{2}{3}$ of 18 kg, you divide 18 kg by 3, then multiply by 2.

$$18 ÷ 3 = 6, 6 × 2 = 12. \text{ So } \frac{2}{3} \text{ of 18 kg} = 12 \text{ kg.}$$

Worked example 7.6

Work these out.   **a** $\frac{1}{3}$ of 15 cm   **b** $\frac{2}{5}$ of 20 kg

c $\frac{4}{7}$ × 105

> If you can't work out part **c** in your head, use a written method or a calculator.

a 15 ÷ 3 = 5 cm   Divide the quantity (15 cm) by the denominator (3).

b 20 ÷ 5 = 4   First of all find $\frac{1}{5}$ by dividing the quantity (20 kg) by the denominator (5).

   4 × 2 = 8 kg   Then multiply the answer by 2 to find $\frac{2}{5}$.

> 'Of' and '×' mean <u>exactly</u> the same thing, so use the same method.

c 105 ÷ 7 = 15   First of all find $\frac{1}{7}$ by dividing the number (105) by the denominator (7).

   15 × 4 = 60   Then multiply the answer by 4 to find $\frac{4}{7}$.

> There are no units in this answer.

◆ Exercise 7.6

1 Work these out mentally.

   a $\frac{1}{2}$ of $8   **b** $\frac{1}{6}$ of 18 km   **c** $\frac{4}{9}$ × 18   **d** $\frac{3}{7}$ × 28

2 Use a written method or a calculator to work these out.

   a $\frac{2}{7}$ of $182   **b** $\frac{4}{13}$ of 195 miles   **c** $\frac{3}{8}$ × 192   **d** $\frac{13}{15}$ × 345

3 Which of these cards is different from the others? Explain your answer.

   $28 × \frac{4}{7}$ $27 × \frac{2}{3}$ $26 × \frac{9}{13}$

4 At a rugby match in the Ellis Park Stadium in Johannesburg there were 58 476 rugby fans.

   $\frac{7}{12}$ of the fans were supporting South Africa. The rest were supporting Australia.

   How many fans were supporting Australia? How can you tell if your answer is likely to be correct?

7.7 Finding remainders

When you are working out a division, the number you are dividing by is called the **divisor** and the number you are dividing into is called the **dividend**.

Example: In the division $163 \div 12$, 12 is the divisor and 163 is the dividend.

When the answer to a division is not an exact whole number, there will be a **remainder**.

Example: $163 \div 12 = 13$ remainder 7

The remainder can be written as a fraction of the divisor.

Example: $163 \div 12 = 13\frac{7}{12}$

When you are solving a problem and you have a remainder, you may need to decide whether to round up or down. Whether you round up or down depends entirely on the question.

> You can check this answer using inverse operations like this:
> $12 \times 13 = 156$, $156 + 7 = 163$

> You can think of this as changing an improper fraction to a mixed number (see Topic 7.4).
> $\frac{163}{12} = 13\frac{7}{12}$

Worked example 7.7

a Work out these divisions. Write the remainders as fractions.
  i $16 \div 3$ ii $90 \div 8$
b Raul shares 50 sweets equally between his 3 children.
  How many sweets do they each get?
c 276 children are going on a school trip by bus. Each bus holds 48 children.
  How many buses do they need?

a i $5\frac{1}{3}$ $16 \div 3 = 5$ remainder 1

  ii $11\frac{2}{8} = 11\frac{1}{4}$ $90 \div 8 = 11$ remainder 2; $\frac{2}{8}$ cancels to $\frac{1}{4}$

b $50 \div 3 = 16$ remainder 2   Here you have to round down so they have 16 sweets each
  16 sweets each   There are not enough sweets for them to have 17 each.

c $276 \div 48 = 5$ remainder 36   In this question you have to round up so they can take everyone on
  6 buses are needed.   the trip. 5 buses would not be enough for everyone.

Exercise 7.7

1 Work out these divisions. Write the remainders as fractions.
  a $19 \div 7$ b $35 \div 11$ c $41 \div 6$ d $65 \div 9$

2 Work out these divisions. Write the remainders as fractions in their simplest form.
  a $6 \div 4$ b $20 \div 8$ c $26 \div 6$ d $38 \div 10$
  e $50 \div 12$ f $33 \div 9$ g $55 \div 15$ h $52 \div 20$

3 Angel uses this method to work out some harder divisions. Use Angel's method, or a similar method of your own, to work these out.
  a $225 \div 4$ b $363 \div 5$ c $373 \div 3$
  d $447 \div 6$ e $758 \div 8$ f $920 \div 12$

> _Question_ Work out $257 \div 3$
>
> _Solution_ 85 remainder 2
> $3\overline{)2\,^2 5\,^1 7}$
>
> $257 \div 3 = 85\frac{2}{3}$

4 Ethan uses his calculator to work out some harder divisions. This is the method he uses. Use Ethan's method to work these out.

    a 558 ÷ 12   **b** 342 ÷ 24   **c** 895 ÷ 25
    d 882 ÷ 23   **e** 852 ÷ 13   **f** 767 ÷ 17

> _Question_ Work out 778 ÷ 15
>
> _Solution_ 778 ÷ 15 = 51.866...
> 15 goes into 778, 51 times
> 15 × 51 = 765
> 778 − 765 = 13 (remainder)
>
> Answer = $51\frac{13}{15}$

5 Eleri has 97 cents credit on her mobile phone.
It costs her 6 cents to send a text message.
How many text messages can Eleri send?
Explain how you worked out your answer.

6 Mrs Gupta has 250 sweets to share among her class of 32 children.
Each child gets the same number of sweets. Mrs Gupta keeps the sweets that are left over.
How many sweets does Mrs Gupta keep?
Use an inverse operation to check your answer.

7 A farmer can fit 12 bales of hay on his trailer.
He has 187 bales of hay to move.
How many trips will he have to make with his trailer?
Use a method of your own choice to check your working.

Summary

You should now know that:

★ Equivalent fractions are equal.

★ When a fraction is in its simplest form, it cannot be cancelled further.

★ To write a fraction in its simplest form you divide both the numerator and denominator by the highest common factor.

★ A terminating decimal is a decimal that comes to an end.

★ A recurring decimal is a decimal that goes on forever.

★ In a proper fraction the numerator is smaller than the denominator.

★ In an improper fraction the numerator is bigger than the denominator.

★ A mixed number contains a whole-number part and a fractional part.

★ You can only add and subtract fractions when the denominators are the same.

★ Finding a fraction <u>of</u> a quantity is the same as working out the fraction × the quantity.

★ When the answer to a division is not an exact whole number, you can write the remainder as a fraction of the divisor.

You should be able to:

★ Simplify fractions into equivalent fractions.

★ Cancel a fraction to its lowest terms or simplest form.

★ Write a terminating decimal as a fraction.

★ Write a percentage as a fraction.

★ Recognise commonly used equivalent fractions, decimals and percentages.

★ Compare fractions, using diagrams or a calculator.

★ Write improper fractions as mixed numbers and vice versa.

★ Add and subtract fractions when the denominators are the same.

★ Add and subtract fractions when one denominator is a multiple of the other.

★ Find fractions of quantities and whole numbers.

★ Write the answer to a division as a mixed number, when the answer isn't a whole number.

★ Round an answer up or down when solving a problem involving remainders.

★ Solve word problems in context.

★ Work logically and draw simple conclusions.

End of unit review

1 Write each fraction in its simplest form. **a** $\frac{2}{6}$ **b** $\frac{15}{20}$ **c** $\frac{12}{15}$

2 Copy and complete the table.

	Fraction	Decimal	Percentage
a		0.5	
c			25%
e		0.1	
g	$\frac{3}{4}$		

	Fraction	Decimal	Percentage
b	$\frac{1}{5}$		
d		0.8	
f			90%
h	$\frac{3}{5}$		

3 Write the symbol < or > between these: **a** $\frac{3}{5}$ ☐ $\frac{5}{11}$

4 **a** Write $3\frac{2}{3}$ as an improper fraction. **b** Write $\frac{32}{5}$ as a mixed number.

5 Emmy made four apple pies for a party. She cut each pie into eight pieces.

At the end of the party there were three pieces of apple pie that had <u>not</u> been eaten.
Write the amount of apple pie that <u>was</u> eaten as:
a mixed number **b** an improper fraction.

6 Work out the answers to these additions and subtractions.
Write each answer in its simplest form.

a $\frac{5}{9} - \frac{3}{9}$ **b** $\frac{4}{15} + \frac{1}{15}$ **c** $\frac{8}{9} - \frac{2}{3}$ **d** $\frac{11}{12} + \frac{3}{4}$

7 Work these out mentally.

a $\frac{1}{2}$ of \$12 **b** $\frac{2}{3}$ of 21 kg **c** $\frac{1}{4} \times 24$ **d** $\frac{4}{5} \times 30$

8 Use a written method or a calculator to work these out.

a $\frac{1}{8}$ of \$336 **b** $\frac{6}{7}$ of 168 mg **c** $\frac{4}{5} \times 215$ **d** $\frac{7}{9} \times 288$

9 In the New York marathon there were 45 360 runners.

$\frac{7}{10}$ of the runners were women. How many of the runners were men?

10 Work out these divisions. Write the remainders as fractions in their
simplest form. **a** $38 \div 5$ **b** $42 \div 8$

11 Aiden has \$135 to spend on DVDs. Each DVD costs \$16.
a How many DVDs can he buy?
b How much money will he have left?
Use a method of your own choice to check your working.

DVDs
only \$16 each!

8 Symmetry

Throughout history, symmetry has played a major part in people's everyday life.

Granada is a city in the south of Spain. It is the capital of the province of Andalusia. The Alhambra Palace in Granada is full of symmetrical designs.

It was built in the thirteenth century and, although it was originally designed as a military area, it became the residence of royalty and of the court of Granada.

You can see symmetry everywhere you look, from the design of the gardens and buildings to the tile patterns on the walls.

Look around you at gardens, buildings, windows and tile designs and see how many symmetrical patterns you can see. They are everywhere!

In this unit you will look at the symmetry of shapes and patterns.

Key words

Make sure you learn and understand these key words:

2D shape
square
rectangle
parallelogram
rhombus
kite
trapezium
scalene triangle
isosceles triangle
equilateral triangle
right-angled triangle
side
parallel
equal
angle
solid shape
3D shape
cube
cuboid
square-based pyramid
triangular-based pyramid
triangular prism
cylinder
cone
sphere
face
edge
vertex (vertices)
symmetrical
line of symmetry
rotational symmetry
order

8.1 Recognising and describing 2D shapes and solids

You need to be able to recognise and describe 2D shapes and solids.

These are some of the **2D shapes** that you should know.

Quadrilaterals

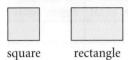

square   rectangle   parallelogram   rhombus   kite   trapezium

Triangles

  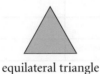 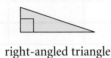

scalene triangle   isosceles triangle   equilateral triangle   right-angled triangle

You should be able to use the words **sides, parallel, equal** and **angles** to describe 2D shapes.

Look at the rectangle to the right.

You can see that all the angles are right angles (90°).

You can also see that <u>opposite</u> sides are both equal in length and parallel.

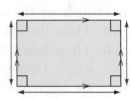

These are the **solid shapes** that you should know.

cube   cuboid   square-based pyramid   triangular-based pyramid

> Solid shapes are also called **3D shapes**, as they have three dimensions: length, width and height.

triangular prism   cylinder   cone   sphere

You should be able to use the words **faces, edges** and **vertices** to describe solid shapes.

Look at the triangular-based pyramid to the right.

You can see that it has **4 faces**, **6 edges** and **4 vertices**.

> Vertices are corners of the shapes. Each corner is a **vertex**.

> The mathematical name for a triangular-based pyramid is <u>tetrahedron</u>.

Worked example 8.1

Write down the name of the shape that is described below.

a 'I am a 2D shape. I have four sides that are all the same length. My opposite angles are the same size but I have no right angles.'

a Rhombus   The sides are the same length, so it could be a square or a rhombus. As the opposite angles are not 90° it is not a square. Opposite angles are equal so it is a rhombus.

◆ Exercise 8.1

1   Copy and complete the table to show a description of the 2D quadrilaterals.
    The parallelogram has been done for you.

Quadrilateral	Four equal sides	Two pairs of equal sides	One pair of parallel sides	Two pairs of parallel sides	All angles 90°	One pair of opposite angles equal	Two pairs of opposite angles equal
Square							
Rectangle							
Parallelogram		✓		✓			✓
Rhombus							
Kite							
Trapezium							

2   Write down the name of each 2D shape that is described.
    a   'I have three sides. All my angles are different sizes and all my sides are different lengths.'
    b   'I have four sides. Two of my sides are the same length. The other two sides are the same
        length. Opposite sides are different lengths. Two of my angles are the same, but the other two
        are different.'

3   This card has an isosceles triangle and a circle drawn on it.

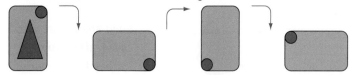

    The card is turned three times. Copy the diagram and draw the missing triangle on each of the cards.

4   Copy and complete the table to show a description of the 3D solids.
    The cone has been done for you.

Solid	Number of faces	Number of edges	Number of vertices
Cube			
Cuboid			
Square-based pyramid			
Triangular-based pyramid	4	6	4
Triangular prism			

5   Write down the name of the solid shape that is being described.
    'When you cut me in half, the number of faces on one of my halves is double the number of faces
    that I started with.'

6   Which two solid shapes can be joined together to form a
    new shape that has three faces, two edges and one vertex?

> Vertices is the plural of vertex, so
> one vertex means one corner.

8.2 Recognising line symmetry

This trapezium is **symmetrical**.
It has one **line of symmetry**.

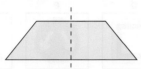

You use dashed lines to show lines of symmetry on a shapes.

If you fold a shape along a line of symmetry, one half of the shape will fit exactly on top of the other half.

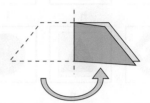

Worked example 8.2

How many lines of symmetry does each of these shapes have?

a   b

a 2 This shape has a vertical line of symmetry and a horizontal line of symmetry.
b 0 This shape has no lines of symmetry.

◆ Exercise 8.2

1 Each of these shapes has one line of symmetry.
   Copy the shapes and draw the lines of symmetry on your diagrams.

   a   b  c   d

2 Each of these shapes has two lines of symmetry.
   Copy the shapes and draw the lines of symmetry on your diagrams.

   a   b   c   d

3 Write down the number of lines of symmetry for each of these shapes.

   a   b   c   d

4 Copy and complete the table for these triangles. The first one is done for you.

   a   b  c

   d   e

	Type of triangle				Number of lines of symmetry
	Isosceles	Equilateral	Scalene	Right-angled	
a	✓			✓	1
b					
c					
d					
e					

5 Here are some road signs.

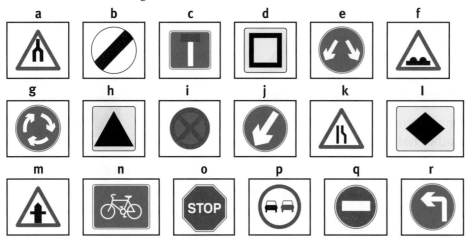

In part **b** the lines of symmetry are not horizontal or vertical but are <u>diagonal</u>, at an angle, as shown.

Copy and complete the table to record their lines of symmetry.
Parts **a** and **b** have been done for you.

Type of line symmetry	a	b	c	d	e	f	g	h	i	j	k	l	m	n	o	p	q	r
Horizontal line of symmetry																		
Vertical line of symmetry	✓																	
Diagonal line of symmetry		✓																
No lines of symmetry																		

6 In each diagram the dashed blue lines are lines of symmetry.
Copy and complete each diagram.

a 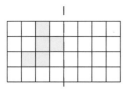   **b** 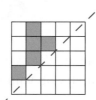   **c**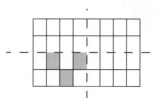

 7 Copy these patterns onto squared paper.

i   **ii**   **iii**   **iv**

a Add one blue square to each pattern to make a new pattern that has a line of symmetry.
b Draw the line of symmetry onto each of your patterns.
c Write down whether each line of symmetry is a horizontal, vertical or diagonal line of symmetry.

 8 Sofi has a box of tiles.
All the tiles have the same pattern.
This is what one of the tiles looks like.
Sofi uses four of the tiles to make a square pattern that has four lines of symmetry.
Draw two different patterns that Sofi could make.

8.3 Recognising rotational symmetry

A shape has **rotational symmetry** if it can be rotated about a point to another position and still look the same.

The **order** of rotational symmetry is the number of times the shape looks the same in one full turn.

A rectangle has rotational symmetry of order 2. This button has rotational symmetry of order 4.

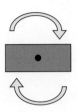

Worked example 8.3

Write down the order of rotational symmetry of each of these shapes.

a  **b**

a Order 2   The parallelogram looks the same after a half-turn and a full turn, so has order 2.
b Order 1   The trapezium only looks the same after a full turn so has order 1.

◆ Exercise 8.3

1 Write down the order of rotational symmetry of these shapes.

a   **b**   **c**

d   **e**   **f**

2 Sort these cards into their correct groups.
Each group must have one blue, one green and one yellow card.

A   Rectangle

a   Order of rotational symmetry is 3

B   Scalene triangle

C   Equilateral triangle

i

b   Order of rotational symmetry is 2

ii

ii

c   Order of rotational symmetry is 1

3 Write down the order of rotational symmetry of each of these road signs.

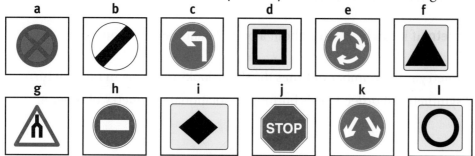

4 Copy this table.

		Number of lines of symmetry				
		0	1	2	3	4
Order of rotational symmetry	1					
	2					
	3	a				
	4					

Write the letter of each of the shapes below in the correct space in the table. Shape **a** has been done for you.

a   **b**   **c**   **d**

e   **f**   **g**   **h**

 5 Samir has five red tiles and four white tiles.

Draw two different ways that Samir could arrange these tiles so that he has a shape with an order of rotational symmetry of 4.

 6 Alex is making a pattern by colouring squares.
This is what he has drawn so far. He has coloured seven squares.

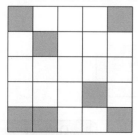

Make two copies of the diagram.
  a In the first diagram, colour one more square so that the new pattern has rotational symmetry of order 2.
  b In the second diagram, colour five more squares so that the new pattern has rotational symmetry f order 4.

8.4 Symmetry properties of triangles, special quadrilaterals and polygons

You should know these symmetry properties of triangles, quadrilaterals and some regular polygons.

<table>
<tr>
<td rowspan="2">Triangles</td>
<td>A scalene triangle has:
• different length sides
• different size angles
• no lines of symmetry
• order 1 rotational symmetry.</td>
<td>An isosceles triangle has:
• 2 sides the same length
• 2 angles the same size
• 1 line of symmetry
• order 1 rotational symmetry.</td>
<td>An equilateral triangle has:
• all sides the same length
• all angles the same size
• 3 lines of symmetry
• order 3 rotational symmetry.</td>
</tr>
<tr>
<td></td>
<td></td>
<td></td>
</tr>
<tr>
<td rowspan="6">Quadrilaterals</td>
<td>A square has:
• all sides the same length
• 2 pairs of parallel sides
• all angles 90°
• 4 lines of symmetry
• order 4 rotational symmetry.</td>
<td>A rectangle has:
• 2 pairs of equal length sides
• 2 pairs of parallel sides
• all angles 90°
• 2 lines of symmetry
• order 2 rotational symmetry.</td>
<td>A rhombus has:
• all sides the same length
• 2 pairs of parallel sides
• opposite angles equal
• 2 lines of symmetry
• order 2 rotational symmetry.</td>
</tr>
<tr>
<td></td>
<td></td>
<td></td>
</tr>
<tr>
<td>A parallelogram has:
• 2 pairs of equal length sides
• 2 pairs of parallel sides
• opposite angles equal
• no lines of symmetry
• order 2 rotational symmetry.</td>
<td>A trapezium has:
• different length sides
• 1 pair of parallel sides
• different-sized angles
• no lines of symmetry
• order 1 rotational symmetry.</td>
<td>An isosceles trapezium has:
• 2 sides the same length
• 1 pair of parallel sides
• 2 pairs of equal angles
• 1 line of symmetry
• order 1 rotational symmetry.</td>
</tr>
<tr>
<td></td>
<td></td>
<td></td>
</tr>
<tr>
<td>A kite has:
• 2 pairs of equal length sides
• no parallel sides
• 1 pair of equal angles
• 1 line of symmetry
• order 1 rotational symmetry.</td>
<td></td>
<td></td>
</tr>
<tr>
<td></td>
<td></td>
<td></td>
</tr>
<tr>
<td rowspan="2">Regular polygons</td>
<td>A regular pentagon has:
• 5 sides the same length
• 5 lines of symmetry
• order 5 rotational symmetry
• 5 angles the same size.</td>
<td>A regular hexagon has:
• 6 sides the same length
• 6 lines of symmetry
• order 6 rotational symmetry
• 6 angles the same size.</td>
<td>A regular octagon has:
• 8 sides the same length
• 8 lines of symmetry
• order 8 rotational symmetry
• 8 angles the same size.</td>
</tr>
<tr>
<td></td>
<td></td>
<td></td>
</tr>
</table>

Worked example 8.4

a 'I am a quadrilateral with one line of symmetry and rotational symmetry of order 1.
I have two pairs of sides of equal length, no parallel sides and one pair of equal angles.
What shape am I?'

b Describe the similarities and differences between a square and a rhombus.

a Kite — One line of symmetry and rotational symmetry of order 1 could be a kite or an isosceles trapezium. The other information tells you it could only be a kite.

b All sides the same length — Opposite angles in a square are equal, but they are all 90°.
This is not the case in the rhombus. They also have different symmetry properties.

Similarities	Differences
Opposite angles are equal	All angles in a square are 90°. This is not the case for a rhombus.
All sides the same length	A square has four lines of symmetry. A rhombus has two lines of symmetry.
Two pairs of parallel sides	A square has order 4 rotational symmetry. A rhombus has order 2 rotational symmetry.

Exercise 8.4

1 Name the shapes that are being described.
  a 'I have three sides that are all the same length.
    I have three equal angles.
    I have three lines of symmetry and rotational symmetry of order 3.'
  b 'I have four sides.
    I have one line of symmetry and rotational symmetry of order 1.
    Two of my angles are equal.
    I have two pairs of equal length sides.'
  c 'I have six sides.
    All my sides are the same length.
    I have six lines of symmetry and rotational symmetry of order 6.'

2 Describe the <u>similarities</u> between a rectangle and a parallelogram.

3 Describe the <u>differences</u> between an isosceles trapezium and a kite.

4 Match each description with the correct shape from the box.
  a 'I have five lines of symmetry and order 5 rotational symmetry.'
  b 'I have no lines of symmetry and order 2 rotational symmetry.'
  c 'I have one line of symmetry and order 1 rotational symmetry.'
  d 'I have eight lines of symmetry and order 8 rotational symmetry.'
  e 'I have no lines of symmetry and order 1 rotational symmetry.'
  f 'I have four lines of symmetry and order 4 rotational symmetry.'
  g 'I have two lines of symmetry and order 2 rotational symmetry.'

square isosceles triangle
regular pentagon parallelogram
rectangle scalene triangle
regular octagon

5 Put each shape through this classification flow chart.
Write down the letter where each shape comes out.

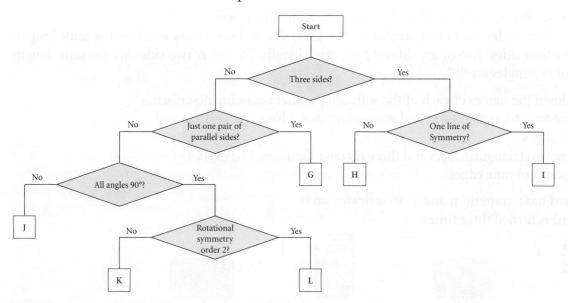

    a trapezium   **b** square   **c** scalene triangle
    d rectangle   **e** rhombus   **f** isosceles triangle

6 A, B and C are three points on this grid.
D is another point on the grid.
When D is at (7, 4) quadrilateral ABDC is a square.
    a Point D moves so that quadrilateral ABCD is a parallelogram.
    What are the coordinates of point D?
    b Point D moves so that quadrilateral ABDC is a kite.
    Write down two possible sets of coordinates for the point D.

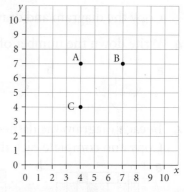

Summary

You should now know that:

★ To describe 2D shapes you need to use the words 'sides', 'parallel', 'equal' and 'angles'.

★ To describe solid or 3D shapes you need to use the words 'faces', 'edges' and 'vertices'.

★ If you fold a shape along a line of symmetry, one half of the shape will fit exactly on top of the other half.

★ The order of rotational symmetry is the number of times the shape looks the same in one full turn.

★ You can describe triangles, quadrilaterals and polygons by using their side, angle and symmetry properties.

You should be able to:

★ Identify and describe 2D shapes.

★ Draw 2D shapes in different orientations.

★ Recognise and describe common solid or 3D shapes.

★ Recognise line symmetry in 2D shapes and patterns.

★ Draw lines of symmetry and complete patterns with two lines of symmetry.

★ Identify the order of rotational symmetry.

★ Name and identify side, angle and symmetry properties of special quadrilaterals and triangles and regular polygons with five, six and eight sides.

★ Recognise and use spatial relationships in two and three dimensions.

★ Draw accurate mathematical diagrams.

End of unit review

1   Write down the name of the 2D shapes that are being described.
   a I have three sides. Two of my angles are the same size and two of my sides are the same length.
   b I have four sides. Two of my sides are the same length. The other two sides are the same length. All of my angles are 90°.

2   Write down the names of each of the solid shapes that are being described.
   a I have four triangular faces and one square face. I have five vertices and eight edges.
   b I have two triangular faces and three rectangular faces. I have six vertices and nine edges.

3   This card has a trapezium and a circle drawn on it.
   The card is turned three times.

   Copy the diagram and draw the missing trapezium on each of the cards.

4   Write down the number of lines of symmetry that each of these shapes has.

   a   **b**   **c**   **d**

5   In each diagram the dashed blue lines are lines of symmetry.
   Copy and complete each diagram.

   a   **b**

6   Write down the order of rotational symmetry of the shapes in question 4.

7   Write a sentence to describe a regular hexagon.
   You must use the words in the box.

  8   Diya has four blue, four white and one yellow tile.

   Draw two different ways that Diya could arrange these tiles so that she has a shape with rotational symmetry of order 2.

  9   A and B are two points on this square grid.
   C is another point on the grid.
   When C is at (3, 6) triangle ABC is a scalene triangle.
   a Point C moves so that triangle ABC is an isosceles triangle.
      Write down two possible sets of coordinates for the point C.
   b Point C moves so that triangle ABC is a right-angled isosceles triangle.
      Write down two possible sets of coordinates for the point C.

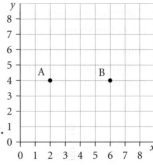

9 Expressions and equations

An equation contains letters and numbers and it <u>must</u> have an equals sign.

An expression can contain numbers and letters, but it does <u>not</u> have an equals sign.

For example, $3x + 2 = 8$ is an equation, whereas $3x + 2$ is an expression.

The equals sign, =, that we use today, was invented by a mathematician called Robert Recorde.

Robert Recorde.

Robert Recorde was born in Tenby in Pembrokeshire in 1510. He studied medicine at university and went on to work as a doctor.

Throughout his life he wrote many mathematical textbooks in the order in which he thought they should be studied. He wrote all these books in English, instead of Latin or Greek, as he wanted them to be available to everyone. He also used clear and simple expressions to try to make them easy to follow.

In 1557 he wrote *The Whetstone of Witte* and it is in this book that he used the modern equals sign (=) for the first time. Other mathematicians were using the letters *ae* or *oe* or two vertical lines, ||, to mean equals.

Today Tenby is a bustling holiday town on the coast of West Wales. Little do the holidaymakers know, while they enjoy an ice cream on the beach, that they are in the place where the inventor of the equals sign was born!

In this unit you will learn more about expressions and equations, and how to solve them.

Key words

Make sure you learn and understand these key words:

equation
expression
like terms
simplify
collecting like terms
brackets
expand
solve
inverse operations
solution
change side, change sign

Tenby Harbour.

9.1 Collecting like terms

Here are two different bricks.

The length of the red brick is x.

The length of the blue brick is y.

When you join together three red bricks, the total length is $3x$.

When you join together two blue bricks, the total length is $2y$.

When you join together three red bricks and two blue bricks
the total length is $3x + 2y$.

You can add, subtract or combine **like terms**.

You cannot combine terms that contain different letters.

You can **simplify** an expression by **collecting like terms**.

This means that you re-write the expression in as short a
way as possible.

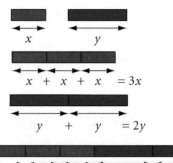

> Like terms are terms that contain the same letter.

Worked example 9.1

Simplify each expression.

a $2x + 3x$ **b** $7y - 2y$ **c** $4p + 3q + 2p - q$ **d** $5t + 7 - 3t + 3$

a $2x + 3x = 5x$ $2x$ and $3x$ are like terms, so add them to get $5x$.
b $7y - 2y = 5y$ $7y$ and $2y$ are like terms, so subtract to get $5y$.
c $4p + 3q + 2p - q = 6p + 2q$ $4p + 2p = 6p$ and $3q - q = 2q$, but $6p$ and $2q$ are not like terms so
                                    you cannot simplify any further.

d $5t + 7 - 3t + 3 = 2t + 10$ $5t - 3t = 2t$ and $7 + 3 = 10$, but $2t$ and 10 are not like terms so you
                                    cannot simplify any further.

◆ Exercise 9.1

1   Erik has yellow, green and blue bricks.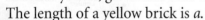
The length of a yellow brick is a.
The length of a green brick is b.
The length of a blue brick is c.
Work out the total length of these arrangements of bricks.
Give your answer in its simplest form.

a 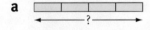   **b**

c 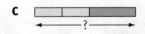   **d**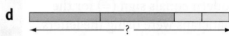

e 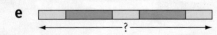   **f**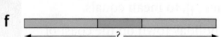

2   Simplify each of these.

     a $x + x + x + x + x$ **b** $2y + 4y$ **c** $5d + 3d$ **d** $6t + 3t + 4t$

     e $8g + 5g + g$ **f** $9p + p + 6p$ **g** $7w - 4w$ **h** $8n - n$

     i $9b - 5b$ **j** $6f + 2f - 3f$ **k** $9j + j - 7j$ **l** $8k - 5k - 2k$

3 In an algebraic pyramid, you find the expression in each block by <u>adding</u> the expressions in the two blocks below it.
Copy and complete these pyramids.

a
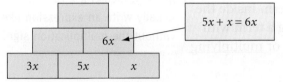

| | 6x | |
| 3x | 5x | x |

5x + x = 6x

b
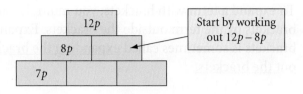

	12p	
	8p	
7p		

Start by working out 12p − 8p

4 Simplify these expressions by collecting like terms.
   a 2a + 3a + 5b
   b 3c + 5c + 2d + d
   c 4x + 5y + 3x + 2y
   d 7h + 8g + 2h + g
   e 4t + 1 + 3t + 9
   f 6m − 2m + 7n − 3n
   g 10q − 5q + 17 − 9
   h 6t + 3v − 4t + v
   i 9k + 5f − 3k − 2f
   j 7r + 2s + 3t − 2r + s + 2t
   k 11q + 6y + 9 − 3y − 7
   l 12 + 6h + 8k − 6 − 3h + 3k

5 Write each expression in its simplest form.
The first one is done for you.
   a 2ab + 3ab + 5pq + 7qp = 5ab + 12pq
   b 3st + 5st + 9pu + 7up
   c 4vb + 2bv + 6ad − 4da
   d 11rt + 9gh − 2rt − 7hg
   e 8xy + 12xz + 3yx − 9zx
   f 6a + 7ac − 2a + ac
   g 4mn − 3nm + 7gh − 7hg

> 2ab and 3ab are <u>like terms</u> so you can add them to give 5ab.
>
> 7qp means 7 × q × p which is the same as 7 × p × q, so 5pq and 7qp are <u>like terms</u>. When you write your answer, put the letters in alphabetical order, so write 12pq and not 12qp.

6 This is part of Dai's homework.
Dai has made several mistakes.
Explain what Dai has done wrong.

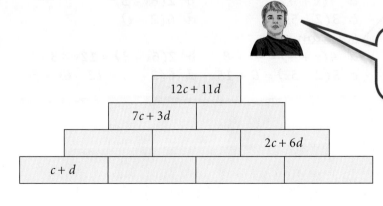

> <u>Question</u>   Write these expressions in their simplest form.
> *a* 2x + 8 + 6x − 4   *b* 3bc + 5bd − 2bc + 3db
> <u>Solution</u>   *a* 2x + 8 + 6x − 4 = 8x + 4 = 12x
>   *b* 3bc + 5bd − 2bc + 3db = 5bc + 5bd + 3db

7 Copy and complete this algebraic pyramid.

> Remember, you find the expression in each block by <u>adding</u> the expressions in the two blocks below it.

		12c + 11d		
	7c + 3d			
			2c + 6d	
c + d				

9.2 Expanding brackets

Some algebraic expressions include **brackets**.

To **expand** a term with brackets, you multiply each term inside the brackets by the term outside the brackets. Expanding a term with brackets is sometimes called <u>expanding the brackets</u> or <u>multiplying out the brackets.</u>

> $4(n + 3)$ means $4 \times (n + 3)$, but you usually write an expression like this without the multiplication sign.

Worked example 9.2

Expand the brackets.
a $4(n + 3)$ **b** $2(x - 5)$ **c** $3(2g + h)$

a	$4(n + 3) = 4 \times n + 4 \times 3$ $\qquad\quad = 4n + 12$	Multiply the 4 by the n then the 4 by the 3. Simplify the $4 \times n$ to $4n$ and the 4×3 to 12.
b	$2(x - 5) = 2 \times x - 2 \times 5$ $\qquad\quad = 2x - 10$	This time there is a minus sign before the 5, so you need to take away the 10 from the $2x$.
c	$3(2g + h) = 3 \times 2g + 3 \times h$ $\qquad\qquad = 6g + 3h$	The first term is $3 \times 2g$, which is the same as $3 \times 2 \times g$ which simplifies to $6g$.

◆ **Exercise 9.2**

1 Expand the brackets.
   a $2(x + 5)$ **b** $3(y + 6)$ **c** $4(w + 2)$ **d** $5(z + 5)$
   e $3(b - 1)$ **f** $7(c - 4)$ **g** $6(d - 9)$ **h** $2(e - 8)$
   i $6(2 + f)$ **j** $2(1 + g)$ **k** $5(7 + h)$ **l** $9(3 + i)$
   m $6(2 - x)$ **n** $2(1 - y)$ **o** $5(7 - p)$ **p** $9(3 - q)$

2 Multiply out the brackets.
   a $3(2x + 1)$ **b** $4(3y + 5)$ **c** $5(2w + 3)$ **d** $6(4z + 7)$
   e $2(3b - 4)$ **f** $4(2c - 3)$ **g** $6(5d - 1)$ **h** $8(3e - 6)$
   i $3(1 + 2f)$ **j** $5(3 + 4g)$ **k** $7(6 + 7h)$ **l** $9(5 + 4i)$
   m $8(3 - 5x)$ **n** $12(2 - 3y)$ **o** $6(5 - 8p)$ **p** $2(13 - 4q)$

3 This is part of Bethan's homework. Bethan has made a mistake on every question. Explain what Bethan has done wrong.

> <u>Question</u>   Multiply out the brackets.
> a $4(x + 4)$ b $2(6x - 3)$
> c $3(2 - 5x)$ d $6(2 - x)$
> <u>Solution</u>
> a $4(x + 4) = 4x + 8$ b $2(6x - 3) = 12x - 3$
> c $3(2 - 5x) = 6 + 15x$ d $6(2 - x) = 12 - 6x = 6x$

4 Which one of these expressions is different from the others? Explain your answer.

    $2(12x + 15)$ $6(5 + 4x)$

    $3(10 + 8x)$ $4(6x + 26)$

9.3 Constructing and solving equations

To **solve** an equation, you need to find the value of the unknown letter.

Take the equation: $x + 5 = 12$

If you take away 5 from both sides of the equation: $x + 5 - 5 = 12 - 5$

you have found the **solution** to the equation. $x = 7$

> You can use **inverse operations** to solve an equation.

Worked example 9.3

a Solve these equations and check your answers.
  i $x - 3 = 12$ **ii** $2x + 4 = 16$
b Mari thinks of a number, she divides it by 2, then adds 3 and her answer is 7.
  i Write an equation for Mari's unknown number.
  ii Solve the equation to find the value of Mari's number.

a i $x = 12 + 3$ — Add 3 to both sides.
  $x = 15$ — Work out the value of x then substitute this value back
  Check: $15 - 3 = 12$ ✓ into the equation to check the answer is correct.
  ii $2x = 16 - 4$ — Subtract 4 from both sides.
  $2x = 12$ — Simplify the right-hand side.
  $x = \frac{12}{2}$ — Divide both sides by 2.
  $x = 6$ — Work out the value of x then substitute this value back
  Check: $2 \times 6 + 4 = 12 + 4 = 16$ ✓ into the equation to check the answer is correct.

b i $\frac{n}{2} + 3 = 7$ — Let Mari's unknown number be n.
  ii $\frac{n}{2} = 7 - 3$ — Subtract 3 from both sides.
  $\frac{n}{2} = 4$ — Simplify the right-hand side.
  $n = 4 \times 2$ — Multiply both sides by 2.
  $n = 8$ — Work out the value of n.

Exercise 9.3

1 Solve each of these equations and check your answers.
  a $x + 4 = 11$ **b** $x + 3 = 6$ **c** $2 + x = 15$ **d** $7 + x = 19$
  e $x - 4 = 9$ **f** $x - 2 = 8$ **g** $x - 12 = 14$ **h** $x - 18 = 30$
  i $3x = 12$ **j** $5x = 30$ **k** $7x = 70$ **l** $12x = 72$
  m $\frac{x}{2} = 4$ **n** $\frac{x}{3} = 5$ **o** $\frac{x}{7} = 3$ **p** $\frac{x}{9} = 7$

2 Dayita uses this method to solve an equation when the unknown is on the right-hand side of the equation. Use Dayita's method to solve these equations.

> Solve the equation: $12 = y + 3$
> Write this as: $y + 3 = 12$
> Solve as normal: $y = 12 - 3$
> $y = 9$

  a $15 = y + 3$ **b** $9 = y + 2$ **c** $13 = y - 5$ **d** $25 = y - 3$
  e $24 = 8y$ **f** $42 = 6y$ **g** $5 = \frac{y}{2}$ **h** $7 = \frac{y}{5}$

3 Solve each of these equations and check your answers.

a $2a + 3 = 13$ **b** $4a + 1 = 17$ **c** $3a - 2 = 13$ **d** $2a - 8 = 4$

e $\frac{b}{2} + 1 = 5$ **f** $\frac{b}{4} + 3 = 7$ **g** $\frac{b}{3} - 2 = 2$ **h** $\frac{b}{5} - 1 = 5$

i $14 = 3c + 2$ **j** $29 = 4c - 3$ **k** $9 = \frac{c}{3} + 2$ **l** $1 = \frac{c}{6} - 6$

4 Write an equation for each of these. Solve each equation to find the value of the unknown number.

a 'I think of a number and add 3. The answer is 18.'

b 'I think of a number and subtract 4. The answer is 10.'

c 'I think of a number and multiply it by 4. The answer is 24.'

d 'I think of a number and divide it by 6. The answer is 12.'

e 'I think of a number, multiply it by 4 and then add 2. The answer is 26.'

f 'I think of a number, divide it by 3 and then subtract 8. The answer is 4.'

5 The total length of each set of bricks is shown.
Write an equation involving the lengths of the bricks, then solve your equation.

a
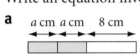

b
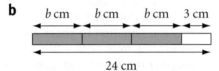

6 Kenji has these cards.

| $4m + 4$ | $2m - 6$ | $6m + 2$ | $=$ | 32 | 44 | 20 |

He chooses one pink card, the purple card and one blue card to make an equation.
Which pink and blue card should he choose to give him the equation with:

a the largest solution for m **b** the smallest solution for m?

Summary

You should now know that:

★ Terms that contain the same letter or letters are called like terms.

★ To expand a term with brackets you multiply each term inside the brackets by the term outside the brackets.

★ To solve an equation you find the value of the unknown letter.

★ You can check the solution of an equation is correct by substituting the number back into the equation.

You should be able to:

★ Simplify an expression by collecting like terms.

★ Expand a term that includes brackets.

★ Construct and solve linear equations.

★ Manipulate numbers, algebraic expressions and equations.

★ Identify and represent unknown numbers in problems.

★ Work logically and draw simple conclusions.

End of unit review

1 Simplify these expressions.
  a $n + n + n$ **b** $3c + 5c$ **c** $4b + b$
  d $8v - 2v$ **e** $9x - x$ **f** $11k - 10k$

2 Simplify these expressions by collecting like terms.
  a $5c + 6c + 2d$ **b** $6c + 5k + 5c + k$
  c $7x + 6w - 3x + 3w$ **d** $9p + 12q - 6p - 10q$
  e $4ad + 7bn + 5ad - 2bn$ **f** $3xy + 5yz - 2xy + 3yz$

 3 Copy and complete this algebraic pyramid.

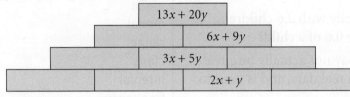

> Remember that you find the expression in each block by <u>adding</u> the expressions in the two blocks below it.

4 Expand the brackets.
  a $3(x + 2)$ **b** $4(y - 5)$ **c** $2(3 + z)$ **d** $6(3 - w)$

5 Multiply out the brackets.
  a $4(3x + 2)$ **b** $2(2y - 3)$ **c** $5(5 + 3z)$ **d** $3(7 - 4v)$

 6 Which one of these expressions is the odd one out?
Explain your answer.

  $3(16x + 12)$ $2(18 + 24x)$ $4(12x + 8)$ $6(6 + 8x)$

7 Solve each of these equations and check your answers.
  a $n + 3 = 8$ **b** $m - 4 = 12$ **c** $3p = 24$ **d** $\frac{x}{5} = 3$

8 Solve each of these equations and check your answers.
  a $3b + 2 = 17$ **b** $4c - 1 = 19$ **c** $\frac{d}{3} + 2 = 9$ **d** $\frac{b}{7} - 1 = 4$

9 Shen and Zalika have set some puzzles. Write an equation for each of them. Solve your equations to find the values of the unknown numbers.

  a
  > I think of a number and add 3. The answer is 22.

  b
  > I think of a number. I multiply it by 2 then add 4. The answer is 28.

 10 The total length of each set of bricks is shown.
Write an equation involving the lengths of the bricks, then solve your equation.

  a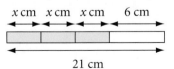

  b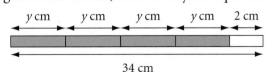

10 Averages

average
height

You often hear people talking about 'average height', 'average income', 'average mass' and 'average age', but what do they mean? What other examples can you think of?

You may even hear about an 'average' family with 2.6 children. What does that mean? How can you have 0.6 of a child?

You need to remember that an average may not actually be a real value. It is just a number, calculated from real data, and is used to represent a typical value for the data.

There are several ways to work out an average. Deciding which method to use can depend on the data you have. Sometimes the values are very close together, and sometimes they are very spread out.

The heights of one group are very similar. The heights of the other group are very varied.

In this unit, you will look at three kinds of average. You will also learn how to measure how spread out the data values are.

10.1 Average and range

A **statistic** is a value that you calculate from a set of data. A statistic that you will often see is the **average**.

An average is a representative value. It is a single number that gives a general idea about a set of numbers.

You need to know about three types of average: the **mode**, the **median** and the **mean**.

Think about the ages of the people in the audience at a concert.

The mode is the most common value. If there are more 19-year-olds than people of any other age at the concert, then the mode, or the **modal** age, is 19 years.

The median is the middle number if you put all the numbers in order. If you lined up all the members of the audience in order of age, the age of the middle person is the median.

> You will learn about the mean in the next section.

The mean is one value that could represent the whole audience.

Another useful statistic is the difference between the largest and smallest numbers. This is the **range**. It shows how spread out the numbers are. If the oldest person at the concert is 75 and the youngest is 13, the range is 62 years.

Worked example 10.1

Here are the times, in seconds, that 16 students took to run 200 metres. Work out the mode and the median.

30	39	32	35	32	37	32	37
44	30	32	38	38	41	39	32

The mode is 32 seconds.
The median is 36 seconds.

There are five 32s, 32 occurs more times than any other number.
The numbers, in order, are:

30 30 32 32 32 32 32 35 37 37 38 38 39 39 41 44

They must be written in order, to find the median.
The middle is halfway between the 8th and 9th number.
There is no middle number.

Here is an example of a large set of data recorded in a table. It shows the masses of 118 people.

The masses are arranged in groups, called **classes**. The **frequency** is the number of people in each class. The table above, called a **frequency table**, shows that 26 people have a mass that is in the interval from 40 to 49 kg and 39 people have a mass in the interval from 50 to 59 kg. You don't know the actual mass of each of the 118 people so you can't find the real median or mode.

You can find the class that includes the greatest number of people. This is called the **modal class**. The modal class for this data is 50–59 kg.

Mass (kg)	40–49	50–59	60–69	70–79	80–89
Frequency	26	39	28	19	6

◆ Exercise 10.1

1   The ages, in years, of a group of students are given in the box.

11	11	12	13	13	14	15	15	15	15	15

Work out: **a** the mode   **b** the median   **c** the range.

2 Tom recorded the midday temperatures, in degrees
   Celsius, each day for three weeks. His results are shown
   on the right.

| 7 | 2 | –1 | 3 | 2 | –2 | 0 | 2 | 6 | 6 |
| 3 | 4 | 6 | 6 | 5 | 3 | 8 | 9 | 6 | 6 | 2 |

   Work out: **a** the mode   **b** the median   **c** the range.

3 These are the masses, in kilograms, of nine members of
   a slimming club.

| 75 | 78 | 82 | 83 | 85 | 88 | 90 | 92 | 93 |

   a Work out the median mass.   **b** Work out the range.
   c After three months, they had all lost 4 kg. Work out the new median and the new range.
   d How will the median change if everyone loses 10 kg?
   e How will the range change if everyone loses 10 kg?

4 The table shows the populations of seven countries. The numbers are in millions.

Country	Nigeria	Saudi Arabia	Egypt	India	Indonesia	Malaysia	New Zealand
Population (millions)	112	22	69	1013	213	22	4

   a Which country has the median population?
   b Work out the range of the populations.

5 The ages of ten students are shown in the box.

| 9 | 11 | 11 | 11 | 11 | 12 | 12 | 13 | 14 | 14 |

   Work out: **a** the mode   **b** the median   **c** the range.

6 These are the heights (in metres) of six members of
   a swimming club.

| 1.40 | 1.45 | 1.55 | 1.65 | 1.65 | 1.80 |

   a Work out: **i** the median height   **ii** the range.
   b One more person joins the club. The range is now 0.45 m and the median is 1.55 m. Find the
   height of the seventh person.

7 This table shows how long a group of 92 holiday-makers are planning to stay in New Zealand.

Length of stay (days)	1–7	8–14	15–21	22–28	29–42
Frequency	6	14	22	35	15

   a Find the modal class. Give a reason for your answer.
   b It is not possible to find the range.
      i Explain why the smallest possible value of the range is 22 days.
      ii What is the largest possible value of the range?

8 A group of 25 children were asked how many sisters they had.
   The frequency table shows the results.

Number of sisters	0	1	2	3	4	5
Frequency	4	8	6	2	4	1

   a From the table, four children have no sisters. How many children have more than two sisters?
   b What is the modal number of sisters?   **c** What is the median number of sisters?

10.2 The mean

You have been using two sorts of average: the mode and the median. The third type of average you need to know about is the mean.

To find the mean of a set of numbers, you <u>add up</u> all the values and then <u>divide</u> by the number of values.

Example: To find the mean of five masses: 12 kg, 14 kg, 15 kg, 20 kg and 23 kg, first find the total mass. Then divide by 5. The mean is $\frac{12+14+15+20+23}{5} = \frac{84}{5} = 16.8$ kg.

For a large set of numbers, you may need to use a frequency table.

Worked example 10.2

An ordinary six-sided dice was thrown 100 times. The table shows the frequencies for each possible score.
Work out: **a** the mode **b** the mean.

Score	1	2	3	4	5	6
Frequency	12	19	15	11	24	19

a Mode = 5   The mode is the score with the highest frequency.

b Mean = 3.73   Total score = 1 × 12 + 2 × 19 + 3 × 15 + 4 × 11 + 5 × 24 + 6 × 19 = 373

Mean = $\frac{373}{100}$ = 3.73.

> The mean is the total ÷ 100 because the dice was thrown 100 times.

Notice that the mean is not one of the actual values. This is because it has been calculated to represent all the values. You can think of it as the score that would have resulted if every throw of the dice had given the same number. This is very unlikely when you actually throw a dice, but in statistics anything might happen!

◆ Exercise 10.2

1 Mia measured the lengths of six pieces of string.   12 cm   9 cm   14 cm   20 cm   13 cm   10 cm
   a Work out the mean length.
   b How many pieces are longer than the mean length?
   c How many pieces are shorter than the mean length?

2 Rex recorded the numbers of people who visited his cinema on several   68   85   31   38   103
   different days.
   Work out the mean number of visitors per day.

3 Leo wrote down the ages of ten members of his family.   18   18   19   20   24   26   30   32   38   45
   a Work out their mean age.
   b Leo has written his uncle's age as 45 instead of 55.
     Work out the correct mean age.

4 Last season Rio's football team scored 50 goals in 20 matches.
This season they scored 60 goals in 25 matches.
Work out the mean number of goals per match for each season.

5 Shona recorded the number of hours of sunshine for eight days.
Work out: **a** the mean   **b** the mode   **c** the median.

| 6 | 0 | 5 | 8 | 2 | 9 | 9 | 9 |

6 25 students in a class each estimated the size of an angle.
Their answers are recorded in this frequency table.

Estimate°	50°	55°	60°	65°
Frequency	6	10	7	2

a Find the mode.
b Work out the mean of all the estimates.
c How many estimates were below the mean?
d How many estimates were above the mean?

7 This table shows the numbers of cars owned by 20 different families living in one street.

Number of cars	0	1	2	3	4
Number of families	5	8	4	2	1

a Work out the modal number of cars.
b Work out the mean number of cars per family.

8 The mean age of five children in a family is 12 years.
Work out the total age of the children.

9 The mean mass of four women is 60 kg.
Another woman has a mass of 70 kg.
Work out the mean mass of the five women.

10 In a group of four children, their mean height is 1.40 m.
In another group of six children, their mean height is 1.60 m.
Work out the mean height of all ten children.

11 A student carries out a survey of favourite colours.
a Can she find the average colour? Give a reason for your answer.
b Can she find the range of colours?

12 Here is a set of numbers:
10, 10, 10, 10, 11, 12, 13, 15, 17
a Find (i) the mode, (ii) the median, (iii) the mean.
b There is a mistake in the set of numbers. The 17 should be 26.
Find the correct value for (i) the mode, (ii) the median, (iii) the mean.

10.3 Comparing distributions

You can use an average and the range to summarise a set of data.

You need to choose which average to use: the mode, the median or the mean.

The range measures the spread of the data.

You can also use the same statistics to compare two sets of data.

> An average is a representative or typical value.

Worked example 10.3

A slimming club recorded the masses (in kilograms) of eight men and six women.
Calculate the mean and the range of each set of data and use them to compare the two sets.

Men: 65, 79, 68, 72, 77, 77, 81, 67

Women: 68, 52, 47, 49, 50, 58

The mean for the men is 73.25 kg.

$$\frac{65+79+68+72+77+77+81+67}{8}$$

$$= \frac{586}{8} = 73.25$$

The mean for the women is 54 kg.

$$\frac{68+52+47+49+50+58}{6} = \frac{324}{6} = 54$$

On average the men are 19.25 kg heavier than the women. $73.25 - 54 = 19.25$

The range for the men is 16 kg. $81 - 65 = 16$

The range for the women is 21 kg. $68 - 47 = 21$

The women's masses are more varied than the men's.   21 is greater than 16.

In the example you compared:

- the average of each group, using the mean (you could also use the median for this)
- the variation within each group, using the range.

◆ Exercise 10.3

1 A primary PE teacher measured the heights of two groups of young children. The results are shown on the right.

   Group A: 84 cm, 73 cm, 89 cm, 80 cm, 77 cm
   Group B: 77 cm, 85 cm, 75 cm, 69 cm, 82 cm, 67 cm, 72 cm

   a Work out the median height for each group.
   b Use the medians to state which group is taller, on average.

2 The test marks of two groups of students are shown on the right.

   Maths: 77, 89, 75, 80, 80, 91, 78, 76, 76, 76
   Science: 72, 78, 77, 87, 86, 79, 66, 75

   a Work out the range for each test.
   b Which test has a greater variation in the marks?

3 In the 2010 football World Cup, Spain won and Brazil was knocked out in the quarter finals. The numbers of goals they scored in their matches are shown on the right.
   Work out the mean scores and state which team scored more goals per match, overall.

   Spain: 0, 2, 2, 1, 1, 1, 1
   Brazil: 2, 3, 0, 3, 1

4 Nils recorded the temperatures in two experiments.

First experiment (°C)	29, 28, 21, 33, 30
Second experiment (°C)	28, 29, 28, 33, 32, 31, 32, 29

   a Work out the mean, the median and the range for each experiment.
   b State whether each of these statements is TRUE or FALSE.
     i The temperatures in the first experiment are higher, on average, than the temperatures in the second experiment.
     ii The temperatures in the first experiment are more varied that the temperatures in the second experiment.
   c Can you work out the modal temperature for each experiment? Explain your answer.

5 A nurse measured the total mass of 20 baby boys as 64 kg. The total mass of 15 baby girls was 51 kg. Which were heavier, the boys or girls? Give a reason for your answer.

6 In a large town there are three sports clubs. Here is some information about the ages of the people who belong to each club.

Club	Number of people	Mean age (years)	Age range (years)	Age of youngest person (years)
Football	46	24	23	9
Swimming	32	29	32	7
Athletics	23	18	11	12

Use the information in the table to answer these questions. Give reasons for your answers.
   a Work out the age of the oldest person in each club.
   b Which club has the highest average age?
   c Which club has the greatest variation in ages?

Summary

You should now know that:

★ Mode, median and mean are three types of average.

★ The mode is the most common value.

★ The modal class is the class with the highest frequency.

★ The median is the middle value when a set of values is listed in order.

★ To find the mean you add all the values and divide by the number of values.

★ The range is the difference between the largest value and the smallest value. It measures variation.

You should be able to:

★ Find the mode, median and range for a set of numbers or values.

★ Find the modal class for a set of grouped data.

★ Calculate the mean of a set of numbers.

★ Calculate the mean from a simple frequency table.

★ Compare two simple distributions, using the range and the mode, median or mean.

★ Work logically and draw simple conclusions.

End of unit review

1 Here are the numbers of students in nine different classrooms.
Work out: **a** the mode   **b** the range   **c** the median.

| 21 18 18 19 24 17 18 19 20 |

2 A set of masses has a range of 28 g. The smallest mass is 102 g.
Work out the largest mass.

3 While she was on holiday, Olga measured the
temperature at the same time every day. Her results are
shown on the right.

| 5 °C   6 °C   –3 °C   –5 °C   –4 °C   3 °C |

Work out: **a** the median   **b** the range of the temperatures.

4 Thse are the ages (in years) of eight children in a holiday club.
  a Work out: **i** the range   **ii** the mode   **iii** the median.

| 8   12   11   10   15   8   8   8 |

  b Now work out what the values will be, in four years' time, of:
     i the range   **ii** the mode   **iii** the median.

5 Bernard recorded the temperature at the same time every day
for five days.

| 8 °C   12 °C   13 °C   13 °C   0 °C |

Work out the mean temperature over these five days.

6 Alexi recorded the numbers of points scored by his favourite basketball
team in six matches.

| 46   51   33   62   48   75 |

  a Calculate the mean number of points per match.
  b Choose the correct answer from those below.
    The team scored <u>more</u> than the mean in ....
    1 match   2 matches   3 matches   4 matches   5 matches

7 This table shows how many goals Red Stars football team scored in each of 30 matches.

Number of goals	0	1	2	3	4	5
Number of matches	3	6	10	4	5	2

  a Complete this sentence: The team scored more than three goals in ☐ matches.
  b Work out the total number of goals scored.
  c Work out the mean number of goals per match.
  d The Green Arrows team scored 56 goals in 16 matches.
    Was their goal average better or worse that that of Red Stars?

8 A class recorded the masses, in grams, of
20 bags of rice.
Their results are shown on the right.

| 490   490   490   490   490   490   495   495   495   495 |
| 500   500   500   505   505   510   510   515   520   535 |

 The average mass is 490 g.

 The average mass is 497.5 g.

 The average mass is 501 g.

Explain how all three students could be correct.

11 Percentages

Percentages are everywhere.

You will see percentages being used if you read a newspaper or watch the news on television. Percentages are used to describe price rises, how well you've done in a test, the chance of bad weather, product sales, and many other things.

-10%   -15%   -20%

-25%   -30%   -35%

-40%   -60%   -70%

There are two particular ways in which you can use percentages.

First, you can use them to compare different things. Suppose you score 14 out of 20 in one test and 60 out of 75 in another one. Which was the better score? It is hard to say because they are marked out of different totals. However, if you change the marks to percentages they become $\frac{14}{20} = 70\%$ and $\frac{60}{75} = 80\%$. You can see immediately that the second mark was better.

Second, you can use percentages to describe increases or decreases. Suppose two items cost 20 dollars and 40 dollars. If both prices are reduced by 10%, one will decrease by 2 dollars and the other by 4 dollars. The <u>percentage</u> decrease is the same in both cases but the <u>actual</u> decrease is different.

In this unit you will learn how to calculate and find percentages of amounts and use them to make comparisons.

11.1 Simple percentages

Per cent just means 'out of 100'.

- 25% means '25 parts out of 100'.
- 25% is another way to write $\frac{1}{4}$.

So a **percentage** is just a different way of writing a **fraction**.

You have already learnt how to write some simple fractions as decimals in Unit 7.

> **Useful conversions**
> $\frac{1}{2} = 50\%$
> $\frac{1}{4} = 25\%$
> $\frac{1}{3} = 33\frac{1}{3}\%$
> $\frac{1}{10} = 10\%$
> $\frac{1}{100} = 1\%$

> **Worked example 11.1**
>
> **a** What percentage of this shape is shaded?
> **b** What percentage is not shaded?
>
>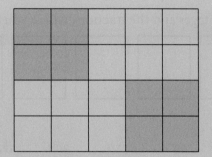
>
> **a** The fraction shaded is $\frac{8}{20}$.   There are 20 identical squares. 8 are shaded.
>
> $\frac{8}{20} = \frac{2}{5}$ 8 and 20 have a common factor of 4. Divide them both by 4.
>
> $\frac{2}{5} = \frac{40}{100} = 40\%$ shaded   Look for a fraction out of 100. 5 × 20 = 100 so multiply by 20.
>
> **b** So 60% is not shaded.   The whole shape is 100%. 100% − 40% = 60%

◆ Exercise 11.1

1 Write down the fraction shaded in each diagram. Then write each fraction as a percentage.

   a 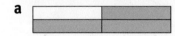   **b**

   c 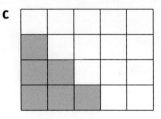   **d**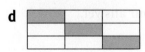

2 Write each percentage as a fraction. Write the answers as simply as possible.
   a 75%   **b** 20%   **c** 30%   **d** 90%   **e** 5%

3 If $25\% = \frac{1}{4}$, what fraction is 12.5%?

4 a Copy this rectangle.
Shade 30%.
b What percentage is un shaded?

5 Write each fraction as a percentage.

a $\frac{1}{4}$ **b** $\frac{3}{10}$ **c** $\frac{3}{20}$ **d** $\frac{3}{5}$ **e** $\frac{9}{10}$ **f** $\frac{1}{20}$ **g** $\frac{19}{20}$

6 $\frac{1}{3} = 33\frac{1}{3}\%$. Use this fact to write $\frac{2}{3}$ as a percentage.

7 Match the percentages and the fractions where you can. What should go on the two blank cards?

| | $\frac{3}{10}$ | $\frac{1}{8}$ | $\frac{4}{5}$ | $\frac{7}{20}$ | $\frac{3}{5}$ |

| | 60% | 40% | 35% | 30% | 12.5% |

8 The label on a new bag of flour states 'Contents 500 grams'. A cake recipe uses 150 g of flour.
a What fraction of a new bag is used?
b What percentage is that?
c What percentage is left?

9 Work out the numbers missing from these percentages.

a 30 metres is ☐ % of 100 metres

b 30 metres is ☐ % of 200 metres

c 30 metres is ☐ % of 50 metres

10 10 people out of a group of 39 watched a movie. Which of these is closest to the percentage that watched the movie? Give a reason for your answer.
5% 15% 25% 35% 45% 55%

11 Work out the numbers missing from these percentages.
a 600 m is ☐ % of one kilometre
b 80 cm is ☐ % of one metre
c 200 ml is ☐ % of half a litre

11.2 Calculating percentages

You should be able to find simple percentages of a **quantity** without using a calculator.

You can easily find 50%, 25% or 10% because they are simple fractions. You can use these to find other percentages.

Worked example 11.2

Find 35% of 80 kg.

Method 1

	35% = 25% + 10%, which are easy percentages to work out.
25% of 80 = $\frac{1}{4}$ of 80 = 20	Divide by 4 to work out $\frac{1}{4}$.
10% of 80 = $\frac{1}{10}$ of 80 = 8	Divide by 10 to work out $\frac{1}{10}$.
35% of 80 kg = 28 kg	25% + 10% = 20 + 8

> You should be able to use either method.

Method 2

$35\% = \frac{35}{100} = \frac{7}{20}$ Write 35% as a fraction and simplify it, cancelling by 5.

$\frac{7}{20}$ of 80 = 80 ÷ 20 × 7 = 28 kg   Divide by 20 to find $\frac{1}{20}$. Multiply by 7 to find $\frac{7}{20}$.

Exercise 11.2

1 a Write 20% as a fraction in its simplest terms.
   b Work out 20% of: **i** 25   **ii** 40   **iii** 50   **iv** 65   **v** 120.

2 a Write each of these percentages as fractions, as simply as possible.
    i 30%   **ii** 85%   **iii** 64%   **iv** 8%
   b Work out: **i** 30% of 40   **ii** 85% of 20   **iii** 64% of 50   **iv** 8% of 200.

3 Work out the following.
   a 10% of 80 m   **b** 15% of 60 kg   **c** 44% of $200   **d** 85% of 40 cm

4 A man has a mass of 120 kg. He reduces his mass by 15%. How many kilograms is that?

5 30% of the mass of an object is 24 kilograms. Use this fact to find:
   a 60% of the mass   **b** 10% of the mass
   c 50% of the mass   **d** the whole mass of the object.

6 There were 300 people at a football match and 35% were adults. The rest were children.
   a What percentage were children?   **b** How many children were present?

7 Find the missing numbers.
   a 25% of 80 m = ☐ % of 40 m   **b** 60% of $25 = ☐ % of $50   **c** 12% of 300 = 6% of ☐

11.3 Comparing quantities

It is often useful to use percentages to compare proportions.

Here is an example. Two schools both have 40 students gaining the top grade in an exam.

You might think that both schools are similar, but the first school entered 50 students and the second school entered 200.

In the first school 80% achieved the top grade. In the second school only 20% did so.

Schools' results are the same!

Schools' results are different!

Which headline is correct?

Worked example 11.3

A student scored 21 out of 30 in a maths test and 54 out of 75 in a science test. Which was her better score?

Maths score = $\frac{21}{30} = \frac{7}{10}$	Write the maths score as a fraction and simplify it.
$\frac{7}{10} = \frac{70}{100} = 70\%$	Change the fraction to a percentage.
Science score = $\frac{54}{75} = \frac{18}{25} = \frac{72}{100} = 72\%$	Do the same with the science score
The scores were similar.	The science score is slightly better, but there is only a difference of 2%.

◆ **Exercise 11.3**

1 a Change these test marks to percentages.
   i 4 out of 10 **ii** 17 out of 25 **iii** 24 out of 80 **iv** 20 out of 60
   b Which was the best mark?

2 In class A, 17 out of 25 students were absent at least one day this year.
   In class B the figure was 14 out of 20. In class C it was 18 out of 24.
   a Work out the percentage who were absent in each class
   b Which class had the worst record for absences?

3 A 400 g pack of couscous contains 116 g of carbohydrate.
   A 250 g bag of maize flour contains 195 g of carbohydrate.
   A 1 kg bag of wheat flour contains 640 g of carbohydrate.
   Use percentages to work out the amount of carbohydrate in each.

4 Mujib has $40 and Prakash has $120. Each of them spends $24.
   Work out the percentage of their money that each of them has spent.

5 In a baby clinic, the nurse weighed 20 baby boys and 30 baby girls.
   Their weights were recorded as 'underweight', 'normal' or 'overweight'.
   The results are in this table.

	Underweight	Normal	Overweight
Boys	5	6	9
Girls	6	12	12

a What percentage of the boys were: **i** underweight **ii** normal **iii** overweight?
b What percentages of the girls were: **i** underweight **ii** normal **iii** overweight?
c Are these statements TRUE or FALSE?
   i More boys than girls were overweight.
   ii A greater percentage of boys were overweight.
   iii More girls than boys were underweight.
   iv A greater percentage of girls than boys were underweight.

6 Ulrika and Jaiyana were two candidates in an election. Here are the votes they received in two areas.
  a Work out the percentages of votes each candidate received in each area.
  b Did Ulrika do better in Area 1 or Area 2?
  c What percentage of votes did Ulrika receive overall?

	Area 1	Area 2
Ulrika	135	94
Jaiyana	165	106

7 The table shows the results when some students were asked if they would like more maths lessons.
  a What percentage of the boys said 'yes'?
  b What percentage of the girls said 'yes'?
  c What percentage of all the children said 'yes'?
  d Who was correct, Xavier or Harsha?

	Boys	Girls
Yes	11	12
No	9	18

Xavier

The answer to **c** should be the sum of the answers to **a** and **b**.

Harsha

The answer to **c** should be halfway between the answers to **a** and **b**.

Summary

You should now know that:
★ Percentages are the number of parts in every 100.
★ Simple fractions, such as $\frac{1}{4}$ and $\frac{3}{10}$, can easily be written as percentages.
★ Equivalent fractions can be used to convert fractions into percentages and vice versa.
★ Simple percentages of a quantity can be found in several different ways.
★ A calculator is not necessary to calculate simple percentages of quantities.
★ A smaller quantity can be represented as a fraction or percentage of a larger one.
★ Percentages can be used to represent and compare different quantities.
★ It is useful to consider whether an answer is reasonable in the context of a problem involving percentages.

You should be able to:
★ Use fractions and percentages to describe parts of shapes, quantities and measures.
★ Calculate simple percentages of quantities (with whole-number answers) and use mental strategies to do so.
★ Express a smaller quantity as a fraction and then as a percentage of a larger one.
★ Find percentages to represent and compare different quantities.
★ Calculate percentages accurately, choosing operations and mental or written methods appropriate to the numbers and context.
★ Consider whether an answer to a problem involving percentages is reasonable in the context of the problem.
★ Solve word problems involving percentages.

End of unit review

1 a Copy this diagram and shade 60% of it.

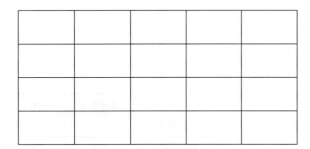

  b Shade half of the unshaded part in a different way. What percentage of the whole shape is this?

2 Write each of these percentages as a fraction in its simplest possible form.
    a 30%   **b** 60%   **c** 90%   **d** 15%   **e** 28%

3 Write these fractions as percentages.
    a $\frac{3}{100}$ **b** $\frac{3}{50}$ **c** $\frac{3}{25}$ **d** $\frac{3}{20}$ **e** $\frac{3}{10}$ **f** $\frac{3}{5}$

4 a What fraction of 40 kg is 16 kg?   **b** Write your answer to part **a** as a percentage.

5 A student had $40 but spent $32. What percentage of his money has he spent?

6 Find 40% of:
    a 20 kg   **b** 35 m   **c** 250 ml   **d** 55 people   **e** 75 hours

7 Find these quantities.
    a 18% of 50   **b** 64% of 25   **c** 65% of 80   **d** 37% of 200

8 Maya has saved $75. This is 30% of what she needs. Explain how you can work out how much she needs.

9 Describe two different ways to calculate 60% of $35.

10 Ma's Mango Chutney is sold in 250 g jars. Each jar contains 135 g of mangoes.
Pa's Mango Chutney is sold in 400 g jars. Each jar contains 248 g of mangoes.
Which brand has the greater percentage of mangoes?

11 In class A, 17 students in a class of 25 passed an exam. In class B, 13 out of 20 passed. In class C, 7 out of 10 passed. Compare the percentage pass rate for each class.

12 Constructions

The word <u>construct</u> means 'to draw accurately'.

In real life it is important for architects to make accurate drawings of the buildings they are planning.

Key words

Make sure you learn and understand these key words:

ruler
straight lines
perpendicular lines
parallel lines
set square
included angle
SAS
included side
ASA
protractor
internal angle

The Louvre museum in Paris, shown on the right, is one of the largest and most visited museums in the world.

It was originally built as a fortress and later converted into a royal palace before becoming a museum.

In 1989 the American architect I. M. Pei designed and built a glass pyramid at the entrance to the Louvre.

The pyramid is a complex steel structure covered with glass pieces. Of these, 603 are rhombus-shaped and 70 are triangular.

You can see why it is important for architects to make accurate drawings of their designs – think what would happen to the glass pyramid if just one of the lengths was wrong!

In this unit you will learn about drawing lines and shapes accurately.

12.1 Measuring and drawing lines

You must be able to use a **ruler** to draw and measure **straight lines** accurately.

This is a centimetre ruler.

> When you are doing mathematical constructions, always use a hard, sharp pencil so that your lines are as thin and clean as possible.

The small divisions that occur in the spaces from one centimetre to the next are millimetres.

You need to be able to measure and draw straight lines to the nearest millimetre.

Worked example 12.1

a Measure the length of this line, correct to the nearest millimetre. _____

Write the measurement in   **i**   cm   **ii**   mm.

b Draw a straight line 2.7 cm long.

a **i** 4.2 cm   Measure the line with a ruler.

ii 42 mm   Make sure that the start of the line is at 0 on the ruler.

The line finishes at 4 cm 2 mm, so the answers are 4.2 cm and 42 mm.

b _____

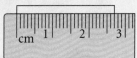

Make sure the start of the line is at 0 on the ruler. Draw the line as far as 2 cm and then 7 mm more.

✦ Exercise 12.1

1 Measure these lines. Give the measurements correct to the nearest millimetre.

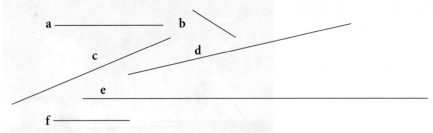

Write each measurement in   **i** ☐ cm   **ii** ☐ mm.

2 Draw straight lines with these lengths. Write the length of each line next to it.

  a 5 cm   **b** 7.3 cm   **c** 0.4 cm   **d** 13.7 cm

3 Alicia has a ruler that is 15 cm long.

Explain to Alicia what she will need to do.

> How can I use my 15 cm ruler to draw a line exactly 22.3 cm long?

12.2 Drawing perpendicular and parallel lines

Perpendicular lines are lines that meet at a right angle (90°).

You show that lines are perpendicular by using a small square symbol in the corner (□). You have already seen this in Unit **5**.

Parallel lines are lines that never meet.

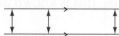

The <u>perpendicular</u> distance between the lines is always the same.

You show that lines are parallel by using an arrow symbol (→) on each line.

You can use a ruler and **set square** to draw parallel and perpendicular lines.

Worked example 12.2

a   Draw a line segment AB 7.5 cm long. Mark the point C on the line AB where C is 4.5 cm from A. Draw a line from C that is perpendicular to the line AB.
b   Draw parallel lines 5 cm long that are a distance of 2 cm apart.

a

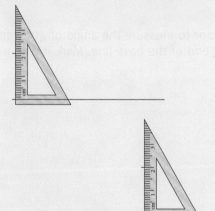

First draw AB, 7.5 cm long.
Mark the point C on the line AB, so that AC is 4.5 cm.
Use the set square to draw a perpendicular line up from C.

b

First draw one line segment 5 cm long.
Place the set square at the end of this line and use it to measure 2 cm up from the first line.

Use the set square to measure another point 2 cm up from the first line.

Join these two points and make sure that the parallel line is also 5 cm long.

Exercise 12.2

1 Draw parallel line segments that are:
  a 7 cm long and 1.5 cm apart   **b** 9.8 cm long and 3.2 cm apart

2 Draw PQ 10 cm long. Mark the point R on PQ so that R is 3 cm from P.
Mark the point S on the line PQ so that S is 4.5 cm from Q.
Draw two lines, one from R and one from S, that are both perpendicular to the line PQ.

3 Draw UV 8 cm long.
  a Draw a 4 cm line perpendicular to UV from the midpoint of UV. Label the ends X and Y.
  b Draw a line, 4 cm long, from the midpoint of XY and perpendicular to XY. Label the ends W and Z.
  c Check by measuring with a ruler that WZ is parallel to UV.

12.3 Constructing triangles

You need to be able to do two types of triangle construction.

In the first, you are given two sides and the angle between them. This angle is the **included angle**. This is known as **SAS**, which stands for <u>S</u>ide <u>A</u>ngle <u>S</u>ide.

In the second, you are given two angles and the side between them. This side is the **included side**. This is known as **ASA**, which stands for <u>A</u>ngle <u>S</u>ide <u>A</u>ngle.

You need a ruler and a **protractor** to draw these triangles accurately.

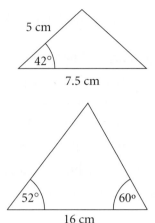

> **Worked example 12.3**
>
> Make an accurate drawing of the following triangles.
>
> **a**
> 4 cm
> 40°
> 6 cm
>
> **b**
> 30°   60°
> 8 cm

a

First, draw the side 6 cm long.

Use a protractor to measure the angle of 40° from the left-hand end of the base line. Mark it with a small point.

Now draw the second side, 4 cm long.

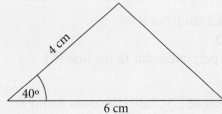

Finally draw the third side of the triangle. Label the sides and angles with their correct measurements.

b

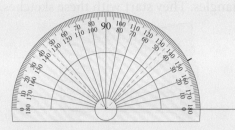

Start by drawing the base line, 8 cm long.

Use a protractor to measure the angle of 30° from the left-hand end of the base line. Mark it with a small point.

Draw a line through the 30° mark

Use a protractor to measure the angle of 60° from the right-hand end of the base line. Mark it with a small point.

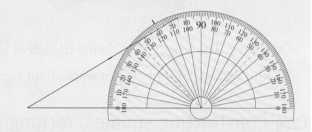

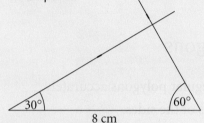

Draw a line through the 60° mark that crosses the 30° line. Label the sides and angles with their correct measurements.

♦ **Exercise 12.3**

1 Draw an accurate copy of each of these triangles.

a   **b**   **c**

2 Draw an accurate copy of each of these triangles.

a 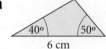   **b** 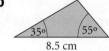   **c**

3 a Draw an accurate copy of triangle ABC.
  b Measure and write down the length of AC.
  c Measure and write down the size of angle BCA.

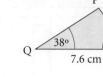

4 a Draw an accurate copy of triangle PQR.
  b Measure and write down the length of PQ.
  c Measure and write down the length of PR.
  d Measure and write down the size of angle QPR.
  e Work out the total of the three angles in the triangle.
  f Have you have drawn your triangle accurately?
    Give a reason for your answer.

5 Draw an accurate copy of each of these triangles.

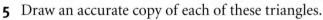

a

b

c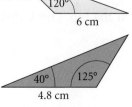

d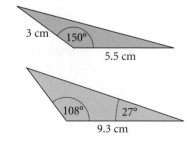

6 Shen and Oditi both make accurate drawings of different triangles. They start with these sketches.

Oditi's sketch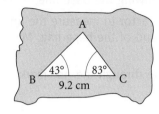

Shen's sketch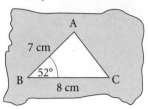

Oditi says: 'The length of AC in my triangle is longer than the length of AC in your triangle.'

Is Oditi correct? Show how you worked out your answer.

12.4 Constructing squares, rectangles and polygons

You need a ruler and a protractor to draw squares, rectangles and regular polygons accurately.

To draw a square or a rectangle, all you need to know are the lengths of the sides.

You already know that all the angles in a square or a rectangle are 90°.

To draw a regular polygon, you need to know the lengths of the sides <u>and</u> the size of the **internal angles**.

Remember that in a regular polygon all the sides are the same length and all the internal angles are the same size.

— internal angle

Worked example 12.4

Make an accurate drawing of:
a a rectangle with a length of 7 cm and a width of 3 cm.
b a regular pentagon with a side length of 5 cm and an internal angle of 108°.

a

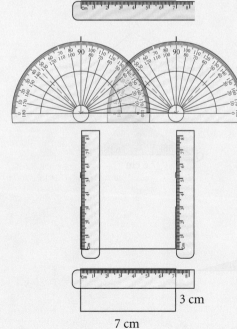

First draw a base of length 7 cm.

Use a protractor to measure angles of 90° at both ends of the base line. Mark them with small points.

Using the points for 90°, draw a perpendicular line, 3 cm long, from each end of the base line to form the sides of the rectangle.

Join the sides of the rectangle at the top. Check that this line measures 6 cm.

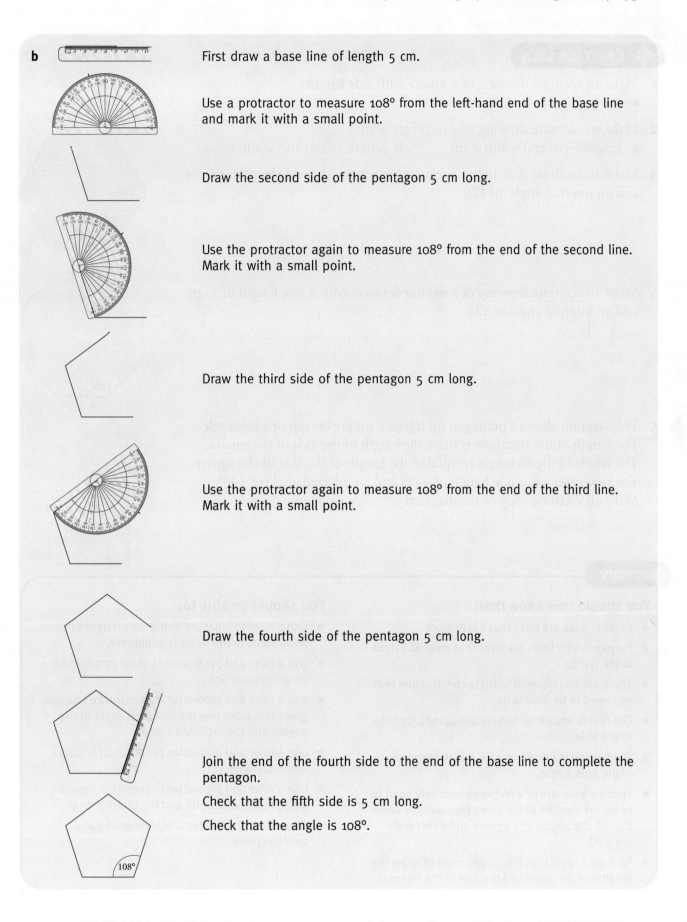

b   First draw a base line of length 5 cm.

Use a protractor to measure 108° from the left-hand end of the base line and mark it with a small point.

Draw the second side of the pentagon 5 cm long.

Use the protractor again to measure 108° from the end of the second line. Mark it with a small point.

Draw the third side of the pentagon 5 cm long.

Use the protractor again to measure 108° from the end of the third line. Mark it with a small point.

Draw the fourth side of the pentagon 5 cm long.

Join the end of the fourth side to the end of the base line to complete the pentagon.

Check that the fifth side is 5 cm long.

Check that the angle is 108°.

◆ Exercise 12.4

1 Make an accurate drawing of a square with side length:
   a 4 cm   **b** 7.2 cm.

2 Make an accurate drawing of a rectangle with:
   a length 5 cm and width 2 cm   **b** length 10 cm and width 6 cm.

3 Make an accurate drawing of a regular hexagon with a side length of 4 cm and an internal angle of 120°.

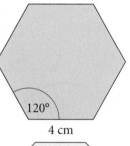
120°
4 cm

4 Make an accurate drawing of a regular octagon with a side length of 5 cm and an internal angle of 135°.

135°
5 cm

 5 The diagram shows a pentagon on top of a square on top of a rectangle. The length of the rectangle is twice the length of the side of the square. The width of the rectangle is equal to the length of the side of the square. The pentagon has a side length of 4 cm and an internal angle of 108°. Make an accurate copy of the diagram.

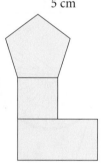

Summary

You should now know that:

★ Parallel lines are lines that never meet.

★ Perpendicular lines are lines that meet at a right angle (90°).

★ There are two types of triangle construction that you need to be able to do.

★ The first is known as SAS, which stands for <u>S</u>ide <u>A</u>ngle <u>S</u>ide.

★ The second is known as ASA, which stands for <u>A</u>ngle <u>S</u>ide <u>A</u>ngle.

★ To draw a square or a rectangle you only need to know the lengths of the sides (you already know that all the angles in a square and a rectangle are 90°).

★ To draw a regular polygon, you need to know the lengths of the sides and the size of the internal angles.

You should be able to:

★ Use a ruler to measure and draw straight lines accurately, to the nearest millimetre.

★ Use a ruler and set square to draw parallel and perpendicular lines.

★ Use a ruler and protractor to construct a triangle, given two sides and the included angle or two angles and the included side.

★ Use a ruler and protractor to construct squares and rectangles.

★ Use a ruler and protractor to construct regular polygons, given a side and the internal angle.

★ Draw accurate mathematical diagrams and constructions.

End of unit review

1 Measure these lines. Give the measurements correct to the nearest mm.
   Write each measurement in   **i**   cm   **ii**   mm.

   a _____   **b**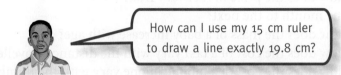

2 Draw straight lines with lengths of:
   a 5.7 cm   **b** 0.8 cm.
   Write the length of each line next to it.

3 Razi has a ruler 15 cm long.
   Explain what Razi will need to do.

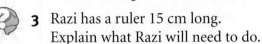

> How can I use my 15 cm ruler
> to draw a line exactly 19.8 cm?

4 Draw two parallel line segments that are 8 cm long and 2.5 cm apart.

5 Draw XY which is 9 cm long. Mark the point Z on XY so that Z is 4 cm from X. Draw a line from Z, which is perpendicular to XY.

6 Draw an accurate copy of each of these triangles.

a

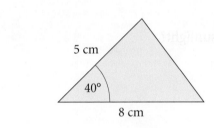

5 cm
40°
8 cm

b

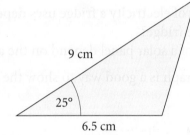

9 cm
25°
6.5 cm

c

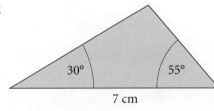

30° 55°
7 cm

d

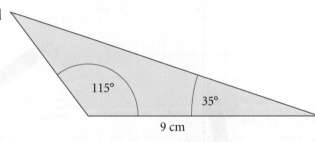

115°
35°
9 cm

7 **a** Look at the sketch of triangle ABC.
       What do you need to do before you can
       draw this triangle?
   b Draw an accurate copy of triangle ABC.
   c Measure and write down the length of AB.
   d Measure and write down the length of AC.

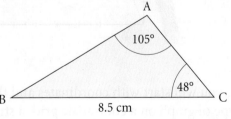

A
105°
48°
C
B
8.5 cm

8 Make an accurate drawing of a square with sides of length 5.5 cm.

9 Make an accurate drawing of a rectangle with length 7 cm and width 4.2 cm.

10 Make an accurate drawing of a regular hexagon with a side
   length of 3.5 cm and an internal angle of 120°

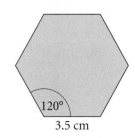

120°
3.5 cm

13 Graphs

A graph is a useful way to show the connection between two variables.

Graphs are a way of showing information as images that are easy to understand.

- How does the price of fuel vary from one month to the next?
- How does the mass of a baby increase with age?
- How does the cost of a taxi vary with the distance travelled?
- How does the cost of a mobile phone vary with the number of calls?
- How does the amount of tax you pay vary with your income?
- How does your healthy mass vary with your height?
- How does the cost of a hotel vary with the length of your stay?
- How does the temperature of water depend on how long you have been heating it?
- How does the amount of electricity a fridge uses depend on the temperature inside the fridge?
- How does the output of a solar panel depend on the amount of sunlight?

In all these examples a graph is a good way to show the connection.

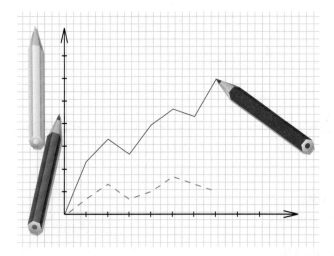

In this unit you will start with coordinates and then look at the simplest type of graph on a coordinate grid: a straight line.

Key words

Make sure you learn and understand these key words:

graph
coordinate grid
axis
origin
x-axis
y-axis
coordinate
mid-point
equation

13.1 Plotting coordinates

Graphs are often drawn on **coordinate grids**, on squared paper.

A coordinate grid is a pair of number lines, called **axes**, at right angles to each other and crossing at the point where the value on both number lines is zero. This point is called the **origin**.

On a basic coordinate grid, based on the values of two variables x and y, the horizontal axis is the x-axis. The vertical one is the y-**axis**.

You can identify any point on a coordinate grid by stating its **coordinates**. These are the x-value and the y-value at the given point. They are written as a pair, in brackets.

- The x-coordinate or x-value is the distance of the point from the origin along the horizontal axis. If the point is to the left of the origin, the x-value will be negative.
- The y-coordinate or y-value is the distance up or down the vertical axis. Up is positive; down is negative.

You should always write the x-coordinate first.

The coordinates of the four points marked on the grid above are:
A(2, 4), B(4, −3), C(−4, −1) and D(−4, 3).

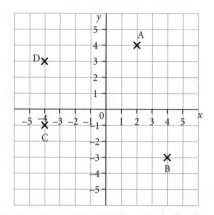

> You may need to use use positive and negative numbers to write coordinates.

Worked example 13.1

The coordinates of three corners of a square are (4, 1), (4, −5) and (−2, −5).
a Find the coordinates of the fourth corner.
b Find the coordinates of the centre of the square.

a

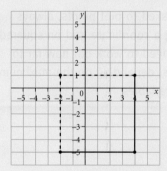

The fourth corner is at (−2, 1).

Draw a coordinate grid.
Plot the three points and join them up to form two lines at right angles.
Draw two more lines to give the other sides of a square.

Write down the coordinates of the fourth corner.

b

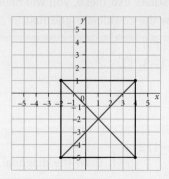

The centre is at (1, −2).

Draw in the diagonals (shown in red).

They cross at the centre of the square.

◆ Exercise 13.1

1 Write down the coordinates of the points D, E, F and G.

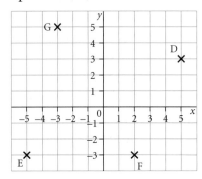

2 **a** Write down the coordinates of the points P and Q.

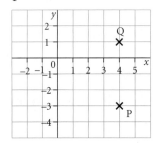

   b M is the mid-point of P and Q.
   Write down the coordinates of M.

   > The **mid-point** of PQ is halfway between P and Q.

3 **a** On a coordinate grid, plot the points $(-2, 4)$ and $(-2, 0)$.
   Join them with a line.
   b Work out the coordinates of the mid-point of the line.

   > When you are asked to plot points, always start by drawing a coordinate grid on squared paper. You will need to work out how far to number the axes, depending on the maximum values of your variables.

4 **a** On a coordinate grid, plot the points $(6, -1)$ and $(2, -5)$. Join them with a line.
   b Work out the coordinates of the mid-point of the line.

5 **a** On a coordinate grid, plot and join the points $(0, -2)$ and $(-6, 0)$.
   b Work out the coordinates of the mid-point.

6 Three corners of a rectangle are at $(3, 5)$, $(3, -3)$ and $(-4, -3)$.
   a Plot these points and draw the rectangle.
   b Find the coordinates of the fourth corner.

   > In questions like these, you will need to draw the coordinate grid first.

7 The four corners of a square are the points $(3, 3)$, $(5, -3)$, $(-1, -5)$ and $(-3, 1)$.
   a Draw the square.
   b Draw the diagonals of the square.
   c Find the coordinates of the centre of the square.

8 **a** Draw the quadrilateral with corners at $(5, 2)$, $(3, -2)$, $(-3, -2)$ and $(-1, 2)$
   b What is the name of this quadrilateral?
   c Find the coordinates of the centre of the quadrilateral.

   > Draw the diagonal.

13.2 Lines parallel to the axes

On this grid, the red line through A(4, 1) and B(4, −5) has been extended in both directions.

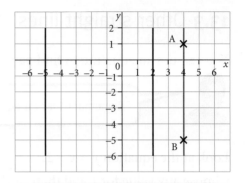

Some other points on the red line are:

(4, 3) (4, 5) (4, −3) (4, 0) (4, −4) (4, 2) (4, −6)

They all have an *x*-coordinate of 4. <u>Every</u> point with an *x*-coordinate of 4 will be on this line.

An **equation** is like a rule connecting *x* and *y*. The equation of the red line is $x = 4$. The line $x = 4$ is perpendicular to the *x*-axis and passes through the 4 on the *x*-axis.

> You learnt about equations in Units 2 and 9.

The diagram also shows the lines $x = 2$ and $x = -5$.

The equation of the *y*-axis is $x = 0$.

These points are on the blue line drawn here:

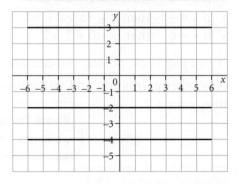

(5, 3) (−4, 3) (2, 3) (−2, 3) (0, 3)

The *y*-coordinate of points on this line is always 3.

The equation of the blue line is $y = 3$.

The equations of the other lines are $y = -2$ and $y = -5$.

The equation of the *x*-axis is $y = 0$.

◆ Exercise 13.2

1 Find the equation of the line through these points.
 a P and Q   **b** Q and R   **c** R and S   **d** S and T

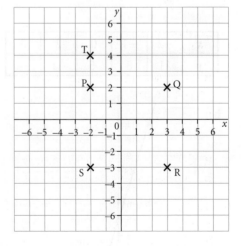

2 a On a coordinate grid, draw and label the lines $x = 7$ and $y = -4$.
 b Write down the coordinates of the point where the lines cross.

3 a On a coordinate grid, draw the rectangle with corners at A(2, 7), B(−6, 7), C(−6, 1) and D(2, 1).
 b Write down the equation of the line through B and C.
 c Write down the equation of the line through A and B.
 d The rectangle has two lines of symmetry. Write down the equation of each of them.

4 Find the equation of the line through these points.
 a (4, −5) and (4, 2)   **b** (−3, 6) and (3, 6)   **c** (−5, 5) and (−5, 0)

5 Three of these points are in a straight line.
 Find the equation of the line.   (4, 2) (2, 4) (−2, 4) (−4, 2) (−4, −2) (2, 2)

6 A rhombus has vertices at the points (−2, 8), (1, 2), (−2, −4) and (−5, 2).
 a Draw the rhombus.
 b The rhombus has two lines of symmetry. Write down the equations of these lines.

13.3 Other straight lines

You can use an equation to find pairs of values of x and y that obey the rule.

Remember that an equation is like a rule connecting x and y.

All the graphs in this unit will be straight lines.

Look at the equation $y = x + 2$.

Choose any value for x and then work out the corresponding values of y. Each time you will get the coordinates of a point.

- If $x = 4$ then $y = 4 + 2 = 6$ This gives the coordinates (4, 6).
- If $x = 1$ then $y = 1 + 2 = 3$ This gives the coordinates (1, 3).
- If $x = -3$ then $y = -3 + 2 = -1$ This gives the coordinates (−3, −1).
- If $x = 0$ then $y = 0 + 2 = 2$ This gives the coordinates (0, 2).

If you plot these points, you can draw a straight line through them.

Any other points you find, using this equation, will be on the same line, $y = x + 2$.

If your line is not straight, check you have worked out the coordinates correctly.

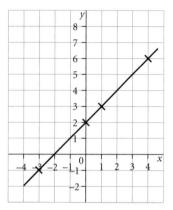

Worked example 13.3

a Complete this table of values for $y = 5 - 3x$.
b Use your table to draw the graph of $y = 5 - 3x$.

x	−2	−1	0	2	3
y		8		−2	

x	−2	−1	0	2	3
y	11	8	5	−1	−4

If $x = -2$ then $y = 5 - 3 \times -2 = 11$
If $x = 0$ then $y = 5 - 3 \times 0 = 5$
If $x = 3$ then $y = 5 - 3 \times 3 = -4$

It is always helpful to put the values in a table, like this.

b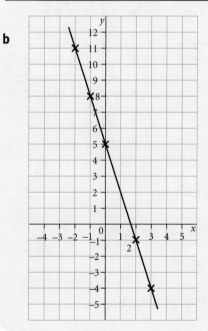

Think carefully about the numbers you put on the axes.
The x-axis must include −2 and 3. The y-axis must include −4 and 11.
Make sure you can plot all five points.
The points are in a straight line. Draw a line through all the points.
Make the line as long as the grid allows.

Exercise 13.3

1 a Copy and complete this table of values for $y = x + 4$.

x	−5	−3	0	2	4
y		1		6	

b Copy these axes. Use your table to draw the graph of $y = x + 4$.

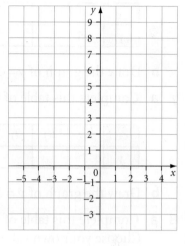

2 a Copy and complete this table of values for $y = 2x + 5$.

x	−4	−2	0	2	3
y		1			11

b Copy these axes. Use your table to draw the graph of $y = 2x + 5$.

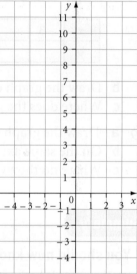

3 a Complete this table of values for $y = x − 3$.

x	−2	−1	2	4	6
y	−5				

b Use your table to draw the graph of $y = x − 3$.
c Where does the graph cross the x-axis?

4 a Complete this table of values for $y = 5 − x$.

x	−3	−1	2	5	6
y		6		0	

b Use your table to draw the graph of $y = 5 − x$.
c Where does the graph cross the x-axis?

5 a Complete this table of values for $y = 2 − x$.

x	−4	−2	0	2	3	5
y		4			−1	

b Draw the graph of $y = 2 − x$.

> When you draw the coordinate grid, look carefully at the table of values so that you will know how to label the axes.

6 a Complete this table of values for $y = 2(x + 1)$.

x	−4	−2	0	2	5
y	−6				

b Draw the graph of $y = 2(x + 1)$.

7 a Complete this table of values for $y = 3 - 2x$.

x	−2	−1	0	1	2	4
y	7				−1	

b Draw the graph of $y = 3 - 2x$.

8 a Complete this table of values for $y = 2x - 4$.
Choose your own values of x between −3 and 5.

x	−3				5
y					6

b Draw the graph of $y = 2x - 4$.
c Where does the graph cross each of the axes?

9 a Draw the graph of $y = 6 - x$ with values of x from −2 to 7.
b On the same axes draw the graph of $y = 2$.
c Where do the two lines cross?

Summary

You should now know that:

★ The x-axis is horizontal and the y-axis is vertical.

★ The first coordinate is the x-coordinate and the second coordinate is the y-coordinate. Coordinates can be positive, negative or zero.

★ Straight lines on a coordinate grid have equations.

★ Lines with equations of the type $x = 2$ or $y = -3$ are parallel to the y-axis or x-axis respectively.

★ An equation such as $y = 2x - 3$ can be used to work out coordinates and draw a straight-line graph.

You should be able to:

★ Read and plot positive and negative coordinates of points determined by geometric information.

★ Recognise straight-line graphs parallel to the x-axis and y-axis.

★ Generate coordinate pairs that satisfy a linear equation, where y is given explicitly in terms of x, and plot the corresponding graphs.

★ Draw accurate mathematical graphs.

★ Recognise mathematical properties, patterns and relationships, generalising in simple cases.

End of unit review

1 a Plot V(−2, 5) and W(4, −1) on a grid and join them with a straight line.

b M is the mid-point of VW. Mark M on the graph and write down its coordinates.

2 The points (−6, 1), (−6, 5) and (−2, 5) are three corners of a square.

a Draw the square and write down the coordinates of the fourth corner.

b Work out the coordinates of the centre of the square.

3 a Draw the parallelogram with vertices at (2, 0), (6, 2), (6, −2) and (2, −4).

b Draw the diagonals of the parallelogram. Write down the coordinates of the point where they cross.

4 Write down the equations of the lines through the points:

a A and B   **b** B and C   **c** C and D   **d** D and A.

5 a Draw the rectangle with vertices at P(−1, 1), Q(5, 1), R(5, −3) and S(−1, −3).

b Find the equation of the line through P and Q.

c Find the equation of the line through P and S.

d The rectangle has two lines of symmetry. Work out the equation of each one.

6 Three of these points are on a straight line.
Work out the equation of the line.

(2, −2)   (2, −5)   (1, 2)   (5, 2)   (−5, 2)   (5, 5)

7 a Complete this table of values for $y = x - 4$.

x	−3	−2	0	3	6
y		−6		−1	

b Use your table to draw the graph of $y = x - 4$.

c Where does the graph cross the x-axis?

8 a Complete this table of values for $y = 2x + 2$.

x	−3	−1	0	2	3
y		0			8

b Use your table to draw the graph of $y = 2x + 2$.

9 a Complete this table of values for $y = 6 - 2x$.

x	−1	0	2	3	5
y		6			

b Use your table to draw the graph of $y = 6 - 2x$.

14 Ratio and proportion

A ratio is a way of comparing two or more numbers or quantities.

The symbol **:** is used to show **ratio**.

Ratios were used long before the symbol we use today was invented.

Pythagoras was a famous Greek mathematician who lived around 500 BC.

Historians and mathematicians believe that he discovered the <u>golden ratio</u>.

Pythagoras (about 570 BC to 495 BC).

Key words

Make sure you learn and understand these key words:

ratio
simplify
simplest form
highest common factor
divide
share
direct proportion
unitary method

If the lengths of the sides of a rectangle are in the golden ratio, the rectangle is called the golden rectangle. Some sizes of paper, such as A4, are based on the golden rectangle.

A rectangle is golden if, when you cut a square from it, the piece left over is mathematically similar to the original. This means that the sides are in the same **proportion**.

If you divide a rectangle in this way several times, you will see that a spiral shape forms.

This spiral shape can be seen in nature, for example, in the shell of a chambered nautilus.

It can also be seen in architecture, such as the Parthenon in Athens.

Today we use ratios in everyday life, often without knowing it! Builders use ratios when mixing sand and cement for concrete. Chefs use ratios when mixing ingredients for cakes.

In this unit you will learn how to use ratio and direct proportion.

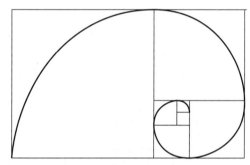

The golden rectangle.

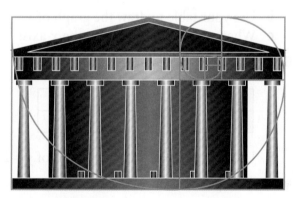

14.1 Simplifying ratios

In this necklace there are two red beads and six yellow beads.

You can write the ratio of red beads to yellow beads as 2 : 6.

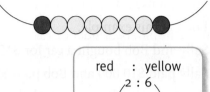

For every one red bead there are three yellow beads, so you can **simplify** the ratio 2 : 6 to 1 : 3.

You write a ratio in its **simplest form** by dividing the numbers in the ratio by the **highest common factor**. Here, the highest common factor of 2 and 6 is 2, so divide both the numbers by 2.

Worked example 14.1

The rectangle is made up of blue squares and green squares.
a   Write down the ratio of blue squares to green squares.
b   Write the ratio in its simplest form.

a   blue : green = 8 : 12   There are 8 blue squares and 12 green squares in the rectangle.
b   8 : 12   The highest common factor of 8 and 12 is 4, so divide both numbers by 4.
       ÷ 4   ÷ 4
              1 : 3

Exercise 14.1

1   For each of these necklaces, write down the ratio of red beads to yellow beads.
    a    b   c   d

2   For each of these necklaces, write down the ratio of green beads to blue beads in its simplest form.
    a    b   c   d

3   Write each of these ratios in its simplest form.
    a 2 : 8   b 2 : 12   c 3 : 6   d 3 : 15   e 4 : 8   f 4 : 12
    g 25 : 5   h 60 : 5   i 36 : 6   j 14 : 7   k 24 : 8   l 54 : 9

4   Write each of these ratios in its simplest form.
    a 4 : 10   b 4 : 14   c 6 : 8   d 6 : 21   e 8 : 10   f 8 : 14
    g 12 : 9   h 24 : 9   i 15 : 10   j 24 : 10   k 28 : 12   l 21 : 9

5   Helena sees this recipe for pastry.
    She says that the ratio of margarine to flour is 4 : 1.
    Is Helena correct? Explain your answer.

Pastry	
200 g flour	pinch salt
50 g margarine	water to mix
50 g lard	

6   Bryn is drawing a scale diagram of a building.
    For every 10 m of the building he draws a line 5 cm long.
    Bryn thinks he is using a ratio of 2 : 1. Alun thinks Bryn is using a ratio of 200 : 1.
    Is either of them correct? Explain your answer.

14.2 Sharing in a ratio

You can use ratios to **divide** things up, or **share** them.

Look at this example.

Sally and Bob bought a car for $15 000.

Sally paid $10 000 and Bob paid $5000.

You can write the amounts they paid as a ratio.

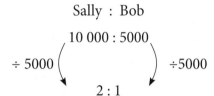

Sally : Bob

10 000 : 5000

÷ 5000   ÷5000

2 : 1

> The highest common factor of 10 000 and 5000 is 5000, so divide by 5000 to simply the ratio.

So, Sally paid twice as much as Bob.

Five years later they sold the car for $9000.

They need to share the money fairly between them.

Sally paid twice as much as Bob, so she should get twice as much as him.

How do you work out how much each of them gets?

To share in a given ratio

- Add the numbers in the ratio to find the total number of parts.
- Divide the amount to be shared by the total number of parts to find the value of one part.
- Use multiplication to work out the value of each share.

Worked example 14.2

Share $9000 between Sally and Bob in the ratio 2 : 1.

Total number of parts:	2 + 1 = 3	Add the numbers in the ratio to find the total number of parts.
Value of one part:	$9000 ÷ 3 = $3000	Divide the amount to be shared by the total number of parts to find the value of one part.
Sally gets:	$3000 × 2 = $6000	Multiply by 2 to get Sally's share.
Bob gets:	$3000 × 1 = $3000	Multiply by 1 to get Bob's share.

◆ Exercise 14.2

1   Copy and complete the workings to share $45 between Ethan and Julie in the ratio 1 : 4.

Total number of parts: 1 + 4 = ☐

Value of one part: $45 ÷ ☐ = ☐

Ethan gets: 1 × ☐ = ☐

Julie gets: 4 × ☐ = ☐

2 Share these amounts between Dong and Chul in the ratios given.
    a $24 in the ratio 1 : 2   **b** $65 in the ratio 1 : 4   **c** $48 in the ratio 3 : 1
    d $30 in the ratio 5 : 1   **e** $21 in the ratio 1 : 6   **f** $64 in the ratio 7 : 1

3 Share these amounts between Lin and Kuan-yin in the ratios given.
    a $35 in the ratio 2 : 3   **b** $56 in the ratio 2 : 5   **c** $49 in the ratio 3 : 4
    d $32 in the ratio 5 : 3   **e** $66 in the ratio 6 : 5   **f** $90 in the ratio 7 : 3

4 Raine and Abella share an electricity bill in the ratio 5 : 4. The electricity bill is $72.
    How much does each of them pay?

5 A tin of biscuits contains shortbread and choc-chip biscuits in the ratio 2 : 3.
    The tin contains 40 biscuits.
    How many shortbread biscuits are there in the tin?

6 A school choir is made up of girls and boys in the ratio 4 : 3.
    There are 35 students in the choir altogether.
    How many of the students are boys?

7 Brad and Lola bought a painting for $120.
    Brad paid $80 and Lola paid $40.
    a Write the ratio of the amount they each paid in its simplest form.
    b Ten years later they sold the painting for $630.
        How much should each of them get?

8 William and Emma buy a racehorse.
    William pays $3000 and Emma pays $4000.
    a Write the ratio of the amount they each pay in its simplest form.
    b The horse wins prize money of $12 600.
        How much should each of them get?

9 In a wood there are oak trees and beech trees.
    In one section of the wood there are 35 oak trees and 49 beech trees.

    In the whole wood there are 7200 trees.
    Show how Mia worked out this estimate.

> I estimate that there are 3000 oak trees in the wood altogether.

10 Agwe and Kai are going to share $240, <u>either</u> in the ratio of their ages,
    <u>or</u> in the ratio of their weights.
    Agwe is 14 years old and weighs 58 kg.
    Kai is 16 years old and weighs 62 kg.
    Which ratio would be better for Agwe?
    Explain your answer.

11 Every New Year Auntie Bea gives $320 to be shared between her nieces in
    the ratio of their ages.
    This year the nieces are aged 3 and 7.
    How much <u>more</u> will the younger niece receive, in five years' time, than
    she receives this year?

14.3 Using direct proportion

Two quantities are in **direct proportion** when their ratio stays the same as the quantities increase or decrease.
One packet of rice costs $3.25, so two packets of rice would cost twice as much.
Two packets of rice would cost $2 \times \$3.25 = \$6.50$.
Six tickets to a concert cost $120, so three tickets would cost half as much.
Three tickets would cost $\$120 \div 2 = \$60$.

Worked example 14.3

a Three books cost $12. Work out the cost of 10 books.
b A recipe uses two eggs to make 12 cupcakes.
How many eggs are needed to make 36 cupcakes?

a $\$12 \div 3 = \$4$	First of all, work out the cost of one book by <u>dividing</u> the total cost of the books by 3.
$10 \times \$4 = \$40$	Now work out the cost of 10 books by <u>multiplying</u> the cost of one book by 10.
b $36 \div 12 = 3$	You can see that to make 36 cupcakes you need to multiply the recipe by 3.
$2 \times 3 = 6$ eggs	So, multiply the number of eggs by 3.

This is called the **unitary method**, because you find the cost of 1 book before finding the cost of 10.

◆ Exercise 14.3

1 Tony buys one bag of chips for $1.20.
 Work out the cost of:
 a two bags of chips   **b** five bags of chips.

> In this type of question, if you can see the connection between the numbers, you don't need to use the unitary method.

2 Rob goes to the gym three times a week.
 Work out how many times he goes to the gym in:
 a four weeks   **b** one year.

> Remember that there are 52 weeks in a year.

3 Three bananas weigh 375 grams.
 Copy and complete the working to find the weight of eight bananas.
 1 banana weighs: $375 \div 3 = \square$
 8 bananas weigh: $8 \times \square = \square$

4 Five apples weigh 320 grams.
 Work out the weight of: **a** one apple   **b** seven apples.

5 Ivan buys four shirts for $37.80.
 Work out the cost of nine shirts.

6 A recipe for four people uses 800 g of chicken.
 Copy and complete the workings to find the weight of chicken needed for:
 a 20 people   **b** 6 people.
 a Weight of chicken for 4 people: 800 g
     The connection between 4 and 20 is: $20 \div 4 = \square$
     Weight of chicken for 20 people: $800\,\text{g} \times \square = \square\,\text{g}$

b Weight of chicken for 4 people: 800 g
Weight of chicken for 2 people: 800 g ÷ 2 = ☐ g
Weight of chicken for 6 people: 800 g + ☐ g = ☐ g

7 Bo is paid $65 for 10 hours work. How much does she earn when she works for:
a 5 hours **b** 15 hours?

8 A catering company charges $960 for a meal for 120 people.
How much do they charge for a meal for:
a 60 people **b** 300 people?

9 This is part of Li-Ming's homework.

Question   A recipe for 6 people uses 300 g of rice.
How much rice is needed for 15 people?

Solution   The recipe is for 6 people, 6 + 9 = 15
6 people need 300 g of rice
3 people need 300 g ÷ 2 = 150 g rice
6 + 3 = 9, so 300 + 150 = 450 g
Altogether 450 g of rice is needed.

Explain what she has done wrong and work out the right answer.

10 A teacher orders homework books for her class of 30 students.
The total value of the order is $135.
Two more students join her class, so she orders two extra books.
What is the total value of the order now?

Summary

You should now know that:

★ A ratio is a way of comparing two or more numbers or quantities.

★ The symbol : is used to show ratio.

★ To write a ratio in its simplest form you divide both the numbers by the highest common factor.

★ To share in a given ratio you need to:
  1 find the total number of parts
  2 find the value of one part
  3 find the value of each share.

★ Two quantities are in direct proportion when their ratios stay the same as the quantities increase or decrease.

You should be able to:

★ Use ratio notation.

★ Write a ratio in its simplest form.

★ Divide a quantity into two parts in a given ratio.

★ Recognise the relationship between ratio and proportion.

★ Use direct proportion in context.

★ Solve simple problems involving ratio and direct proportion.

★ Understand everyday systems of measurement and use them to calculate.

★ Solve word problems involving whole numbers, money or measures.

End of unit review

1 For each of these shapes, write down the ratio of red squares to yellow squares.
   a   b

2 For each of these shapes, write down the ratio of green squares to blue squares.
   Write each ratio in its simplest form.

   a ▢▢▢▢▢▢▢▢▢▢   b ▢▢▢▢▢▢▢▢▢▢▢▢▢▢▢

3 Write each of these ratios in its simplest form.
   a 2 : 6   b 18 : 3   c 6 : 9   d 24 : 16

4 Chaska sees these ingredients for a concrete mix.
   He says that the ratio of cement to sand is 2 : 1.
   Is Chaska correct? Explain your answer.

   > **Concrete mix**
   >
   > 2 sacks cement
   >
   > 4 sacks sand

5 Share these amounts between Tao and Chris in the ratios given.
   a $15 in the ratio 1 : 2   b $25 in the ratio 4 : 1
   c 45 kg in the ratio 3 : 2   d 24 litres in the ratio 5 : 3

6 A tin of sweets contains toffees and chocolates in the ratio 3 : 4.
   The tin contains 35 sweets.
   How many chocolates are in the tin?

7 Mia and Gianna are going to share $180 <u>either</u> in the ratio of the number of brothers they each have,
   <u>or</u> in the ratio of the number of sisters they each have.
   Mia has two brothers and three sisters.
   Gianna has one brother and five sisters
   How much more would Gianna get if they shared the money in the ratio of the number of sisters
   rather than the ratio of brothers?

8 Sham buys one packet of peanuts for $1.60.
   Work out the cost of:
   a two packets of peanuts   b seven packet of peanuts.

9 Four tins of beans weigh 1.6 kg.
   Work out the weight of:
   a 12 tins of beans   b 10 tins of beans.

10 The total length of three fence panels is 5.4 m.
   Work out the total length of ten fence panels.

11 A coach orders shirts for her netball team.
   There are seven players in the team.
   The total value of the order is $89.60.
   She remembers at the last minute to order three extra shirts for the
   reserve players.
   What is the total value of the order now?

Nowadays the units used for measuring are almost always decimal, based on 10, 100 or 1000. For example, there are 100 cents in a dollar, 10 millimetres in a centimetre and 1000 grams in a kilogram. Using decimal systems makes calculation easy.

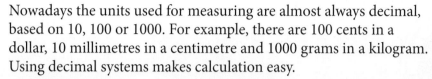

Key words

Make sure you learn and understand these key words:

time
12-hour clock
24-hour clock

There is an important exception to this. Time is not measured in a decimal system. The system of measuring time, in hours and minutes, is very ancient. There are 60 minutes in an hour, 24 hours in a day and 7 days in a week. This can make calculations more awkward.

Although some countries may still use different units for some measures, the passage of time is one thing that everyone in the world measures in exactly the same way. It would make life very difficult if that were not the case!

Of course the actual time varies in different countries. For example, because of the Earth turning, it is evening in Australia while it is midday in the UK. This is something you need to remember if you travel from one country to another, or you want to talk on a phone or computer to someone in a different country.

There are two ways of writing time. These are the 12-hour clock system and the 24-hour clock system. In everyday conversation, people generally use the 12-hour system. Timetables almost always use the 24-hour system to avoid confusion.

Alarm clock (12-hour system). Digital clock (24-hour system).

Astronomical clock.

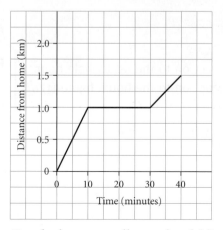

Graph shows a walk to school (distance travelled against time).

15.1 The 12-hour and 24-hour clock

These are different ways to describe the **time** shown on the clock.

> It is a quarter to four.

> It is 45 minutes past 3.

> 24-hour clock times are sometimes written with a colon (:). There may be a gap between hours and minutes of they may be closed up. 03:45, 0345 and 03 45 are all correct ways of writing the same time.

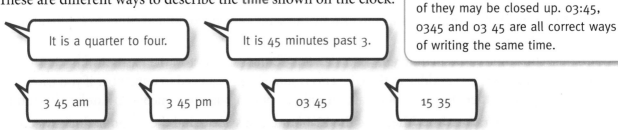

> 3 45 am

> 3 45 pm

> 03 45

> 15 35

In the **12-hour clock** system, 3 45 am is in the morning and 3 45 pm is in the afternoon.

In the **24-hour clock** system, 03 45 is in the morning and 15 45 is in the afternoon.

The 24-hour system is usually used for timetables, because it is clear whether the time is in the morning or afternoon.

> 24-hour times always have four numerals.

You need to understand both the 12-hour and the 24-hour systems.

Worked example 15.1

An aeroplane takes off at 14 40 and lands at 17 25. How long does the journey take?

Method 1

14 40 → 15 40 → 16 40 is 2 hours   Count on in hours. Stop at 16 40 because 17 40 is after 17 25.
16 40 → 17 25 is 45 minutes   16 40 to 17 00 is 20 minutes; 17 00 to 17 25 is another 25 minutes.

Time taken is 2 hours 45 minutes

Method 2

14 40 → 15 00 is 20 minutes   Count on to the next whole hour.
15 00 → 17 00 is 2 hours   Count on to the hours figure (17).
17 00 → 17 25 is 25 minutes

> Be careful. You can't use a calculator for subtractions like the one in the example.

Time taken is 2 hours 45 minutes   20 minutes + 2 hours + 25 minutes.

◆ Exercise 15.1

1 Write these as 24-hour clock times.
   a 7 15 am   **b** 10 45 am   **c** 3 35 pm   **d** 8 pm   **e** 11 30 am   **f** 11 30 pm

2 Write these times using the 12-hour clock
   a 09 30   **b** 16 00   **c** 21 40   **d** 00 45   **e** 23 10   **f** 12 05

3 How long is it:
   a from 08 30 to 09 15   **b** from 13 49 to 14 22   **c** from 17 42 to 18 11?

4 How long is it:
   a from 8 25 am to 11 08 am   **b** from 11 30 am to 2 45 pm   **c** from 9 30 am to 7 15 pm?

5 A train left at 10 35 and arrived at 12 10. How long did the journey take?

6 A car left at 13 50 and arrived at 18 15.
   a How long did the journey take?

   b The driver took one break, for $1\frac{1}{2}$ hours. How long was she driving?

7 A train left at 22 47 and arrived at its destination the next morning at 06 33. How long did the journey take?

8 A car left at 09 45. The journey took 25 minutes. Work out when it arrived.

9 A plane took off at 11 55 and arrived 2 hours 40 minutes later. What time did it arrive?

10 A traveller arrived at 17 25. The journey took 5 hours and 50 minutes. What time did the traveller start?

11 The time in Wellington is 11 hours ahead of the time in London. What time is it in Wellington when it is 6 15 am in London?

12 The time in Abuja is $4\frac{1}{2}$ hours behind the time in Delhi.

   a What time is it in Abuja when it is 18 20 in Delhi?
   The time in Jakarta is $1\frac{1}{2}$ hour ahead of the time in Delhi:
   b What time is it in Abuja when it is 01 05 in Jakarta?

> When it is midday in Delhi it will be early morning in Abuja.

13 A plane left Cairo at 16 45 and arrived in Abu Dhabi 3 hours and 40 minutes later. Abu Dhabi is 2 hours ahead of Cairo. What time did the plane arrive?

15.2 Timetables

Travel timetables are usually written in 24-hour clock times.
In a timetable, each column shows a different journey. Each row shows a different stop.

> Timetables are written in the same way, whether they are for buses, trains or aeroplanes.

Worked example 15.2

This is part of a bus timetable.

a How many bus journeys are shown?

b Eesha arrives at the station at 15 55. How long must she wait for a bus to the airport?

c How long does the 15 47 from the zoo take to get to the airport?

Bus 6X departive times				
Station	15 33	15 48	16 08	16 23
Zoo	15 47	16 02	16 22	16 37
Factory	16 05	16 20	16 40	16 55
Airport	16 19	16 34	16 54	17 09

d Mahdi must be at the factory by 16 30. What time should he catch a bus at the station?

a 4   Each column shows a separate bus journey.

b 13 minutes   The next bus is at 16 08, which is 13 minutes after 15 55.

c 32 minutes   It arrives at 16 19; 15 47 → 16 19 is 13 + 19 = 32 minutes.

d 15 48   It arrives at 16 20. The next bus arrives at 16 40, which is too late.

Exercise 15.2

1 Here is part of a bus timetable.
   a What time does the bus leave the bus station?
     Write the answer in the 12-hour clock.
   b How long is the journey from the town centre to the harbour?
   c Masha gets to the museum bus stop at 14 20.
     How long will she have to wait for the bus?
   d The next bus leaves the bus station 35 minutes later than the time shown on the timetable.
     What time is that?

	Departure times
Bus station	14 10
Town centre	14 26
Museum	14 33
Park	14 45
Harbour	15 08

2 Here is part of a ferry timetable.
   a Hassan arrives at City Bridge at 11 50. How long will he wait for a ferry?
   b What time will Hassan get to Tower Bridge?
   c How long does the 13 25 from City Bridge take to get to Old Bridge?
   d How long does the second ferry take for the whole journey?

	Departure times		
City Bridge	11 35	12 15	13 25
Dock	11 52	12 26	13 42
Tower Bridge	12 14	12 50	14 04
Old Bridge	12 26	13 21	14 16

3 This table shows the departure times of planes at an airport.
  a It is now 15 50. Work out the time until the Bangkok departure.
  b Work out the time between the Abu Dhabi departure and the Cairo departure.
  c The Tokyo flight is delayed by 85 minutes. Work out the new departure time.

Departure times	
18 25	**Bangkok**
18 40	**Abu Dhabi**
18 45	**Hyderabad**
18 55	**Tokyo**
19 10	**Delhi**
19 15	**Cairo**

4 This is a train timetable.

	Departure times				
Ayton	10 40	11 25	12 50	14 05	15 12
Caply	11 15	–	13 25	14 40	–
Denby	11 42	–	–	15 07	–
Filsea	12 18	12 32	14 15	15 43	16 09

  a How many trains stop at Caply?
  b How long does the 10 40 from Ayton take to reach Filsea?
  c What is the fastest journey time from Ayton to Filsea?
  d A man arrives at Ayton Station at 12 30. What is the earliest time he can reach Denby?
  e A woman has an appointment in Filsea at 4 pm. What train from Ayton should she catch?

5 This timetable shows flights in New Zealand from Christchurch to Auckland. Some flights stop in Wellington.

Christchurch depart	08 40	10 30	13 35	14 45	18 45
Wellington arrive		11 15			19 30
Wellington depart	↓	13 00	↓	↓	20 00
Auckland arrive	10 00	14 00	14 55	15 05	21 00

  a Write the arrival and departure times of the 13 35, using 12-hour clock times.
  b How long does the flight on the 08 40 take?
  c How long does the journey on the 18 45 take?
  d Melissa takes the 10 30 from Christchurch. How long does she wait in Wellington?

6 Yusef is going to watch a football match in the park.
He will catch a bus and then a train.
It takes Yusef 10 minutes to walk from his home to the Statue bus stop.
The walk from Park Station to the football pitch takes 15 minutes.
The match starts at 4 pm.
Here are the bus and train timetables.

Bus timetable

Statue	13 35	13 50	14 05	14 20	14 35
Hospital	13 55	14 10	14 25	14 40	14 55
Lake	14 11	14 26	14 41	14 56	15 11
Main Station	14 27	14 38	14 53	15 12	15 27

Train timetable

Main Station	14 00	14 30	15 00	15 30
Park Station	14 25	14 55	15 25	15 55

  a What is the latest time Yusef can leave home?
  b Which bus and train should he catch?

15.3 Real-life graphs

Graphs can tell stories.

This graph shows Ari's journey from home.

First look at the two axes.

The horizontal axis shows time (in minutes).

The vertical axis shows Ari's distance from home (in kilometres).

The graph is in three parts.

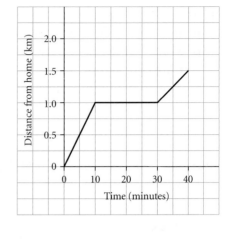

- He walks for 10 minutes and travels 1 km.
- He waits for a bus for 20 minutes. You can tell he is not moving because the line is horizontal.
- The bus does not come. He starts walking again. After a total of 40 minutes he is 1.5 km from home.

In the first part, Ari took 5 minutes to walk 0.5 km. In the third part he took 15 minutes to walk 0.5 km. He walked more slowly in the third part. You can see this on the graph. When the graph is steeper (first part) he is walking faster. When the graph is less steep (third part) he is walking more slowly.

◆ Exercise 15.3

1 This graph shows a car journey.
The journey was in two stages with a rest break.
  a Work out the time taken for the first part of the journey.
  b Work out the distance the car travelled in the first part.
  c Work out the time taken for the rest break.
  d Work out the time taken for the whole journey.
  e Work out the total distance travelled.
  f Did the car travel more quickly in the first stage or the last stage? Give a reason for your answer.

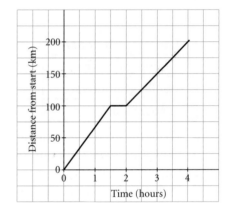

2 Luis drove to Overton.
He stayed there for a while and then he drove back home. The graph shows his journey.
  a Work out the distance from Luis's home to Overton.
  b Work out how long Luis was at Overton.
  c Find: **i** the time taken to reach Overton
             ii the time taken to get back home from Overton.
  d Did Luis drive faster travelling to Overton or going home?

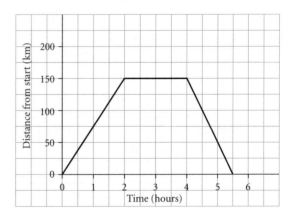

3 Maya likes to run from home to school.
This graph shows her journey one morning.
  a How far from school is Maya's home?
  b When did Maya leave home?
  c Maya stopped for a rest on the way.
    i When did she stop?
    ii How long did she stop for?
  d When did she get to school?

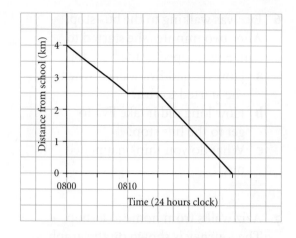

4 In an experiment Salman heated some water.
The graph shows how the temperature changed.
  a What was the temperature at the start?
  b What was the temperature after 2 minutes?
  c What was the highest temperature?
  d What happened after 4 minutes?

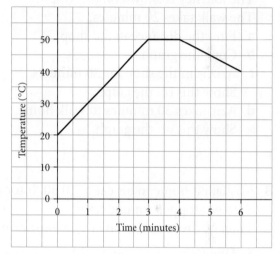

5 Leia went on a cycle ride.
This graph shows her progress.
  a What time did Leia start?
  b How far had Leia travelled at 10 30?
  c Leia had two rest stops. What times were these?
  d How far did Leia travel in the first five hours?
  e How far did Leia cycle?
  f How long did the journey take her?

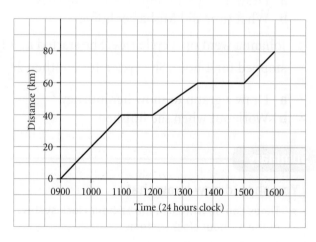

6 Eva was walking to the bus stop. After two minutes she started to run. She stopped at the bus stop.

a How far had Eva walked when she started to run?

b How long did it take Eva to get to the bus stop?

c What do you think happened next?

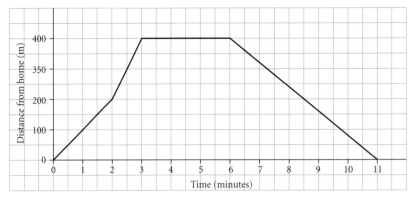

7 Aziz walks from home to a shop. The journey is shown on the graph. The walk takes 20 minutes.

a Find the distance to the shop.

b Copy the graph.

c Aziz is in the shop for 20 minutes. Show this on the graph.

d Aziz takes 30 minutes to walk home. Show this on the graph.

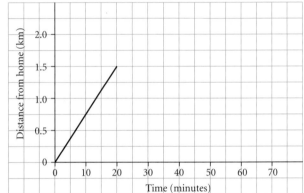

8 Misha left home in his car at 10 30. It took 2 hours to drive 50 km and then he stopped for one hour.
Then he drove back home. The journey home took $1\frac{1}{2}$ hours.

a Draw a graph to show Misha's journey.

b What time did Misha get home?

9 Johanna went on a cycle ride. She started at 9 15 am. She rode for 2 hours and travelled 30 km. She stopped for 1 hour. She cycled for another $2\frac{1}{2}$ hours and travelled another 40 km.

a Draw a graph to show her journey.

b Work out when she finished.

Summary

You should now know that:

★ Times can be written in the 12-hour clock system or the 24-hour clock system.

★ Timetables usually use the 24-hour system. Each column shows a different journey.

★ You must be careful calculating the difference between two times because time does not use a decimal system: there are 60 minutes in an hour.

★ Graphs can be used to show journeys. Time is shown on the horizontal axis.

You should be able to:

★ Understand and use the 12-hour and 24-hour clock systems.

★ Interpret timetables.

★ Calculate time intervals.

★ Draw and interpret graphs in real-life contexts involving more than one stage, such as travel graphs.

★ Understand and use everyday systems of measuring time.

★ Solve word problems involving time.

End of unit review

1 Write these as 24-hour clock times.
   a 5 50 am   **b** 10 17 pm   **c** half past 3 in the afternoon   **d** 12 35 pm

2 Write these as 12-hour clock times.
   a 04 27   **b** 16 35   **c** 23 05   **d** 07 07

3 a A train leaves Thane at 14 21 and arrives at Panvel at 15 15.
      Work out the time the journey takes.
   b A train leaves Thane at 17 48. It takes 32 minutes to get to Nerul.
      What time will it arrive?

4 A car journey begins at 19 50 and arrives at 01 17 the following day.
   How long does it take?

5 This is part of a bus timetable.
   a What time does the 13 29 from the station reach the castle?
      Write this as a 12-hour clock time.
   b Amon just misses the 13 54 from the station.
      How long will he wait for the next bus?
   c Work out the time it takes for the earliest bus
      to get from the castle to New Bridge.
   d Anisa wants to get to the football ground
      by 2 30 pm.
      What time will she catch a bus at the station?

	Departure times			
Station	13 29	13 54	14 19	14 44
Castle	13 46	14 11	14 36	15 01
Football ground	14 08	14 33	14 58	15 23
New Bridge	14 22	14 47	15 12	15 37

6 Mina is cycling home. This graph shows her journey.
   a Find her distance from home after 2 hours.
   b How long did she take to cycle home?
   c Work out how far she travelled in the first 3 hours.
   d Work out how far she travelled in the second
      3 hours.
   e Mina said: 'I cycled more quickly in the second
      3 hours than I did in the first 3 hours.' Is this true?
      Give a reason for your answer.

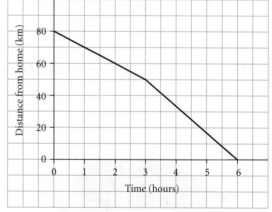

7 Meril starts driving at 14 00.
   a How far had she travelled at 14 30?
   b Copy the graph.
   c At 15 00 she stopped for half an hour.
      Show this on your graph.
   d She continued her journey. She took 90 minutes to
      travel another 100 km. Show this on your graph.

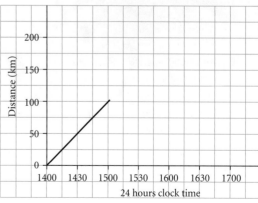

There are aspects of uncertainty and chance in everybody's life.

Although it may not always be important to know whether the sun will shine tomorrow, for example, it might matter very much if you are planning a big outdoor activity.

It would be useful to be able to work out how likely it is that particular situations occur.

- Is it likely to rain? Should I take an umbrella?
- Will my team win their next match?
- What is the chance of an earthquake?
- What is the likelihood of having an accident on a particular road?
- If I throw two dice, will I score a double 6?
- Is it safe to go skiing?
- Will I get caught if I don't do my homework?
- Will my train be late?
- What are my chances of getting a top exam grade?
- Am I likely to live to be 100 years old?

Working out the likelihood of something can be difficult – but mathematics can help.

Probability is the branch of maths that measures how likely it is that something will happen.

You can use it to find the probability of a particular outcome of an event.

In this unit you will learn how to calculate and use probabilities in simple situations.

Key words

Make sure you learn and understand these key words:

likely
unlikely
certain
chance
even chance
very unlikely
very likely
probability
probability scale
event
outcome
equally likely
random
mutually exclusive
estimate
experimental probability
theoretical probability

16.1 The probability scale

Words such as **likely**, **unlikely** and **certain** are used to describe the **chance** that something will happen.

Sometimes a result can be associated with a number from 0 to 1.

This is the **probability** of the result.

> Probabilities can be written as fractions, decimals or percentages.

- Something that is certain to happen has probability 1.
- Something that is impossible has probability 0.

Probabilities can be shown on a **probability scale**, as worked example **16.1** shows.

Worked example 16.1

United and City are two football teams. The probability that City will win their next match is 25%.

The probability that United will win their next match is $\frac{2}{3}$.

a Which team is more likely to win their next match?
b Show the probabilities on a probability scale.

a United is more likely to win their next match.   25% is $\frac{1}{4}$, which is less than $\frac{2}{3}$.

b
```
       City              United
        ↓                  ↓
   ├────┼──┼──────┼─────┼──┼──────────┤
   0    1/4 1/3   1/2   2/3 3/4        1
```

The scale goes from 0 to 1.

Mark $\frac{1}{4}$ and $\frac{2}{3}$ on the scale.

> It helps to mark a few fractions on the probablity scale.

◆ Exercise 16.1

1 Choose the best word or phrase from the box to describe each situation.
   a If you drop a fair coin it will land showing 'heads'.
   b The day after Monday will be Tuesday.
   c You have the same birthday as the President of the United States.
   d You will do well in your next maths exam.

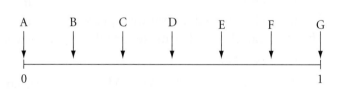

heads   tails

> likely unlikely impossible
> very likely very unlikely
> even chance certain

2 Match each statement to the most appropriate letter on the probability scale.
   a A new-born baby will be a girl.
   b A plane will fly from New York to Hong Kong in two hours next week.
   c A dice will show a 2 when it is rolled.
   d There will be an earthquake in Asia in the coming year.

```
   A     B     C     D     E     F     G
   ↓     ↓     ↓     ↓     ↓     ↓     ↓
   ├─────┼─────┼─────┼─────┼─────┼─────┤
   0                                   1
```

3 Draw a probability scale. Mark these probabilities in the correct places on your diagram.
   a It will rain tomorrow: 25%.
   b A hurricane will reach a town: 50%.
   c Your team will win the match: $\frac{1}{5}$.
   d A plant will flower: 70%.
   e Mia will study maths at university: 0.9.
   f Razi's train will be late: 5%.

16.2 Equally likely outcomes

For some simple activities or **events**, such as spinning a coin, throwing a dice or picking a card from a pack, there are various results, or **outcomes**, that are all **equally likely**. With a coin the two outcomes are 'heads' and 'tails'. With a dice the numbers 1, 2, 3, 4, 5 and 6 are all **equally likely outcomes**.

But how can you assign a probability to a particular outcome?

Worked example 16.2

Here are eight number cards.   2   5   5   8   10   10   10   13

The cards are placed face-down on a table. One card is chosen at random. What is the probability that the number chosen is:
a 5   **b** greater than 9   **c** an even number?

> If the card is chosen at **random** it means that all the cards have the same chance of being chosen.

a $\frac{2}{8} = \frac{1}{4}$ There are eight cards, so there are eight equally likely outcomes.

Two of the cards are 5s so there are two chances out of eight of choosing a 5.
Write this as a fraction.

b $\frac{4}{8} = \frac{1}{2}$ There are four cards with numbers greater than 9.

c $\frac{5}{8}$ The even numbers are 2, 8 and 10. Five cards have even numbers so the probability is $\frac{5}{8}$.

◆ Exercise 16.2

1 There are 20 picture cards in a set. Six show flowers, four show trees, three show birds, five show antelopes and two show lions.
   Bryn picks a card at random. What is the probability that it is:
   a a bird   **b** a lion   **c** a plant   **d** an animal with four legs?

2 Alicia throws a dice. What is the probability that she scores:
   a 4   **b** more than 4   **c** less than 4   **d** an odd number?

3 There are six girls and ten boys in a class. Three of the girls and four of the boys wear glasses.
   a The teacher chooses one person at random. What is the probability that the teacher chooses:
   i   a girl   **ii**   a girl wearing glasses
   iii   a boy who does not wear glasses   **iv**   a child wearing glasses?
   b How can the teacher make sure that the choice is random and each child has an equal chance of being chosen?

4 Each letter of the word MATHEMATICS is written on a separate card.

   | M | A | T | H | E | M | A | T | I | C | S |

> The vowels are A, E, I, O and U.

   Jake picks one card at random. What is the probability that the letter is:
   a M   **b** not T   **c** a vowel   **d** not a vowel
   e X   **f** in the word CHANCE?

5 What is wrong with Anders' argument?

> A football team can win, lose or draw a match.
>
> These are the only three possible outcomes and winning is one of those outcomes.
>
> The probability that the team will win is $\frac{1}{3}$.

6 In a game of snooker there are 15 red balls and seven other balls coloured yellow, green, brown, blue, pink, black and white. Gianni takes one ball at random.

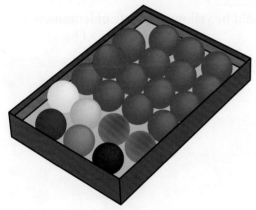

What is the probability that the ball Gianni takes is:
a red   **b** not red   **c** yellow   **d** red, white or blue   **e** orange?

7 A ten-sided dice has the numbers from 1 to 10 on its faces.

Jiao rolls the dice once.
Find the probability of each of these outcomes. Write your answers as percentages.
a 3   **b** more than 3   **c** a multiple of 3
d a factor of 12   **e** more than 12   **f** less than 12

8 A teacher has 12 red pens, 8 blue pens, 5 black pens and 7 green pens.
She hands one, at random, to each student in the class.
a Find the probability that the first student is given a red pen.
b Deshi wants to have a red pen. By the time the teacher gets to Deshi she has given out two pens of each colour. Has Deshi's chance of getting a red pen increased or decreased? Give a reason for your answer.

16.3 Mutually exclusive outcomes

A bag contains sweets of different colours.

One sweet is taken from the bag. This is an event.

Here are two possible outcomes.

| A red sweet is taken out. | | A green sweet is taken out. |

These are **mutually exclusive** outcomes. They cannot both happen at the same time.

Here are two more possible outcomes.

| A yellow sweet is taken. | | The sweet taken tastes of lemons. |

These are <u>not</u> mutually exclusive outcomes. The sweet could be yellow <u>and</u> taste of lemons.

Worked example 16.3

A wallet contains $5, $10, $20 and $50 notes. One note is taken from the wallet. Here are three possible outcomes.
  Outcome A: An amount of $5 is taken.
  Outcome B: An amount of $10 or less is taken.
  Outcome C: An amount of $20 or more is taken.
Which of these pairs of outcomes are mutually exclusive?
a A and B   **b** A and C   **c** B and C

a	A and B are not mutually exclusive.	A means a $5 note is taken. B means a $5 or a $10 note is taken. $5 could be taken in either case.
b	A and C are mutually exclusive.	A means a $5 note is taken. C means a $20 or $50 note is taken. These have nothing in common.
c	B and C are mutually exclusive.	B means a $5 or a $10 note is taken. C means a $20 or $50 note is taken. These have nothing in common.

◆ **Exercise 16.3**

1 Aiden has these coins in his pocket.
  He takes out one coin at random.
  Here are four possible outcomes.
  A: He takes out 10 cents.
  B: He takes out 20 cents or less.
  C: He takes out 20 cents.
  D: He takes out 50 cents or more.

  a Find the probability of:
    i outcome A   **ii** outcome B   **iii** outcome C   **iv** outcome D.
  b Which of these are mutually exclusive?
    i A and B   **ii** A and C   **iii** B and C   **iv** B and D   **v** A, C and D

2 Jessica throws a normal six-sided dice. Here are four different outcomes.

    A: an even number   **B:** an odd number   **C:** more than 5   **D:** less than 4

    a Which outcome is least likely?

    b Write down three different pairs of mutually exclusive outcomes.

3 People are invited to compete to be a contestant in a television quiz show.
Here are some possible outcomes for the person who is chosen.

    A: The contestant is a woman over 25 years old.   **B:** The contestant is a man.

    C: The contestant is 21 years old.   **D:** The contestant is a 30-year-old man.

    a List the possible pairs of mutually exclusive outcomes.

    b List three of the outcomes that are all mutually exclusive.

    c What can you say about the probabilities of B and D?

4 These are some possible outcomes for an aeroplane that is due to arrive at midday tomorrow.

    A: It is late.   **B:** It arrives at 12 35.   **C:** It arrives before 11 45.

    D: It arrives after 11 50.   **E:** It is early.

    a Are any pairs of these outcomes mutually exclusive?
If so, which pairs?

    b Write down three mutually exclusive outcomes for
when the aeroplane lands, one of which must happen.

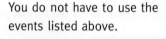

You do not have to use the events listed above.

5 A fair spinner has four colours: red, green, blue and yellow.
It is spun once.

    a List two possible outcomes that are mutually exclusive.

    b List two outcomes that are not mutually exclusive.

    c Find the probabilities of your outcomes in part **b**.

6 This 20-sided dice has the numbers from 1 to 20 on its faces.
All numbers are equally likely. Gavin throws the dice once.

    a What is the probability that the outcome is a single-digit number?

    b Find an outcome that is mutually exclusive to the outcome in part **a**
but has the same probability.

    c Here are three different outcomes.

        T: a multiple of 3   **F:** a multiple of 5   **S:** a multiple of 7

        i Find the probability of each of these outcomes. Write your answer as a percentage in each case.

        ii Which of these three outcomes are mutually exclusive?

16.4 Estimating probabilities

If you drop a thumb tack it can land point up or point down.

You <u>cannot</u> assume these two outcomes are equally likely.

You <u>cannot</u> use equally likely outcomes to find the probabilities.

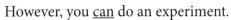

However, you <u>can</u> do an experiment.

The table shows the outcomes when 80 thumb tacks were dropped.

Outcome	point up	point down	total
Frequency	31	49	80

An **estimate** of the probability of 'point up' is $\frac{31}{80}$ = 0.39 or 39%.

An estimate of the probability of 'point down' is $\frac{49}{80}$ = 0.61 or 61%.

These are **experimental probabilities**. Probabilities found by using equally likely outcomes are **theoretical probabilities**.

What are the theoretical probabilities if the two outcomes are equally likely? They will both be 0.5.

> The outcomes of tossing a coin, either 'heads' or 'tails', are equally likely.

- Different experiments on the same event could give different experimental probabilities.
- Theoretical probabilities do not depend on an experiment and they do not change.

◆ Exercise 16.4

1 A survey of 40 cars on a particular length of road showed that 14 were speeding.
   Find the experimental probability that the next car will be:
   a speeding **b** not speeding.

2 There are 320 students in a school. 16 come to school by car. 96 walk to school.
   Estimate the probability that a particular student:
   a arrives by car **b** walks to school **c** does not walk to school **d** does not walk or come by car.

3 Mrs Patel goes to work by car each day. Sometimes she has to stop at a set of traffic lights.
   In the past 25 working days she has had to stop 16 times.
   a Find the experimental probability that she will have to stop at the lights tomorrow.
   b Find the experimental probability that she will not have to stop at the lights next Wednesday.

4 Jasmine goes to school five days a week. In the last four weeks she has been late for school
   on three days.
   Estimate the probability that she will not be late for school tomorrow.

5 Carlos looks at the weather records for his town in November.
   Over the last five years (150 days) there has been rain on 36 days
   in November.
   a Use this information to estimate the probability that it will rain on 1 November next year.
   b Use the information to estimate the probability that it will not rain on 30 November next year.

> Write your answer as a percentage or a decimal.

6 Why might Razi's method not be a good way to estimate the probability?

> My team has won 18 of their last 20 matches, so the probability
> that they will win their next match is $\frac{18}{20}$ = 90%.

7 Here are the results of a survey of 240 students in a school.

Item	Mobile phone	Computer in bedroom	Wants to be in a band	Member of sports team
Number of students	232	164	92	68

   a Estimate the probability that a student chosen at random from the school:
     i has a mobile phone   **ii** is not a member of a sports team.
     Give your answers as percentages.

   b Why is the following argument incorrect?
     A good estimate of the probability that a student wants to be in a band or is a member of a sports

     team is $\frac{92+68}{240} = \frac{160}{240} = \frac{2}{3}$ or 67%.

8 Raj is tossing a coin. The two possible outcomes are 'heads' and 'tails'.
   a If the outcomes are equally likely, what are the probabilities of each outcome?
   b Raj records his results in a table.
     Use the results to find the experimental probability of
     each outcome.

Outcome	heads	tails	total
Frequency	24	16	40

   c Raj's friend Xavier says that Raj is not throwing fairly because the probabilities from the
     experiment are wrong.
     Raj says that you should not expect an experiment to give exactly the same results as the 'equally
     likely' method.
     Who do you think is correct?

9 A bag contains one white ball, one black ball and some red balls.
  Biyu takes one ball out, records the colour and replaces it.
  She does this 50 times.
  Biyu records his results in a table.

Outcome	white	black	red	total
Frequency	6	8	36	50

   a Use the results of the experiment to estimate the probability of picking each of the three colours.
   b If there are 3 red balls, calculate the probability of each colour.
   c If there are 5 red balls, calculate the probability of each colour.
   d If there are 7 red balls, calculate the probability of each colour.
   e Biyu knows that there are an odd number of red balls. What is the most likely number? Give a
     reason for your answer.

Summary

You should now know that:

★ Words such as 'likely' and 'unlikely' can be used to describe results involving chance.

★ The probability of an outcome is a number from 0 to 1.

★ Probabilities can be calculated using equally likely outcomes.

★ Some outcomes are mutually exclusive.

★ Probabilities can be estimated using experimental data.

★ Experimental and theoretical probabilities may be different.

You should be able to:

★ Choose appropriate words to describe likelihood.

★ Write a probability as a fraction, a percentage or a decimal.

★ Use equally likely outcomes to calculate a probability.

★ Identify mutually exclusive outcomes.

★ Use experimental data to estimate a probability.

★ Compare experimental and theoretical probabilities.

End of unit review

1 Choose the correct word or phrase from the box to describe each outcome.
   a A coin will come up heads each time when it is spun three times.
   b The number shown when a dice is thrown will be less than 8.
   c It will rain in the next month.
   d The population of the world will be less in 20 years' time than it is now.

   | likely   certain |
   | unlikely   even chance |
   | very likely   impossible |
   | very unlikely |

2 Mark these probabilities on a probability scale.

   A: Passing an exam: $\frac{2}{3}$.   **B:** Failing the exam: $\frac{1}{3}$.

   C: A good harvest: 95%.   **D:** Jo's horse winning the race: 0.2.

   0 ─────────────── 1

3 Omar lays out ten cards, numbered from 1 to 10, face down. He takes one card at random. What is the probability that the number on his card is:

   Write your answers as decimals.

   a 7   b less than 4   c an even number   d a multiple of 3   e not the 10?

4 A large jar of sweets has equal numbers of red, yellow, green and orange sweets and no other colours.
   Anil takes out a sweet without looking. What is the probability that it is:
   a yellow   b either red or green   c not orange?

5 What is wrong with Zalika's argument?

   If I throw two dice and add the scores together I can get any total from 2 to 12.

   That's 11 different numbers, so the probability of getting a total of 3 is $\frac{1}{11}$.

6 Tamsin throws a single dice.
   a Find the probability of each outcome.
      T: She scores 3.   **M:** She scores more than 3.   **L:** She scores less than 3.   **N:** She does not score 3.
   b State whether each of these statements is true or false.
      i   **M** and **L** are mutually exclusive events.   ii   **T** and **N** are mutually exclusive events.
      iii **M** and **N** are mutually exclusive events.

7 Aisha chooses a whole number from 1 to 20, at random. Here are three possible outcomes.
   F: a multiple of 4   **S:** a multiple of 7   **P:** a prime number
   a Find the probability of each of the outcomes **F**, **S** and **P**.
   b Explain why **F** and **P** are mutually exclusive outcomes but **S** and **P** are not.

8 Tanesha throws two dice and adds the scores together.
   Here are her results after 80 throws.

Total	less than 5	from 5 to 10	more than 10
Frequency	16	56	8

   a Find the experimental probability that the total is:
      i   less than 5   ii   more than 10   iii   5 or more.
   b In 20 more throws, two scores are less than 5. Find the new experimental probability of 'less than 5'.

A **transformation** happens when you move a shape by **reflecting**, **translating** or **rotating** it.

The shape you start with is called the **object**. The shape you finish with, after a transformation, is called the **image**.

You see transformations in everyday life.

Look in a lake, a river or the sea on a calm day and you will see a **reflection**. In the picture below you can see the mountains, clouds, jetty, trees and stone wall all reflected in the lake.

Key words

Make sure you learn and understand these key words:

transformation
reflect
translate
rotate
object
image
reflection
translation
rotation
congruent
mirror line
line of symmetry
centre of rotation
clockwise
anticlockwise

In the picture on the right you can see someone firing an arrow in an archery competition. When the arrow hits the target it will have undergone a **translation** from where it started to where it finished.

In the bottom picture you can see the *Singapore Flyer*. It is one of the largest Ferris wheels in the world. It is 165 metres tall, has 28 capsules and can carry a maximum of 784 people at a time.

The wheel turns or rotates about its centre. Each complete **rotation** takes about 32 minutes.

When a shape undergoes a transformation it only changes its position. It doesn't change its shape and size. An object and its image are always identical or **congruent**.

In this unit you will learn more about transformations of plane shapes.

17.1 Reflecting shapes

When you draw the reflection of a shape, you use a **mirror line**.

Each point of the shape moves across the mirror line to the point that is the same distance away from the mirror line on the other side.

The mirror line is a **line of symmetry** for the whole diagram.

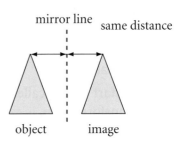

mirror line   same distance

object   image

> **Worked example 17.1**
>
> **a** Draw a reflection of this shape in the mirror line.
>
> **b** Draw a reflection of this shape in the line with equation $x = 4$.
>
>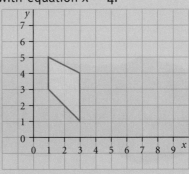

a

object

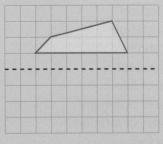

image

Take one corner of the shape at a time and plot its reflection in the mirror line. Remember that each point on the image must be the same distance away from the mirror line as its corresponding point on the object. Use a ruler to join the reflected points with straight lines, to produce the image.

b

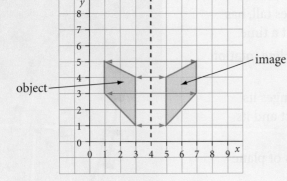

object

image

First draw the mirror line $x = 4$ on the grid. Take each corner of the shape, one at a time, and plot its reflection in the mirror line. Use a ruler to join the reflected points with straight lines, to produce the image.

Exercise 17.1

1 Which drawings show a correct reflection of triangle A?

a 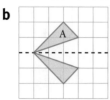 b 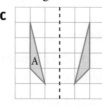 c 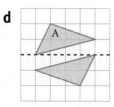 d

2 Copy each diagram and reflect the shape in the mirror line.

a b c 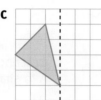 d

3 Copy each diagram and reflect the shape in the diagonal mirror line.

a b 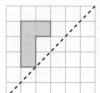 c d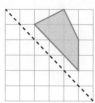

The first one has been started for you.

4 Copy each diagram and reflect the shape in the mirror line with the given equation.

mirror line $x = 3$ mirror line $y = 4$ mirror line $x = 4$ mirror line $y = 3$

a 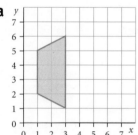 b 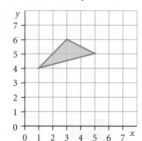 c 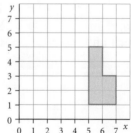 d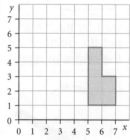

5 Copy each diagram and draw in the correct mirror line for each reflection.

a b c

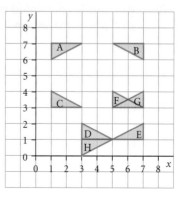

6 The diagram shows eight triangles, labelled A to H.
Write down the equation of the mirror line that reflects:
a triangle A to triangle B   b triangle A to triangle C
c triangle B to triangle E   d triangle D to triangle E
e triangle F to triangle G   f triangle D to triangle H.

17.2 Rotating shapes

When you rotate a shape you turn it about a fixed point called the **centre of rotation**.

You can rotate a shape **clockwise** or **anticlockwise**.

You must give the fraction of a whole turn, or the number of degrees, by which you are rotating the object.

The turns that are most often used are a quarter-turn (90°), a half-turn (180°) or a three-quarters turn (270°).

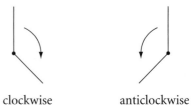

clockwise   anticlockwise

Worked example 17.2

a Draw the image of this shape after a rotation of 90° clockwise about the centre of rotation marked C.

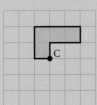

b Describe the rotation that takes shape A to shape B.

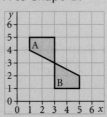

---

a

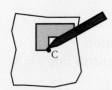

Start by tracing the shape, then put the point of your pencil on the centre of rotation.

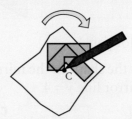

Start turning the tracing paper 90° (a quarter-turn) clockwise.

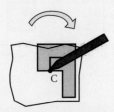

Once the turn is completed make a note of where the image is.

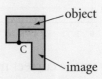

Draw the image onto the grid.

b Rotation is 180° (or a half-turn).

The centre of rotation is at (3, 3).

When you describe the rotation, give the number of degrees and the coordinates of the centre of rotation. Note that when the rotation is 180° you don't need to say clockwise or anticlockwise as both give the same result.

◆ **Exercise 17.2**

1 Copy each diagram and rotate the shape about the centre C by the given number of degrees.

a 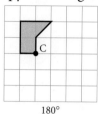   **b** 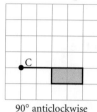   **c** 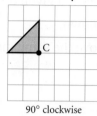   **d**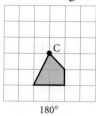

180°   90° anticlockwise   90° clockwise   180°

2 Copy each diagram and rotate the shape about the centre C by the given fraction of a turn.

a 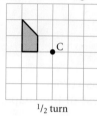   **b** 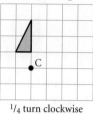   **c** 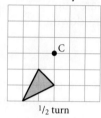   **d**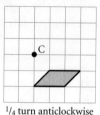

½ turn   ¼ turn clockwise   ½ turn   ¼ turn anticlockwise

3 Copy each diagram and rotate the shape, using the given information.

a 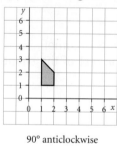   **b** 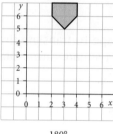   **c** 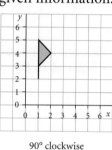   **d**

90° anticlockwise   180°   90° clockwise   180°
centre (1, 3)   centre (3, 3)   centre (1, 1)   centre (4, 3)

4 The diagram shows seven triangles. Describe the rotation that takes:

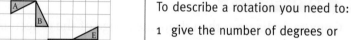

a triangle A to triangle B
b triangle B to triangle C
c triangle C to triangle D
d triangle C to triangle E
e triangle F to triangle G.

To describe a rotation you need to:

1 give the number of degrees or fraction of a turn

2 if the turn is not 180°, say whether the turn is clockwise or anticlockwise

3 give the coordinates of the centre of rotation.

5 a Copy this diagram.
Follow these instructions to make a pattern.

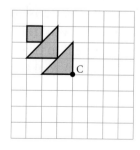

i Rotate the pattern a quarter-turn clockwise about the centre C.
ii Draw the image.
iii Rotate this new image a quarter-turn clockwise about the centre C.
iv Draw the image.
v Rotate the third image a quarter-turn clockwise about the centre C.
vi Draw the image.

b What is the order of rotational symmetry of the completed pattern?

17.3 Translating shapes

When you translate a shape you move it a given distance.

It can move right or left, and up or down.

All the points on the shape must move the <u>same</u> distance in the <u>same</u> direction.

Worked example 17.3

Translate this shape:
a 2 squares to the right and 3 squares up
b 5 squares to the left and 1 square down.

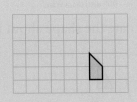

a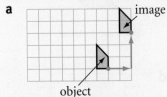

Pick one corner of the shape to translate first. Move this corner 2 squares to the right and 3 squares up. Draw in the rest of the shape.

b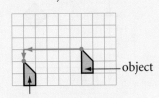

Pick one corner of the shape to translate first. Move this corner 5 squares to the left and 1 square down. Draw in the rest of the shape.

Exercise 17.3

1 Copy each diagram then draw the image of the object, using the translation given.

a 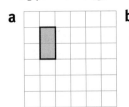   **b**   **c** 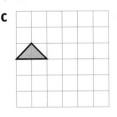   **d**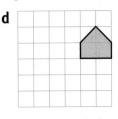

2 squares right   3 squares left   4 squares right   1 square left
2 squares down   4 squares up   1 square up   3 squares down

2 The diagram shows three triangles.
Describe the translation that takes:
a triangle A to triangle B
b triangle B to triangle C
c triangle A to triangle C.

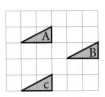

In part **c** the translation doesn't involve any movement left or right, so you only need to give the number of squares down.

3 Copy the diagram.
  a Translate shape A 2 squares right and 1 square up.
  Label the image B.
  b Translate shape B 3 squares right and 2 squares up.
  Label the image C.
  c Describe the translation that takes shape A to shape C.
  d Explain how you could work out the answer to part **c** without drawing shapes B and C.

4 Xavier is giving Harsha some instructions for a translation.

Move the shape 3 squares left and 4 squares up, then 5 squares left and 3 squares down.

Is Harsha correct?
Explain your answer.

Why don't you just say move the shape 8 squares left and 1 square up. The image will end up in the same position!

5 Dakarai shows this diagram to Harsha.

Can you translate the shape 2 squares across and 3 squares down?

No, it's not possible. Your instructions are not good enough.

Explain why Harsha is right.

6 a Copy these coordinate axes.
  Plot and join the points A(1, 4), B(2, 5) and C(3, 3).
  b Draw the image of ABC after a translation of 3 squares right and 2 squares down. Label the image PQR.
  c Describe the translation that would take PQR back to ABC.
  d What do you notice about your answers to parts **b** and **c**?
  e Mari draws triangle DEF onto the coordinate grid.
  She draws the image of DEF onto the grid after a translation of 2 squares left and 1 square up. She labels the image JKL.
  Describe the translation that would take JKL back to DEF.

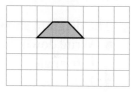

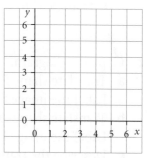

Summary

You should now know that:

★ Shapes remain congruent after a reflection, rotation or a translation.

★ When you draw the reflection of a shape, you use a mirror line.

★ When you draw a rotation you need to know:
  1 the number of degrees or fraction of a turn
  2 (if the turn is not 180°) whether the turn is clockwise or anticlockwise
  3 the coordinates of the centre of rotation.

★ When you translate a shape you can move it right or left and up or down.

You should be able to:

★ Transform 2D points and shapes by a: reflection in a given line rotation about a given point translation.

★ Recognise and use spatial relationships in two dimensions.

★ Draw accurate mathematical diagrams.

★ Communicate findings effectively.

End of unit review

1 Copy each diagram and reflect the shape in the mirror line.

a 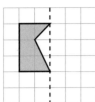 **b** 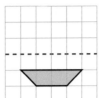 **c** 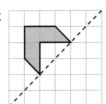 **d**

2 Copy each diagram and rotate the shape using the given information.

a 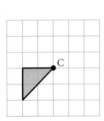 **b** 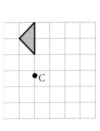 **c** 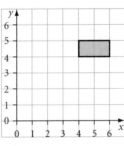 **d**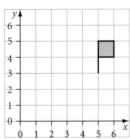

half-turn
centre C

quarter-turn
clockwise centre C

180° turn
centre (4, 3)

90° turn anticlockwise
centre (5, 2)

 3 The diagram shows triangles A, B, C and D.
  a Write down the <u>equation</u> of the mirror line that reflects:
     i triangle A to triangle B   **ii** triangle A to triangle C.
  b Describe the rotation that transforms:
     i triangle C to triangle D   **ii** triangle B to triangle C.

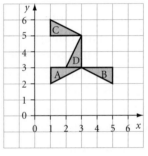

 4 Copy the diagram.
  a Translate shape P 5 squares left and 4 squares down.
     Label the image Q.
  b Translate shape Q 4 squares right and 1 square up.
     Label the image R.
  c Describe the translation that takes shape P to shape R.
  d Explain how you could work out the answer to part **c** without
     drawing shapes Q and R.

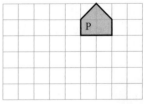

 5 Mia draws a shape on a coordinate grid. She labels the shape X.
  She draws the image of shape X after a translation of 5 squares left and 3 squares up.
  She labels the image Y.
  She draws the image of shape Y after a translation of 2 squares right and 5 squares down.
  She labels the image Z.
  a Write down the translation that takes shape X directly to shape Z.
  b Write down the translation that takes shape Z directly back to shape X.

18 Area, perimeter and volume

The **area** of a shape is the amount of space that a shape takes up.

Imagine a square piece of land that is exactly 1 km long and exactly 1 km wide. The area of this piece of land is 1 **square kilometre**, which you can write as 1 **km²** or 1 sq km.

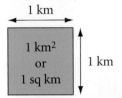

The square kilometre is a very large unit of area. You will also use much smaller units, when you are measuring smaller items. The unit you will use must always be suitable for what you are measuring.

Here are some interesting area facts about places in the world.

The smallest ocean in the world is the Arctic. It has a total area of just over 15 millon sq km.

The largest country in the world is Russia. It has a total area of just over 17 million sq km.

The largest island in the world is the Greenland. It has a total area of just over 2 million sq km.

The largest freshwater lake in the world is Lake Superior in North America. It has a total area of 82 100 sq km.

One of the smallest island in the world is the Grenada. It has a total area of just over 344 sq km.

The largest saltwater lake in the world is the Caspian Sea in Asia. It has a total area of 371 000 sq km.

The smallest country in the world is the Vatican City. It has a total area of 0.44 sq km.

The largest ocean in the world is the Pacific. It has a total area of over 155 million sq km.

In this unit you will learn how to work out the area and perimeter of squares and rectangles. You will also learn how to work out the surface area and volume of cubes and cuboids.

18.1 Converting between units for area

The diagram shows three squares.

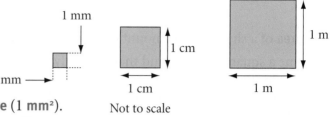

- The first has a side length of 1 mm.
- The second has a side length of 1 cm.
- The third has a side length of 1 m.
- The first square has an area of 1 **square millimetre** (1 mm²).
- The second has an area of 1 **square centimetre** (1 cm²).
- The third has an area of 1 **square metre** (1 m²).

To convert between units of area you need to know the **conversion factors.**

Look at the square with a side length of 1 cm and area 1 cm².
If you divide it up into squares with side length 1 mm
you get 10 × 10 = 100 of these smaller squares.

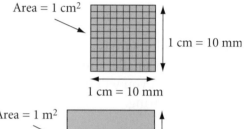

This shows that: 1 cm² = 100 mm²

You can do the same with the square with a side length
of 1 m and area 1 m².
If you divide it up into squares with side length 1 cm
you get 100 × 100 = 10 000 of these smaller squares.

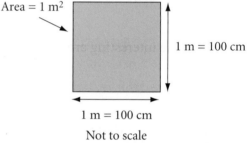

This shows that: 1 m² = 10 000 cm²

Worked example 18.1

a What units for area would you use to measure the area of a football pitch?
b A shape has an area of 5 cm². What is the area of the shape, in square millimetres?

a Square metres, m²   You would measure the length of a football pitch in metres, so the area
                          would be in square metres.
b 5 × 100 = 500 mm²   1 cm² = 100 mm², so 5 cm² would be 5 times as much.

Exercise 18.1

1 What units would you use to measure the area of:
   a a postage stamp   **b** a bank note   **c** a tennis court   **d** a cinema screen?

2 Copy and complete the following area conversions.
   a 6 cm² = ☐ mm²   **b** 7.2 cm² = ☐ mm²   **c** 3 m² = ☐ cm²
   d 5.4 m² = ☐ cm²   **e** 900 mm² = ☐ cm²   **f** 865 mm² = ☐ cm²
   g 20 000 cm² = ☐ m²   **h** 48 000 cm² = ☐ m²   **i** 125 000 cm² = ☐ m²

3 Is Maha correct? Explain your answer.

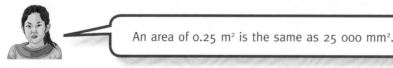

An area of 0.25 m² is the same as 25 000 mm².

18.2 Calculating the area and perimeter of rectangles

When you draw a rectangle on a centimetre square grid, you can work out the area of the rectangle by counting squares.

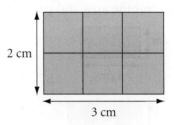

Area = 6 cm²

Instead of counting squares, you can multiply the length of the rectangle by its width to work out the area.

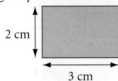

Area = 3 × 2 = 6 cm²

The formula for working out the area of any rectangle is:

area = length × width

or $A = l \times w$

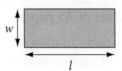

The **perimeter** of a shape is the total distance around the outside of the shape.

You find the perimeter of a shape by adding the lengths of all the sides together.

The perimeter of this rectangle is:

3 + 2 + 3 + 2 = 10 cm

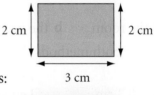

You can see that you are adding two lengths and two widths together.

The formula for working out the perimeter of any rectangle is:

perimeter = 2 × length + 2 × width

or $P = 2l + 2w$

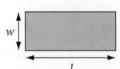

Worked example 18.2

Work out the area and the perimeter of this rectangle.

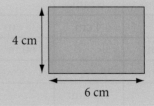

Solution

Area	= 6 × 4	Use the formula: area = length × width.
	= 24 cm²	Remember to write the correct units, cm², with your answer.
Perimeter	= 2 × 6 + 2 × 4	Use the formula: perimeter = 2 × length + 2 × width.
	= 12 + 8	Work out 2 × length and 2 × width first, then add the answers.
	= 20 cm	Remember to write the correct units, cm, with your final answer.

◆ Exercise 18.2

1 Work out the area and perimeter of each of these rectangles.

a
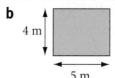
2 cm
4 cm

b
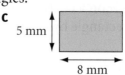
4 m
5 m

c
5 mm
8 mm

d
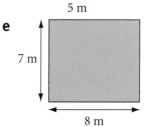
5 cm
5 cm

e
7 m
8 m

f
3 mm
12 mm

2 A sheet of A5 paper is 210 mm long and 148 mm wide.
What is the area of a sheet of A5 paper?

3 Connor is laying a new patio in his garden.
The diagram shows the dimensions of his patio.
Work out:
  a the area of the patio   **b** the perimeter of the patio.

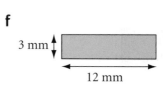
4 m
2.5 m

4 A rectangular room has an area of 12 m².
The length of the room is 4 m.
Work out:
  a the width of the room   **b** the perimeter of the room.

5 Copy and complete both methods shown to find the area of this rectangle.

Method 1
Width = 3 mm = 0.3 cm
Area = 2 × 0.3 = ☐ cm²

Method 2
Length = 2 cm = 20 mm
Area = 20 × 3 = ☐ mm²

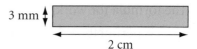
3 mm
2 cm

6 The table shows some information about five rectangles A to E.

Rectangle	Length	Width	Area	Perimeter
A	8 mm	6 mm		
B		4 cm	28 cm²	
C	12 m		60 m²	
D	8 cm			22 cm
E		1.5 mm		20 mm

Copy and complete the table.

7 Keira wants new carpet in her hall.
The hall is a rectangle that measures 4 m long by 90 cm wide.
Work out the area of carpet that she needs.

8 Oditi and Tanesha are drawing rectangles with whole-number lengths and widths.
Who is correct? Explain your answer.

I can only draw three different rectangles with an area of 24 cm².

There are four different rectangles with an area of 24 cm².

18.3 Calculating the area and perimeter of compound shapes

A **compound shape** is one that is made up of simple shapes such as squares and rectangles.

You work out the area of a compound shape using this method.

1 Split the shape up into squares and/or rectangles.

2 Work out the area of each individual square or rectangle.

3 Add together the individual areas to get the total area.

You work out the perimeter of a compound shape by adding the lengths of all the sides.

Worked example 18.3

Work out the area and perimeter of this shape.

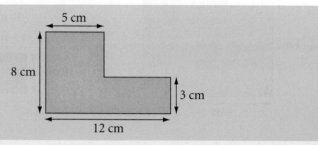

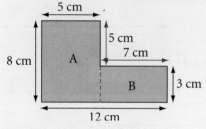

Area A = 8 × 5 = 40 cm²
Area B = 7 × 3 = 21 cm²
Total area = 40 + 21 = 61 cm²
Perimeter = 12 + 8 + 5 + 5 + 7 + 3
= 40 cm

Start by working out the missing two lengths on the shape.
12 − 5 = 7 cm and 8 − 3 = 5 cm
Split the shape up into two rectangles and label them A and B.
Work out the area of rectangle A using area = length × width,
Work out the area of rectangle A using area = length × width,
Work out the area of rectangle B using area = length × width
Work out the area of the compound shape by adding the areas
of the two rectangles. Remember to write the correct units, cm²,
with your answer.
Add together all the lengths to get the perimeter.
Remember to write the correct units, cm, with your answer.

Exercise 18.3

1 a Copy and complete both methods to find the area of this compound shape.

Method 1

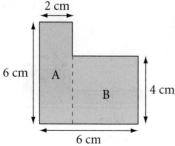

Area A = 6 × 2 = ☐
Area B = 4 × ☐ = ☐
Total area = ☐ + ☐ = ☐

Method 2

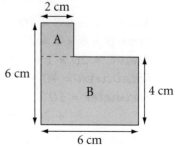

Area A = 2 × ☐ = ☐
Area B = 6 × 4 = ☐
Total area = ☐ + ☐ = ☐

b What do you notice about your answers in part **a**?

2 Work out the area and perimeter of each of these compound shapes.

a 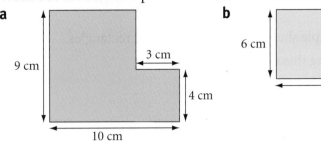 **b**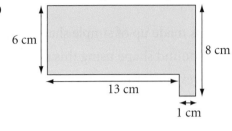

c 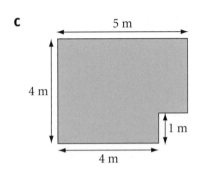 **d**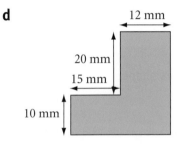

3 Copy and complete the workings to find the area of the blue section in this diagram.

Area of large rectangle = $30 \times \square = \square$ cm²

Area of hole = $8 \times \square = \square$ cm²

Blue area = $\square - \square = \square$ cm²

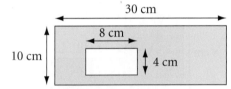

4 Work out the area of the red section in each of these diagrams.

a 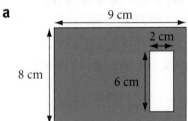 **b**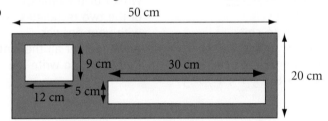

 5 This is part of Vishanthan's homework.

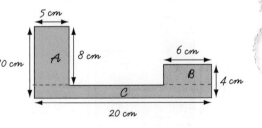

> _Question_ Work out the area and perimeter of this compound shape.
>
> _Solution_ Area A = 5 × 8 = 40
> Area B = 6 × 4 = 24
> Area C = 20 × 1 = 20
> Total area = 40 + 24 + 20 = 84 cm
> Perimeter = 10 + 5 + 8 + 6 + 4
>   + 20 = 53 cm²

Vishanthan has made several mistakes.
Explain what he has done wrong. Work out the correct answers for him.

18.4 Calculating the volume of cuboids

Look at this cube. It has a length, a width and a height of 1 cm.

It is called a centimetre cube. You say that it has a **volume** of one **cubic centimetre** (1 cm³).

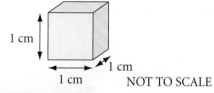

1 cm
1 cm
1 cm
NOT TO SCALE

This cuboid is 4 cm long, 3 cm wide and 2 cm high.

If you divide the cuboid into centimetre cubes, it looks like this.

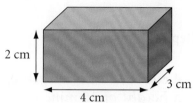

2 cm
4 cm
3 cm

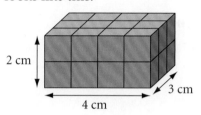

2 cm
4 cm
3 cm

You can see that there are 12 cubes in each layer and that there are two layers. This means that the total number of centimetre cubes in this cuboid is 24.

You say that the volume of the cuboid is 24 cm³.

You can work out the volume of a cuboid, using the formula:

volume = length × width × height

<u>or</u> $V = l \times w \times h$

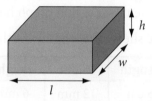

h
w
l

If the sides of a cuboid are measured in millimetres, the volume will be in **cubic millimetres** (mm³).
If the sides of a cuboid are measured in metres, the volume will be in **cubic metres** (m³).

Worked example 18.4

a Work out the volume of this cuboid.
b A concrete cuboid has a length of 5.1 m, a width of 3.2 m and a height of 1.8 m.
  i Work out the volume of the cuboid.
  ii Use estimation to check your answer.

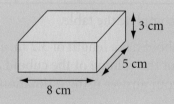

3 cm
5 cm
8 cm

a $V = 8 \times 5 \times 3$ Use the formula: volume = length × width × height.
  $= 120$ cm³   All the lengths are in cm so the answer is in cm³.
b i $V = 5.1 \times 3.2 \times 1.8$ Use the formula: volume = length × width × height.
  $= 29.376$ m³   All the lengths are in m so the answer is in m³.
  ii $V = 5 \times 3 \times 2$ To estimate, round all the lengths to the nearest whole number.
  $= 30$ m³   30 is close to 29.376 so the answer to part **bi** is probably correct.

◆ Exercise 18.4

1 Work out the volume of each of these cuboids.

a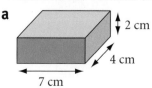

2 cm
4 cm
7 cm

b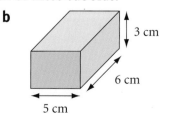

3 cm
6 cm
5 cm

c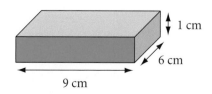

1 cm
6 cm
9 cm

2 Work out the volume of each of these cuboids.

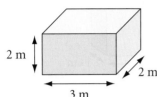

a

2 m

3 m

2 m

b

8 mm

3 mm

15 mm

> Make sure you write the correct units with your answers.

3 This is part of Steph's homework.

> Question A cuboid has a length of 12 cm, a width of 9 cm and
> a height of 35 mm.
> What is the volume of the cuboid?
> Solution Volume = 12 × 9 × 35
> = 3780 cm³

Steph has got the solution wrong.
Explain the mistake that Steph has made and work out the correct answer for her.

4 The table shows the length, width and height of four cuboids.

	Length	Width	Height	Volume
a	5 cm	12 mm	6 mm	☐ mm³
b	12 cm	8 cm	4 mm	☐ cm³
c	8 m	6 m	90 cm	☐ m³
d	1.2 m	60 cm	25 cm	☐ cm³

Copy and complete the table.

5 A metal cuboid has a length of 3.2 m, a width of 4.8 m and a height of 2.1 m.
   a Work out the volume of the cuboid.
   b Check your answer using estimation.

6 Alicia buys a fish tank.
The dimensions of the fish tank are shown in the diagram.

Alicia fills the tank with water to $\frac{4}{5}$ of the height of the tank.

What is the mass of the water in the fish tank?

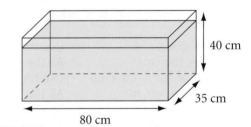

40 cm

35 cm

80 cm

> I know that 1 cm³ of water has a mass of 1 gram.

Give your answer in kilograms.

18.5 Calculating the surface area of cubes and cuboids

The **surface area** of a cube or cuboid is the total area of all its faces.

The units of measurement for surface area are square units, for example, mm^2, cm^2 or m^2.

This cube has six faces.

The area of one face = 2×2

$\qquad = 4 \ cm^2$

The surface area of the cube = 6×4

$\qquad = 24 \ cm^2$

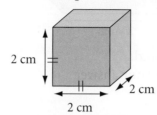

This is a **net** of a cuboid. It can be folded up to make the cuboid shown.

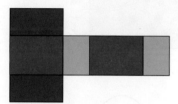

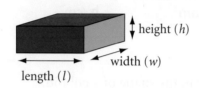

You can see that the cuboid has two blue faces, two red faces and two green faces.

Area of one red face = length × width

Area of one blue face = length × height

Area of one green face = width × height

To work out the surface area you need to add together the areas of all the faces. This cuboid has two faces of each colour so you would need to multiply the area of each face by 2, before adding them all together.

> **Worked example 18.5**
>
> Work out the surface area of this cuboid.
>
>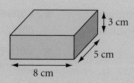
>
> | | |
> |---|---|
> | Area of top face = $8 \times 5 = 40 \ cm^2$ | Use the formula: area = length × width |
> | Area of front face = $8 \times 3 = 24 \ cm^2$ | Use the formula: area = length × height |
> | Area of side face = $5 \times 3 = 15 \ cm^2$ | Use the formula: area = width × height |
> | Surface area = $2 \times 40 + 2 \times 24 + 2 \times 15$ | Multiply the area of each face by 2. |
> | $\quad = 80 + 48 + 30$ | Add the areas to find the total surface area. |
> | $\quad = 158 \ cm^2$ | Remember to include the units in your answer. |

> **Exercise 18.5**

1 Work out the surface area of each of these cuboids.

a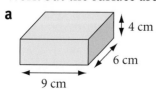

b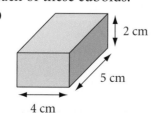

c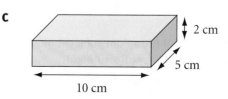

2 Work out the surface area of each of these cuboids.

> Make sure you write the correct units with your answers.

a

4 m, 6 m, 5 m

b

12 mm, 5 mm, 20 mm

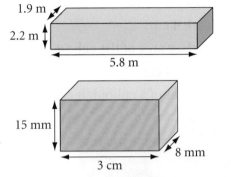

3 a Work out the surface area of this cuboid.
   b Show how to use estimation to check your answer to part **a**.

1.9 m, 2.2 m, 5.8 m

4 Work out the surface area of this cuboid.
   Give your answer in: **a** mm²   **b** cm².

15 mm, 3 cm, 8 mm

5 Michiko has a metal container in the shape of a cuboid.
   The container is 2.4 m long, 1.2 m wide and 0.6 m high.
   Michiko plans to paint all the outside faces of the container with
   two coats of metal paint.
   a How many tins of paint does Michiko need to buy?
   b What is the total cost of the paint?

Metal paint
$8.49

Size of tin: 250 ml
Paint coverage: 4.5 m² per litre

Summary

You should now know that:

★ Area is measured in square units such as square
metres (m²), square centimetres (cm²) and square
millimetres (mm²).

★ The conversion factors for area are:
1 cm² = 100 mm², 1 m² = 10 000 cm².

★ The formula for the area of a rectangle is:
area = length × width.

★ The perimeter of a shape is found by adding the
lengths of all the sides together.

★ To find the area of a compound shape:
   1 split the shape up into squares and/or
   rectangles

   2 work out the area of each individual square or
   rectangle

   3 add together the individual areas to get the total
   area.

★ The formula for the volume of a cuboid is:
volume = length × width × height.

★ The surface area of a cube or cuboid is the total
area of all its faces.

You should be able to:

★ Convert between units for area, for example, m²,
cm² and mm².

★ Derive and use formulae for the area and
perimeter of a rectangle.

★ Calculate the perimeter and area of compound
shapes made from rectangles.

★ Derive and use the formula for the volume of a
cuboid.

★ Calculate the surface area of cubes and cuboids
from their nets.

★ Understand everyday systems of measurement
and use them to estimate and calculate.

★ Work logically and draw simple conclusions.

End of unit review

1 What units would you use to measure the area of:
 a a hockey pitch   **b** a book cover?

2 Copy and complete the following area conversions.
 a $8 \text{ cm}^2 = \square \text{ mm}^2$ **b** $5 \text{ m}^2 = \square \text{ cm}^2$ **c** $420 \text{ mm}^2 = \square \text{ cm}^2$

3 Work out the area and perimeter of each of these rectangles.

a 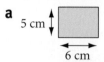 5 cm / 6 cm

b 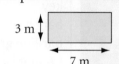 3 m / 7 m

c 8 mm / 5 cm

4 A rectangular room has an area of 24 m².
 The length of the room is 6 m.
 Work out: **a** the width of the room   **b** the perimeter of the room.

5 a Work out the area of these green shapes.

i 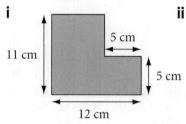 11 cm, 5 cm, 5 cm, 12 cm

ii 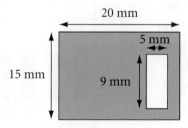 20 mm, 5 mm, 15 mm, 9 mm

> Make sure you write the correct units with your answers.

 b Work out the perimeter of the shape in part **ai**.

6 Work out:
 a the volume of the cuboid
 b the surface area of the cuboid.

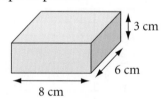 3 cm, 6 cm, 8 cm

7 This is part of Petra's homework.

> _Question_ A cuboid has a length of 15 mm, a width of 8 mm and a height of 12 mm.
> What is the volume of the cuboid?
> _Solution_ Volume = 15 + 8 + 12
> = 35 mm

Petra has got the solution wrong.
Explain the mistakes that Petra has made and work out the correct answer for her.

8 a Work out the surface area of this cuboid.
 b Show how to use estimation to check your answer to part **a**.

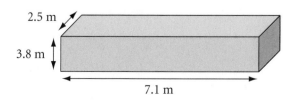 2.5 m, 3.8 m, 7.1 m

19 Interpreting and discussing results

What is the purpose of drawing charts or diagrams, when you can just look at the data?

Imagine you were going to book a holiday. If you look in a holiday brochure you will often see graphs and charts that show you what the weather is usually like at the holiday destinations. It is much easier to get the information you need from a graph or chart than it is from a long list of data.

For example, suppose you want to book a holiday to Rome, but you want to go when there is unlikely to be much rain.

If you look at the chart on the right, you can quickly and easily see that July has the least amount of rain, and also that May, June and August do not have a lot of rain either.

October, November and December are the months to avoid as this is when Rome has most of its rain.

If you also wanted to go to Rome when the temperature wasn't too high, you could use this temperature chart.

Suppose that you wanted the temperature to be lower than 20 °C: you can see that June, July, August and September are too hot, but the other months are suitable.

Looking at both charts you would probably decide to go to Rome in May as there isn't very much rain and the temperature is less than 20 °C.

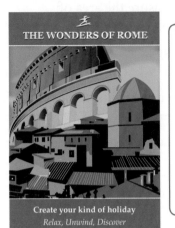

THE WONDERS OF ROME

Create your kind of holiday
Relax, Unwind, Discover

Key words

Make sure you learn and understand these key words:

pictogram
key
bar chart
bar-line graph
frequency diagram
pie chart
sectors

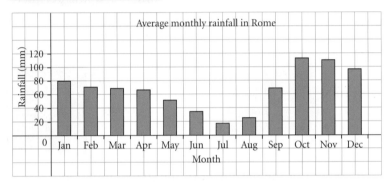

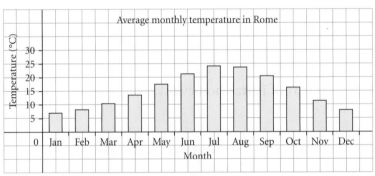

The Colosseum, Rome.

19.1 Interpreting and drawing pictograms, bar charts, bar-line graphs and frequency diagrams

In a **pictogram**, you use pictures to represent data. You can use each picture to represent an item or a number of items. The **key** shows how many items one picture represents. When you draw a pictogram you must make sure that:

- the pictures are all the same size
- the pictures are in line horizontally and vertically
- you include a key.

Worked example 19.1A

The pictogram shows the number of hours of sunshine on 1 July in three cities.
a Which city had the least sunshine?
b How many hours of sunshine were there in:
  i New York   **ii** Manama?

Cape Town	✻ ✻ ✻
Manama	✻ ✻ ✻ ✻ ✻
New York	✻ ✻ ✻ ✻

Key: ✻ represents 2 hours of sunshine

a Cape Town   Cape Town has the fewest pictures, so has the least amount of sunshine.
b i $4 \times 2 = 8$ hours   New York has 4 pictures. The key tells you that 1 picture represents 2 hours. So New York has 8 hours of sunshine.

  ii $5 \times 2 = 10$ hours   Manama has $5\frac{1}{2}$ pictures. 5 pictures represent 10 hours.

  $5\frac{1}{2} \times 2 = 1$ hour   Half a picture represents 1 hour.

  $10 + 1 = 11$ hours   Add 10 and 1 to work out the total number of hours.

In a **bar chart**, you use bars to show data. When you draw a bar chart you must make sure that:

- the bars are all the same width and the gap between bars is always the same
- each bar has a label underneath it
- the bar chart has a title and the axes are labelled
- you use a sensible scale on the vertical axis.

Worked example 19.1B

The table shows the favourite fruit of the students in Mrs Hassan's class.

Fruit	apple	pear	orange	banana
Number of students	7	6	4	8

Draw a bar chart to show this information.

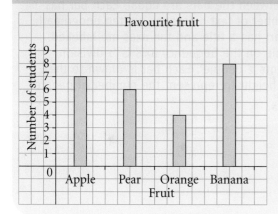

You can see that the bars are the same width and gaps between the bars are equal. Each bar has a label underneath to show which fruit it represents. The chart has a title and the axes are labelled 'Fruit' and 'Number of students'. The scale on the vertical axis is '1 division represents 1 student'. Each bar is drawn to the correct height to represent the number of students who chose that fruit.

A **bar-line graph** is similar to a bar chart, but you use thick lines instead of bars.

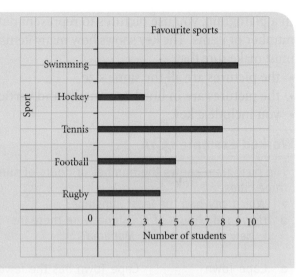

Worked example 19.1C

The bar-line graph shows the favourite sport of the students in Mr Scrivener's class.
a   How many students said rugby was their favourite sport?
b   How many more students chose tennis than chose football?
c   How many students are there altogether in Mr Scrivener's class?

a   4 students   The line for rugby goes up to 4 students.
b   8 – 5 = 3 students   The line for tennis goes up to 8 students. The line for football goes up to halfway between 4 and 6, which is 5. Then calculate the difference between the two.
c   4 + 5 + 8 + 3 + 9 = 29 students   Read off from the graph the number of students for each sport, then add them together to find the total number of students.

A **frequency diagram** is any diagram that shows frequencies. It could be a bar chart or a bar-line graph. The next example shows one used for grouped data.

Worked example 19.1D

The table shows the numbers of text messages sent by 30 people one day.
Draw a frequency diagram to show this information.

Number of text messages sent	Frequency
0–9	8
10–19	12
20–29	7
30–39	3

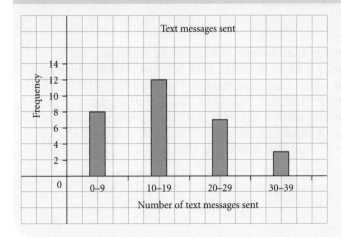

You can see that the bars are the same width and gaps between the bars are equal. Each bar has the number of text messages written underneath. The chart has a title and the axes are labelled. The scale on the frequency axis is '1 division represents 2 people'. Each bar is drawn to the correct height to represent the number of people.

◆ **Exercise 19.1**

1 The pictogram shows the favourite lesson of the students in class 7T.

Science	☺ ☺ ☺ ☺
Maths	☺ ☺ ☺ ☺ ☺
Geography	☺ ☺
History	☺ ☺ ☾
Art	☺ ☺ ☺ ☾

Key: ☺ represents 2 students

    a How many of the students said their favourite lesson was science?

    b How many more students chose maths than chose art?

    c How many students are there in class 7T?

2 The table shows the number of letters Mr Khan received each day during one week.

Day of week	Number of letters
Monday	9
Tuesday	12
Wednesday	6
Thursday	5
Friday	15

Monday	⊞ ⊞ ▫
Tuesday	
Wednesday	
Thursday	
Friday	

Key: ⊞ represents 4 letters

    a Copy and complete the pictogram to show the information. Use the key given.

    b Copy and complete the bar chart below to show the information.

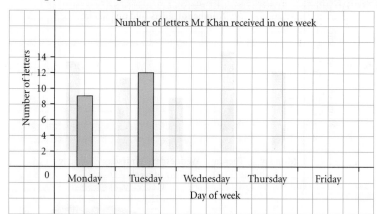

3 The bar-line graph shows the number of drinks sold in a canteen one lunchtime.

    a How many apple juice drinks were sold?

    b How many more teas than coffees were sold?

    c How many drinks were sold altogether?

    d What was the least popular drink?

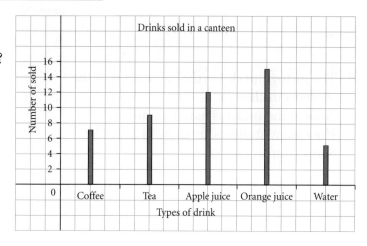

4 The number of runs scored by the batsmen at a cricket match are shown in the table. Copy and complete the frequency diagram to show the information.

Number of runs	Frequency
0 – 19	4
20 – 39	9
40 – 59	6
60 – 79	3

Number of runs scored at a cricket match

Frequency

10
8
6
4
2
0

0–19   20–39   40–59   60–79

Number of runs

5 This is part of Anil's homework.

Has Anil got his homework right? Explain your answer.

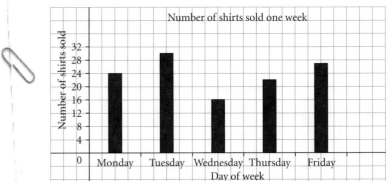

Question Use the bar chart to work out how many more shirts were sold on Tuesday than Monday.

Answer   29 – 24 = 5 shirts

Number of shirts sold one week

Number of shirts sold

32
28
24
20
16
12
8
4
0

Monday   Tuesday   Wednesday   Thursday   Friday

Day of week

6 The pictogram shows the hair colour of the students in class 7V.
Nine of the students have blonde hair.
How many students are there in class 7V?
Show your working.

Black	☺ ☺ ☺ ☺ ☺ ☺
Brown	☺ ☺ ☺
Blonde	☺ ☺ ☺ ☺ ☾
Red	☺ ☾

19.2 Interpreting and drawing pie charts

You can use a **pie chart** to display data showing how an amount is divided or shared. A pie chart is drawn as a circle divided into sections called **sectors**. The angles at the centres of all the sectors add up to 360°. When you draw a pie chart you must make sure that you label each sector and draw the angles accurately.

Worked example 19.2

a The pie chart shows the favourite animal of the students in class 7A.
  i Which animal is the most popular?
  ii Which animal is the least popular?
  iii Can you tell from the pie chart how many students are in class 7A?
b The table shows the favourite animal of the students in class 7B.
  Draw a pie chart to show this information.

Favourite animals of the students in class 7A

Animal	Frequency
dog	8
cat	7
horse	10
donkey	5

a **i** Dog is the most popular.
  ii Cat is the least popular.
  iii No

Dog has the biggest sector of the pie chart.
Cat has the smallest sector of the pie chart.
The pie chart only shows the fraction, or proportion, of the students who like the various animals, not the actual numbers.

b 8 + 7 + 10 + 5 = 30
360° ÷ 30 = 12°
Dog: 8 × 12 = 96°
Cat: 7 × 12 = 84°
Horse: 10 × 12 = 120°
Donkey: 5 × 12 = 60°

First add the frequencies to work out the total number of students in the class. Work out the number of degrees per student by dividing the total number of students into 360°. Multiply each frequency by 12° to get the total number of degrees for each sector.
Check that the total of the degrees does add up to 360°.
96° + 84° + 120° + 60° = 360°
Start by drawing a circle and then draw a line from the centre to the top of the circle. Measure an angle of 96° for the 'dog' sector, then draw a straight line from the centre to the edge of the circle. Repeat for the other sectors. Label each sector with the name of the animal and give the chart a title.

Favourite animals of the students in class 7B

Exercise 19.2

1 The pie chart shows the favourite colours chosen by 40 people.
  a Which colour is the most popular?
  b Which colour is the least popular?
  c Explain how you can tell from the pie chart that blue is the favourite colour of 10 of the people.

Favourite colour

2 The pie chart shows the number of emails Preety received in one week.

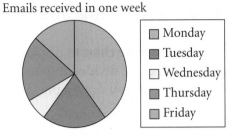

Emails received in one week

- Monday
- Tuesday
- Wednesday
- Thursday
- Friday

   a On which day did she receive the most emails?

   b On which day did she receive the fewest emails?

   c On which two days did she receive the same number of emails?

   d Can you tell from the pie chart how many emails Preety received on Friday? Explain your answer.

3 The table shows the number of different makes of car in a car park.

   a Copy and complete Anna's calculations below to work out the number of degrees for each sector of a pie chart to show this information.

Make of car	Frequency
Ford	12
Vauxhall	18
Toyota	10
Nissan	20

Total number of cars = 12 + 18 + 10 + 20 = ☐ cars
Number of degrees per car = 360 ÷ ☐ = ☐°
Number of degrees for each sector:
Ford = 12 × ☐° = ☐°   Vauxhall = 18 × ☐° = ☐°
Toyota = 10 × ☐° = ☐°   Nissan = 20 × ☐° = ☐°

   b Draw a pie chart to show the information in the table.

4 A group of 40 people were asked which type of music they prefer. The table shows the results.

> Remember to label each sector and give the pie chart a title.

Type of music	Frequency
Soul	5
Classical	20
Pop	8
Other	7

   Draw a pie chart to show the information in the table.

5 Alexi has worked out the number of degrees for each sector of a pie chart, but he has spilt coffee on the table showing his results!
This is what his table looks like now.

Favourite type of film	Frequency	Number of degrees
Action	2	40
Romantic	7	
Science fiction		80
Comedy		100

   a Work out the missing entries in his table.

   b Draw a pie chart to show the information in the table.

19.3 Drawing conclusions

You can use pictograms, bar charts, bar line graphs, frequency diagrams and pie charts to compare two sets of data.

When you are asked to compare two sets of data, follow these steps.

1 Look at the overall total number of items in each graph or chart and see if there is a big difference in the totals.

2 Compare the shapes of the graphs or charts and comment on how they are different.

Worked example 19.3

The pictograms show the number of people using a swimming pool during the first week in January and the first week in July.

First week in January

Monday	🧍 🧍
Tuesday	🧍 🧍 🧍
Wednesday	🧍 🧍 🧍 🧍
Thursday	
Friday	🧍 ⅃

Key: 🧍 represents 10 people

First week in July

Monday	🧍 🧍 🧍
Tuesday	🧍 🧍 🧍 🧍 ⅃
Wednesday	🧍 🧍 🧍 🧍 🧍 🧍 🧍 🧍
Thursday	🧍 🧍 🧍 🧍 🧍 ⅃
Friday	🧍 🧍 🧍 🧍 🧍 🧍 ⅃

Key: 🧍 represents 10 people

a Compare the pictograms and make two comments.
b On which day of the week were twice as many people using the pool in the first week of July than in the first week of January?
c No one used the pool on the Thursday in the first week of January. Give a reason why you think this might have happened.

| a 1 More people used the pool in the first week in July than the first week in January.

2 In January most of the people used the pool in the first three days of the week, but in July most of the people used the pool in the last three days of the week.

b Wednesday

c The pool might have been closed for repair, for cleaning or for a national holiday. | 1 You can see that there are a lot more pictures in the July pictogram than the January pictogram.

2 The January pictogram has more pictures at the start of the week, whereas the July pictogram has more pictures at the end of the week.

In the first week of January 40 people used the pool and in the first week of July 80 people used the pool.

Think of any sensible reason why there were no people using the pool. |

◆ Exercise 19.3

1 Mari and Aiden go to different schools.
   The pictograms show how the students in Mari's class and in Aiden's class travel to school.

Mari's class

Walk	☺ ☺ ☺ ☺ ☺ ☺ ☺
Cycle	☺ ☺ ☺ ☺ ☺
Bus	☺
Car	☺ ☺

Key: ☺ represents 2 students

Aiden's class

Walk	☺
Cycle	☺ ☺ ☺
Bus	☺ ☺ ☺ ☺ ☺ ☺ ☺
Car	☺ ☺ ☺ ☺

Key: ☺ represents 2 students

   a Work out the number of students in: **i** Mari's class   **ii** Aiden's class.
   b Compare the pictograms and make two comments.
   c Do you think that the students in Mari's class live near to their school?
          Explain your answer.
   d Do you think that students in Aiden's class live near to their school?
          Explain your answer.

2 Abeeku carries out a survey on the favourite sport of the students in his year group at school. The
   bar charts show his results.

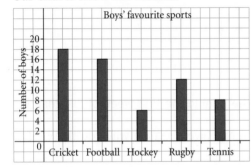
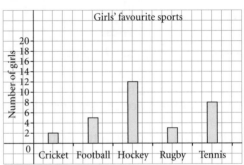

   a Compare the bar charts and make two comments.
   b Which sport is the favourite for the same number of boys as girls?
   c Which sport is the favourite of twice as many girls as boys?
   d Write down the modal sport for   **i** the boys   **ii** the girls.

3 Mrs Kaul gives the students in her class a reading test and a spelling test.
   The frequency diagrams show the results of the tests.

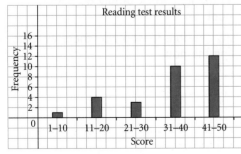
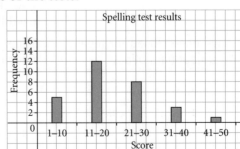

   a Work out the number of students that took: **i** the reading test   **ii** the spelling test.
   b Give a possible reason why your two answers in part **a** are different.
   c Compare the bar charts and make two comments.
   d Write down the modal score for: **i** the reading test   **ii** the spelling test.

4 Zalika sees these bar line graphs in a magazine. They show the average monthly temperatures in Cairo and Harare in January, April, July and October.

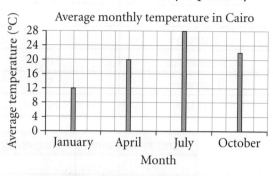

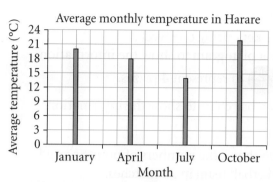

a Is Zalika correct? Explain your answer.

> I can tell it's warmer in Harare in October than it is in Cairo because the October line is longer.

b During which month is the temperature in Cairo double the temperature in Harare?

5 The pie charts show how Akila and Medina spend their money each week.

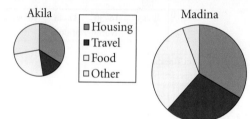

a Medina says: 'I spend a larger proportion of my money on housing, as the housing sector of my pie chart is bigger than Akila's.'
Is Medina correct? Explain your answer.

b Akila says; 'I pay half the amount that Medina does on travel, as the angle of my travel sector is half the size of the angle of Medina's travel sector.'
Is Akila correct? Explain your answer.

Summary

You should now know that:

★ A pictogram uses pictures to represent data.

★ A bar chart uses bars to show data.

★ A bar-line graph is similar to a bar chart, but the bars are replaced with thick lines.

★ A frequency diagram is the same as a bar chart except that the data has been grouped.

★ A pie chart is a way of displaying data to show how an amount is divided or shared.

★ You can use pictograms, bar charts, bar-line graphs, frequency diagrams and pie charts to compare two sets of data.

You should be able to:

★ Draw and interpret
  – pictograms
  – bar charts
  – bar-line graphs
  – frequency diagrams
  – pie charts.

★ Draw conclusions based on the shape of graphs and simple statistics.

★ Work logically and draw simple conclusions.

★ Record and explain methods results and conclusions.

★ Discuss and communicate findings effectively.

End of unit review

1 The table shows the number of pizzas sold in a supermarket during one week.

   a Draw a pictogram to show the information.

      Use 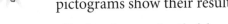 to represent 4 pizzas.

   b Draw a bar chart to show the information.

Day of week	Number of pizzas
Monday	12
Tuesday	8
Wednesday	10
Thursday	5
Friday	19

2 The table shows the numbers of points scored by a basketball team in 20 matches.

   a Copy and complete the frequency diagram to show the information.

   b Draw a pie chart to show this information.

Number of points	Frequency
1–15	2
16–30	3
31–45	8
46–60	7

Number of points scored by basketball team

(frequency diagram with axes: Frequency 0–10, Number of points 1–15, 16–30, 31–45, 46–60)

3 The bar-line graphs show the number of T-shirts sold in a shop on the first Monday and Tuesday in May.

Number of T-shirts sold on Monday

(bar-line graph: Number of sold 0–16, Colour of T-shirt: Red, Blue, Green, Yellow, Black)

Number of T-shirts sold on Tuesday

(bar-line graph: Number of sold 0–16, Colour of T-shirt: Red, Blue, Green, Yellow, Black)

   a Work out the total number of T-shirts sold on: **i** Monday   **ii** Tuesday.

   b Compare the bar-line graphs and make two comments.

   c Write down the modal colour T-shirt sold on: **i** Monday   **ii** Tuesday.

   d Give a reason why you think that sales of blue T-shirts dropped on Tuesday.

4 Alun and Bryn count the number of cars that pass their houses each morning for five days. The pictograms show their results.

Number of cars passing Alun's house

Monday	🚗 🚗 🚗 🚗
Tuesday	🚗 🚗 🚗
Wednesday	🚗 🚗 🚗 🚗 🚗
Thursday	🚗 🚗 🚗 🚗 🚗 🚗
Friday	🚗 🚗 🚗 🚗 🚗

Number of cars passing Bryn's house

Monday	🚗 🚗 🚗
Tuesday	🚗 🚗
Wednesday	🚗 🚗 🚗 🚗
Thursday	🚗 🚗 🚗
Friday	🚗 🚗

Key: 🚗 represents 2 cars

Key: 🚗 represents 4 cars

   a Alun says: 'On Thursday twice the number of cars came past my house as passed your house.' Is Alun correct? Explain your answer.

   b Who do you think lives on the busier road? Explain your answer.

19 Interpreting and discussing results

1 Look at the numbers in the box.
Write down the numbers from the box that are:

| 2 | 5 | 8 | 9 | 12 | 15 | 18 | 29 | 36 | 51 |

a multiples of 4
b factors of 30
c prime numbers
d square numbers.

2 Copy these finite sequences and fill in the missing terms.

a 3, 7, □, 15, □, 23, 27   **b** 31, 28, 25, □, □, 16, □

3 Write down the value shown on each of these scales.

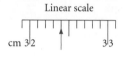
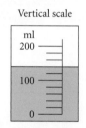
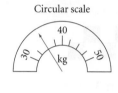

Linear scale   Vertical scale   Circular scale

4 Write these temperatures in order of size, starting with the lowest.

5 °C   −3 °C   2 °C   −6 °C   −15 °C   12 °C   −1 °C   9 °C   −7 °C

5 A card has a right-angled triangle and a circle drawn on it.
The card is turned three times, as shown.

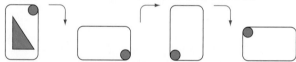

Copy the diagram. Draw the missing triangle on each of the cards.

6 Work these out.

a 34 × 10   **b** 1700 ÷ 100   **c** 2.6 × 100   **d** 27 ÷ 1000

7 A company employs nine people.
The table shows how many days each person was late to work, in one year.

Person	Eleri	Gill	Shona	Sam	Lin	Rao	Sion	Alun	Max
Number of days late to work	2	0	10	0	4	1	6	4	0

a Work out: **i** the mode   **ii** the median.
b Shona says: 'The mean number of days people were late to work is 12.'

   i Without actually working out the mean, how can you tell that Shona is wrong?
   ii Work out the correct mean number of days people were late to work.

c Copy and complete this bar chart to show the information in the table.

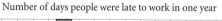
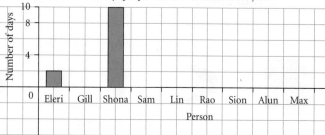

Number of days people were late to work in one year

8 Write the symbol <, > or = between the numbers in each pair.

a 50% ☐ $\frac{1}{2}$ **b** 10% ☐ 0.2   **c** $\frac{1}{4}$ ☐ 0.2   **d** 0.75 ☐ $\frac{3}{4}$

9 Make an accurate drawing of the triangle sketched here.

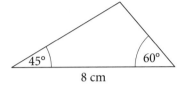

45°   60°

8 cm

10 Work these out.

a $\frac{4}{5} - \frac{1}{5}$ **b** $\frac{2}{3} + \frac{1}{6}$ **c** $\frac{2}{5}$ of 30 kg

11 This pattern is made from squares.

Pattern 1   Pattern 2   Pattern 3

a Draw the next two patterns in the sequence.
b Copy and complete the table to show the number of squares in each pattern.

Pattern number	1	2	3	4	5
Number of squares	3	5	7		

c Write down the term-to-term rule.
d How many squares will there be in:
   i Pattern 8   **ii** Pattern 10?

12 In a supermarket there are four bags of flour.

250 g   2.5 kg   0.8 kg   1500 g

Serena want to buy the bag of flour with mass as close as possible to 1.2 kg.
Which bag of flour do you suggest she buys?
Explain your answer.

13 Copy each of these shapes.
Draw all the lines of symmetry onto each shape.

14 Vishan has a ruler 30 cm long.
Explain how Vishan can use his ruler to draw a line exactly 42.5 cm long.

15 a Round 127 to the nearest 10.
  b Round 423 to the nearest 100.
  c Round 3.452 to one decimal place.

16 Work these out.   **a** 12.4×8 **b** $37.65 \div 5$

17 Solve each of these equations.
  a $x + 3 = 15$ **b** $4x = 12$
  c $3x - 2 = 13$ **d** $\frac{x}{3} + 9 = 14$

18 A train leaves at 14 35 and arrives at 17 12.
  a How long did the journey take?
  b The train arrives 25 minutes late. When was it due to arrive?

19 Olivia makes a journey by car. She draws a graph to illustrate it.

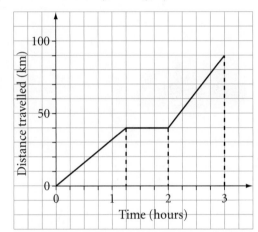

  a How long did it take her to travel the first 40 kilometres?
  b Olivia stopped for a rest during the trip. For how long did she stop?
  c How far did she travel in the last hour?

20 Chris and Mair share a gas bill in the ratio 3 : 2.
The gas bill is £85.
How much does each of them pay?

21 Fahran has a five-sided spinner.
  a He spins the spinner once.
    What is the probability that the spinner lands on:

    i 4
    ii an odd number
    iii a number smaller than 5?

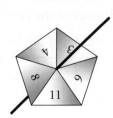

  b Fahran spins the spinner 50 times.
    How many times, out of the 50 spins, would you expect the spinner to land on the number 9?

22 Mrs Sanchez gave her class an algebra test.
These are the students' scores, marked out of 20.

16	17	9	19	12	3	12	1	20	7	10	11	18	2
8	12	3	16	6	7	19	15	15	18	9	12	8	17

a Copy and complete the grouped frequency table.

Score	Tally	Frequency
1–5		
6–10		
11–15		
16–20		

b How many students are there in Mrs Sanchez's class?
c How many students had a score less than 11?
Explain how you worked out your answer.

23 Which of these expressions is the odd one out?
Explain your answer.

$$3(6x + 4) \qquad 6(2 + 3x) \qquad 2(6 + 9x) \qquad 9(2x + 2)$$

24 Look at the coordinate graph.

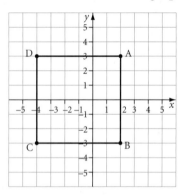

a What are the coordinates of D?
b What is the equation of the straight line through B and C?
c What are the coordinates of the centre of the square ABCD?

25 a Copy and complete this table of values for $y = x - 3$.

x	−3	−1	1	3	5
$y = x - 3$			−2		

b Draw a graph of the line $y = x - 3$.

Glossary and index

195

cuboid   a solid with six rectangular faces   87

cylinder   a solid whose two ends, and its cross-sections, are identical and parallel circles   87

data   facts, numbers or measurements collected about someone or something, used for reference or analysis and to produce useful information   63

data-collection sheet   a table used for data collection, involving tallying   68

decimal number   a number in the counting system based on 10; the part before the decimal point is a whole number, the part after the decimal point is a decimal fraction   32

decimal places   the number of digits after the decimal point   32

decimal point   the dot between the whole-number part and the decimal fraction of any number in the decimal system   32

degree   unit of measure of angles; a whole turn is 360 degrees (360°)   53

denominator   the number below the line in a fraction   73

derive   construct a formula or work out an answer   28

direct proportion   the ratio of quantities stays the same   140

divide   split up into parts   138

dividend   a number that is being divided   83

divisible   one whole number is divisible by another if it is a multiple of it   12

division (of a scale)   the value between successive marks on a scale   50

divisor   the number by which another number is divided   83

edge   the line where two faces of a solid meet   87

equal   being the same   87

equally likely   a set of outcomes with the same chance of happening   154

equation   two different mathematical expressions, both having the same value, separated by an equals sign (=)   26, 97

equation   a way of labelling a line on a grid   131

equilateral   having all sides the same length   54

equilateral triangle   triangle in which all sides are equal and all angles are 60°   87

equivalent fractions   Fractions that represent the same amount, for example, $\frac{3}{6}$ and $\frac{1}{2}$ 73

estimate   approximation of a number or amount, based on a calculation with rounded numbers   42, 49, 158

even chance   an equal chance of happening or not happening; an example is getting a head when you throw a coin   153

event   an action that can have different outcomes; throwing a dice is an event, scoring a six is an outcome   156

expand   (brackets), to multiply all parts of the expression inside the brackets by the term alongside the bracket   100

experimental probability   a probability estimated from data   158

expression   a collection of symbols representing numbers and mathematical operations, but not including an equals sign (=)   26, 97

face   flat side of a solid   87

factor   a factor of a whole number will divide into it without a remainder; 6 and 8 are factors of 24   12

finite sequence   a sequence that has an end   20

formula   an equation that shows the relationship between two or more quantities   28

formulae   plural of formula   28

fraction   a part of a whole, such as $\frac{1}{4}$ or $\frac{2}{3}$ 113

frequency   how many times a number occurs in a set   105

frequency diagram   any diagram that shows frequencies   181

frequency table   a table that lists the number or frequency of items of each category in a set of data   68

function   a relationship between two sets of numbers   24

function machine   a method of showing a function 24

gram (g)   one thousandth of a kilogram 47

graph   a line drawn on a coordinate grid 129

grouped frequency table   a table that lists, in groups, the number or frequency of items of each category in a set of data 68

highest common factor   the largest number that is a factor of two or more other numbers 73, 137

image   a shape after a transformation 161

improper fraction   fraction in which the numerator is larger than the denominator 80

included angle   the angle between two given sides 122

included side   the side between two given angles 122

infinite sequence   a sequence that has no end 22

information   facts, often produced from collected data 63

input   a number to be acted upon by a function 24

integer   the whole numbers …, −3, −2, −1, 0, 1, 2, 3, ….. 7

internal angle   any angle inside a flat shape 124

inverse   the operation that has the opposite effect; the inverse of 'add 5' is 'subtract 5' 16

inverse operation   the operation that reverses the effect of another 42, 101

isosceles triangle   triangle in which two sides are equal in length and the angles opposite equal sides are also equal 60, 87

key   (pictogram), the value of one picture or symbol 181

kilogram (kg)   standard unit of mass 47

kilometre (km)   one thousand metres 47

kite   quadrilateral in which two pairs of adjacent sides are equal, the opposite angles between the sides of different lengths are equal 87

length   measurement of a line, usually in metres 47

like terms   terms containing the same letter(s) 98

likely   more than an even chance 153

line of symmetry   a line dividing a shape into two parts, each part being a mirror image of the other 89, 162

line segment   a part of a straight line between two points 54

litre (l)   standard unit of capacity 47

lowest common multiple   the smallest possible common multiple of two numbers; 24 is the lowest common multiple of 6 and 8 11

lowest terms   a fraction is reduced to its lowest terms by dividing both numerator and denominator by their highest common factor; it cannot be simplified further 73

map   be converted, by means of a function, from a value in one set of numbers into a value in another set of numbers 24

mapping diagram   a diagrammatical representation of a function 24

mass   the amount of substance in an object; sometimes the word weight' is used in everyday speech 47

mean   To find the mean of a set of numbers, add them and divide by how many there are 107

median   The middle number when a set of numbers is put in order 105

metre (m)   unit of length; standard unit of length 47

metric units   measurements based on multiples and divisions of ten; the most common units of measurement 47

mid-point   the centre point of a line segment 129

millilitre (ml)   one thousandth of a litre 47

millimetre (mm)   one thousandth of a metre 47

mirror line   a line dividing a diagram into two parts, each being a mirror image of the other 162